XML:
The Annotated
Specification

ISBN 0-13-082676-6

90000

9 780130 826763

The Charles F. Goldfarb Series on Open Information Management

"Open Information Management" (OIM) means managing information so that it is open to processing by any program, not just the program that created it. That extends even to application programs not conceived of at the time the information was created.

OIM is based on the principle of data independence: data should be stored in computers in non-proprietary, genuinely standardized representations. And that applies even when the data is the content of a document. Its representation should distinguish the innate information from the proprietary codes of document processing programs and the artifacts of particular presentation styles.

Business data bases—which rigorously separate the real data from the input forms and output reports—achieved data independence decades ago. But documents, unlike business data, have historically been created in the context of a particular output presentation style. So for document data, independence was largely unachievable until recently.

That is doubly unfortunate. It is unfortunate because documents are a far more significant repository of humanity's information. And documents can contain significantly richer information structures than data bases.

It is also unfortunate because the need for OIM of documents is greater now than ever. The demands of "repurposing" require that information be deliverable in multiple formats: paper-based, online, multimedia, hypermedia. And information must now be delivered through multiple channels: traditional bookstores and libraries, the World Wide Web, corporate intranets and extranets. In the latter modes, what starts as data base data may become a document for browsing, but then may need to be reused by the reader as data.

Fortunately, in the past ten years a technology has emerged that extends to documents the data base's capacity for data independence. And it does so without the data base's restrictions on structural freedom. That technology is the "Standard Generalized Markup Language" (SGML), an official International Standard (ISO 8879) that has been adopted by the world's largest producers of documents and by the World Wide Web.

With SGML, organizations in government, aerospace, airlines, automotive, electronics, computers, and publishing (to name a few) have freed their documents from hostage relationships to processing software. SGML coexists with graphics, multimedia and other data standards needed for OIM and acts as the framework that relates objects in the other formats to one another and to SGML documents.

The World Wide Web's HTML and XML are both based on SGML. HTML is a particular, though very general, application of SGML, like those for the above industries. There is a limited set of markup tags that can be used with HTML. XML, in contrast, is a simplified subset of SGML facilities that, like full SGML, can be used with any set of tags. You can literally create your own markup language with XML.

As the enabling standard for OIM of documents, the SGML family of standards necessarily plays a leading role in this series. We provide tutorials on SGML, XML, and other key standards and the techniques for applying them. Our books vary in technical intensity from programming techniques for software developers to the business justification of OIM for enterprise executives. We share the practical experience of organizations and individuals who have applied the techniques of OIM in environments ranging from immense industrial publishing projects to websites of all sizes.

Our authors are expert practitioners in their subject matter, not writers hired to cover a "hot" topic. They bring insight and understanding that can only come from real-world experience. Moreover, they practice what they preach about standardization. Their books share a common standards-based vocabulary. In this way, knowledge gained from one book in the series is directly applicable when reading another, or the standards themselves. This is just one of the ways in which we strive for the utmost technical accuracy and consistency with the OIM standards.

And we also strive for a sense of excitement and fun. After all, the challenge of OIM—preserving information from the ravages of technology while exploiting its benefits—is one of the great intellectual adventures of our age. I'm sure you'll find this series to be a knowledgable and reliable guide on that adventure.

About the Series Editor

Dr. Charles F. Goldfarb invented the SGML language in 1974 and later led the team that developed it into the International Standard on which both HTML and XML are based. He serves as editor of the Standard (ISO 8879) and as a consultant to developers of SGML and XML applications and products. He is based in Saratoga, CA.

About the Series Logo

The rebus is an ancient literary tradition, dating from 16th century Picardy, and is especially appropriate to a series involving fine distinctions between things and the words that describe them. For the logo, Andrew Goldfarb incorporated a rebus of the series name within a stylized SGML/XML comment declaration.

The Charles F. Goldfarb Series on Open Information Management

As XML is a subset of SGML, the Series List is categorized to show the degree to which a title applies to XML. "XML Titles" are those that discuss XML explicitly and may also cover full SGML. "SGML Titles" do not mention XML per se, but the principles covered may apply to XML.

XML Titles

Goldfarb, Pepper, and Ensign
■ SGML Buyer's Guide™: Choosing the Right XML and SGML Products and Services

Megginson
■ Structuring XML Documents

Leventhal, Lewis, and Fuchs
■ Designing XML Internet Applications

Goldfarb and Prescod
■ The XML Handbook™

Jelliffe
■ The XML and SGML Cookbook: Recipes for Structured Information

DuCharme
■ XML: The Annotated Specification

SGML Titles

Turner, Douglass, and Turner
■ ReadMe.1st: SGML for Writers and Editors

Donovan
■ Industrial-Strength SGML: An Introduction to Enterprise Publishing

Ensign
■ SGML: The Billion Dollar Secret

Rubinsky and Maloney
■ SGML on the Web: Small Steps Beyond HTML

McGrath

■ ParseMe.1st: SGML for Software Developers

DuCharme

■ SGML CD

General Titles

Martin

■ TOP SECRET Intranet: How U.S. Intelligence Built
Intelink—the World's Largest, Most Secure Network

XML:
The Annotated
Specification

■ Bob DuCharme

Prentice Hall PTR, Upper Saddle River, NJ   07458
http://www.phptr.com

Editorial/Production Supervision: Patti Guerrieri
Acquisitions Editor: Mark L. Taub
Editorial Assistant: Audri Anna Bazlan
Marketing Manager: Dan Rush
Manufacturing Manager: Alexis R. Heydt
Cover Design: Anthony Gemmellaro
Cover Design Direction: Jerry Votta
Series Design: Gail Cocker-Bogusz

© 1999 Prentice Hall PTR
Prentice-Hall, Inc.
A Simon & Schuster Company
Upper Saddle River, NJ 07458

Prentice Hall books are widely used by corporations and government agencies for training, marketing, and resale.

The publisher offers discounts on this book when ordered in bulk quantities.
For more information, contact:

Corporate Sales Department,
Phone: 800-382-3419; FAX: 201-236-7141
E-mail: corpsales@prenhall.com; or write:
Prentice Hall PTR
Corp. Sales Dept.
One Lake Street
Upper Saddle River, NJ 07458

Printed in the United States of America

10 9 8 7 6 5 4 3 2

ISBN 0-13-082676-6

Prentice-Hall International (UK) Limited, London
Prentice-Hall of Australia Pty. Limited, Sydney
Prentice-Hall Canada Inc., Toronto
Prentice-Hall Hispanoamericana, S.A., Mexico
Prentice-Hall of India Private Limited, New Delhi
Prentice-Hall of Japan, Inc., Tokyo
Simon & Schuster Asia Pte. Ltd., Singapore
Editora Prentice-Hall do Brasil, Ltda., Rio de Janeiro

Thanks to: *Charles for his imprimatur and all the work behind it; Mark Taub and Patti Guerrieri at Prentice Hall; Joseph Reagle of the W3C; Peter DuCharme, Stacey Duda, Dave Peterson, and especially Tom Green for pointing out problems in the material they reviewed; everyone at Moody's Systems Development for keeping me grounded in reality with this stuff; and Jennifer, Madeline, and Alice for everything else.*

Contents

Foreword

XML—the Extensible Markup Language—is an approved Recommendation of the World Wide Web Consortium (W3C).

That is a very important statement, as we'll see in a minute.

If you're looking at this book, you are aware that XML is rapidly becoming the base of a Brave New Web of smart data and electronic commerce. Thousands of people are building it into Web sites, products, and industry standards.

And beyond the Web, enterprise software companies like SAP, BAAN, IBM, and Oracle are supporting XML for object repositories, data interchange, and development tools. In short, XML is emerging as the universal format for information exchange.

There are many solid technical reasons for this extraordinary acceptance:

- Powerful expressive capability for data and documents
- Efficient implementations, tuned for networked environments
- Proven track records of XML's parent, SGML, and its sibling, HTML

But that very first statement is perhaps even more important. Even arch competitors like Microsoft, Sun, IBM, and Netscape—who disagree on most things—agree on XML. And they, and the hundreds of other members of the W3C, have documented that agreement in the form of the official text of the XML Recommendation.

That document is the One True Source of information about the XML language. By design, it is expressed in rigorous, elegant (in the mathematical sense, which is to say, "efficient"), formal, and concise language. Parts of it are intended to be read by computers; the rest is intended to be read by people who are comfortable reading things that are intended to be read by computers.

For earth people—even for most programmers—it's a daunting read, indeed!

Which is a shame, because if you really want to understand every detail of a language, you *should* read the original spec. The authors in my *Definitive XML Series* have read the XML spec, and we've done our best to make our books accurate and consistent with it. But for the ultimate reference on the details, only the spec itself will do.

And now, thanks to Bob DuCharme and this book, the XML spec has become much more accessible. Bob is a full-time practicing SGML/XML expert, author, and frequent speaker at industry conferences.

In preparing *XML: The Annotated Specification*, he studied all of the three million bytes of email and scores of supporting documents that were generated during the long development effort for XML. From it, he has created illuminating commentary on every part of the W3C Recommendation, plus more than 170 new usage examples.

With the permission of the W3C, the entire Recommendation is presented verbatim in this book. Intermingled with it—but typographically distinct—are Bob's explanations, hints, insights, and examples. Together they form a marvelous reference to what is fast becoming the Web's most important content standard.

Whatever your interest in XML, as user or implementor, you'll want *XML: The Annotated Specification.*

Charles F. Goldfarb
Saratoga, CA
November, 1998

Annotation
Introduction

Where did XML come from? What are all those other acronyms that people keep mentioning with it? If there's an official specification, what makes it so official? And what good are the strange, numbered pieces of cryptic syntax throughout the specification?

This chapter answers these questions. After giving you a little background It gives you some context to help you understand where XML came from, how the specification specifies what it does, and what you can do with it.

This Book and the XML Specifications

There are many books about XML, but the official W3C specification is the single most important document of all. The official XML specification, as written, edited, and promulgated by the W3C (the organization created to develop common World Wide Web protocols

1

such as HTML) is available for free on the Web. For the reader who lacks a strong background in computer science and SGML, however, the specifications are difficult to understand.

- By providing background on the SGML concepts, the computer science vocabulary (such as "grammar productions", "big-endian", "name spaces", "nonterminal", and "schema"), and the myriad other standards bodies and specifications alluded to (for example, ISO 8879, 639, 10744, 10646, 8859, 3166; UTF-8, UTF-16; RFCs 1738, 1808, and 1766) this book explains exactly what the specs mean.

- In addition to the "what", the book explains the "why"— the debate among the W3C's XML Working Group that led to the final wording of the spec.

If you are accustomed to learning computer languages directly from their formal specifications, this book will be all you need to learn XML. My annotations and my 170 new examples will make the task a lot easier than it would be if you read the spec alone.

However, even if you have such skills—and especially if you don't—I can recommend two other books in this Series. You might want to explore either or both of them before tackling this book.

The XML Handbook, by Series Editor Charles F. Goldfarb and Paul Prescod, contains user-friendly (but technically rigorous) tutorials on XML and related standards, plus extensive coverage of XML applications and tools.

XML by Example: Building E-Commerce Applications, by Sean McGrath, is a programmer's introduction to XML. It uses examples from electronic commerce to illustrate both the XML language and programming techniques for use with XML data.

HTML, SGML, and XML: History and Influences

What is XML's relationship to SGML and HTML? They have one obvious thing in common: the "ML" in their names. It stands for "markup language", a collection of markup codes and rules for adding those codes to documents in order to indicate the structure or appearance of those documents.[†] Using a text editor such as Windows' Notepad or the Macintosh's BBedit (or, more likely, a specialized editor that automates the use of your markup language), you add markup to files so that a program processing the document knows what to do with each part of it.

Early markup languages were usually invented by the companies that sold document processing software. For example, if you used the PageMania program to typeset your books for a printing house, the PageMania documentation would tell you the markup that was developed at PageMania, Inc. to specify margins, fonts, and other page layout details in your books.

As an alternative to these proprietary systems, SGML, or "Standard Generalized Markup Language", was issued as an International Standard in 1986. The "Standard Generalized" part meant that document developers were no longer tied to a particular vendor's markup language, but could instead develop their own markup, ideally in such a way that their documents would easily convert into other formats. Using SGML, they could define new "document types" by specifying certain details about documents of each type:

- The names of their potential components.

[†] We don't ever call any of these "programming languages", because you don't use them to create a series of instructions for a computer. For the same reason, we refer to the markup codes simply as "markup" to avoid confusion with "program code".

- The documents' structure—that is, the allowable ordering of those components.

This makes documents more versatile, because a document processing application that knows a document's structure can do more useful things with it more efficiently, just as a relational database management program can do sophisticated manipulation of a database once it knows the names, sizes, and data types of each column in a database's tables.

HTML and SGML

HTML was developed in 1991 as a specific markup language to identify the structure of Web documents. For the Web browsing programs then under development, HTML markup identified which parts of the document were headings, subheadings, bulleted and numbered lists, hypertext links, and other components of a technical document.

HTML is an SGML application, defining a document type by using SGML syntax to indicate the purpose of each part of an HTML Web page. The "tags" that mark the start and end of HTML document components (or "elements") each begin and end with angle brackets (<>) and include a name identifying the type of element represented. End-tags have a slash after their opening angle bracket to distinguish them from start-tags.

For example, you would code an HTML first-level heading (an h1 element) as shown in Example 1, and a second-level header with the h2 tags shown in Example 2.

Example 1: An HTML first-level heading

```
<h1>HTML, SGML, and XML: History and Influences</h1>
```

Example 2: An HTML second-level heading

```
<h2>HTML and SGML</h2>
```

In addition to the name of the element's type, a start-tag often has one or more labeled pieces of information about the element known as attributes. For example, HTML's a element (like the one in Example 3, which identifies hypertext anchors and links) has an href attribute to tell browsers the Web address of the link's destination.

Example 3: An HTML hypertext link element

```
<a href="http://www.w3.org">World Wide Web Consortium</a>
```

The text between the start- and end-tags of an element describes the element's *content*. Some elements have no content text; these are called "empty" elements.

HTML's most popular type of empty element was not part of the original HTML, but was added by the designers of Mosaic, the first widely popular HTML browser. The empty img element type's src attribute identifies a file that has a picture for the browser to display, and optional attributes specify details such as the alignment of the image in the browser window. Example 4 shows a typical img element; it has no content text or end-tag.

Example 4: HTML img element with src and align attributes

```
<img src="treegraf.gif" align="right">
```

Character-based markup languages have a unique problem: if the "<" character begins tags, what if you really want a "<" to show up in your document? Special characters like this have names assigned to them in HTML (in this case, lt for "less-than"). By using this name in a document, preceded by an ampersand and followed by a semicolon, you tell the processing application to replace this "entity reference" with the actual entity. This is why a Web browser displays "<" when it sees <.

HTML uses entity references to represent many of the characters of Western alphabets not found on the typical keyboard, such as ñ for ñ, È for È and è for è. What if you want to actually display an ampersand? Use its character entity reference: &.

To see how all of these elements and entity references looks when assembled, let's look at the simple HTML file shown in Example 5.

Example 5: Sample HTML document

```
 1. <html>
 2. <head><title>Title of Web Page</title></head>
 3. <body>
 4. <h1>A Sample Web Page</h1>
 5.
 6. <p>Here is the first paragraph of text in the sample Web
 7.  page. It has enough text to wrap to the next line so that
 8.  we can see what the left indentation is like.
 9.
10. <h2>Bulleted Lists</h2>
11. <p>Here is an unordered list. The browser
12. prefixes a bullet to each item:
13. <ul>
14. <li>Here is the first item of the bulleted list. The
15. Spanish word for "Spain" is "Espa&ntilde;a" and the
16. German word for "brew" is "br&auml;u".
17. <li>Here is the second item of the bulleted list.
18. </ul>
19.
20. <h2>Images</h2>
21. <p>Here is a picture:
22. <img src='sample.jpg' alt='face'>
23. <p>This concludes our test.
24. </body>
25. </html>
```

Figure 1 shows how Netscape displays the document from Example 5.

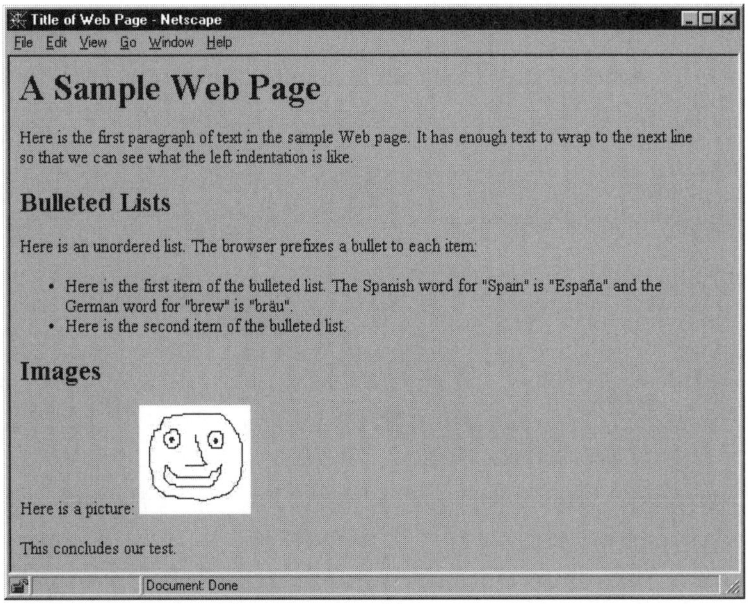

Figure 1 Simple HTML Web page displayed with Netscape.

The HTML document's `<head>` start-tag (line 2) is right after line 1's `<html>` start-tag. The `</head>` end-tag comes at the end of line 2, well before the `</html>` end-tag on line 25, which shows that the `head` element is inside of (or, "is a sub-element of") the `html` element. The `head` element has only one sub-element: line 2's `title` element.

It's easier to understand the different levels of container relationships in the document if we look at the tree graph in Figure 2, which shows each element branching off into the "child" elements it contains.

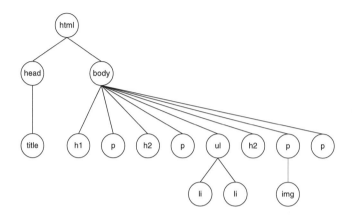

Figure 2 Tree graph of Figure 1's sample HTML file.

After the `html` element's `head` element, it only has a `body` element. The `body` element's structure is fairly flat—of its eight elements, only `ul` and one `p` element have child sub-elements of their own, and those children (the `li` sub-elements and the `p` element's `img` child) have no children themselves. Although the `h1` and `h2` elements should represent different hierarchical levels of information in the document (a head and a subhead), in HTML they're both on the same level of the document "tree", one level below the `body` element.

HTML and Structure

Although HTML was an SGML application, the browsers that displayed HTML documents ignored one important aspect of SGML: valid document structure. HTML came with guidelines for the use of its elements, but popular browsers didn't enforce any particular element ordering. For example, HTML uses `h1`, `h2`, and `h3` elements as the titles of main sections, subsections, and the subdivisions of those subsections in an HTML Web page. It uses the `p` element to represent regular paragraphs of document text. (If this chapter was an HTML Web page, this paragraph would be a single `p` element.) The docu-

ment in Example 6 has no `head` element, no `p` paragraphs of text anywhere, and it has section headings in a meaningless order—and none
of the popular Web browsers would have a problem with it.

Example 6: HTML document with haphazard header ordering

```
<html><body>
<h2>Florida</h2>
<h1>United States</h1>
<h3>Miami</h3>
<h2>California</h2>
</body></html>
```

Was this laxity bad? Was it good? Yes and yes. It was bad because, as
with database programs, a program that can rely on a regular structure
in its input can do much more with it. For example, an outlining program could generate a table of contents from HTML files with properly ordered headings, but would only make a mess of the
"document" in Example 6.

This flexibility was good because, by minimizing the number of
document-crippling mistakes that HTML authors could make, it let
them create Web documents with the simplest of tools. This ease of
document creation played a big role in the Web's tremendous growth
in the mid- and late-nineties.

Some HTML editing programs do enforce structure, but there's
not much to enforce. As the tree graph of Figure 1-1's HTML document showed, `h1`, `h2`, `p`, and `ul` are all at the same hierarchical level.
In more structured documents, subsections are components of their
parent sections, instead of just more text preceded by a different
header, so that treating a specific chapter or section as a unit (for
example, to extract it for use in another publication) means simply
finding a particular start-tag and its matching end-tag.

As an example, let's compare a well-structured document (Example
7) with an equivalent HTML document (Example 8). As SGML and
XML let you do, I've made up my own element type names and struc-

ture for the document in 7, and I indented its elements to show the structure more clearly.

Example 7: A well-structured XML document

```
<chapter>
  <title>Here is the Chapter Title</title>
  <para>This paragraph introduces the chapter.</para>
  <section>
    <title>Section 1</title>
    <para>Here is the first section's first paragraph.</para>
    <para>It has two paragraphs.</para>
    <subsection>
      <title>Section 1's First Subsection</title>
      <para>Here is Section 1's first subsection.</para>
    </subsection>
    <subsection>
      <title>Section 1's Second Subsection</title>
      <para>Here is Section 1's second subsection.</para>
    </subsection>
  </section>
  <section>
    <title>Section 2</title>
    <para>Here is the introduction to section 2.</para>
    <subsection>
      <title>Subsection of Section 2</title>
      <para>Here is a subsection of section 2.</para>
    </subsection>
  </section>
</chapter>
```

For reasons we'll see below, many HTML end-tags are optional, but I included them in 8 to make comparison easier. I also added line numbers so that the discussion that follows the example could more easily refer to specific lines.

Example 8: HTML equivalent of Example 7

```
1. <html><head><title>Sample Structured Document</title>
2. <body>
3. <h1>Here is the Chapter Title</h1>
4. <p>This paragraph introduces the chapter.</p>
5. <h2>Section 1</h2>
```

```
 6. <p>Here is the first section's first paragraph.</p>
 7. <p>It has two paragraphs.</p>
 8. <h3>Section 1's First Subsection</h3>
 9. <p>Here is Section 1's first subsection.</p>
10. <h3>Section 1's Second Subsection</h3>
11. <p>Here is Section 1's second subsection.</p>
12. <h2>Section 2</h2>
13. <p>Here is the introduction to section 2.</p>
14. <h3>Subsection of Section 2</h3>
15. <p>Here is a subsection of section 2.</p>
16. </body></html>
```

If we look at a tree diagram of the non-HTML version (Figure 3) we see more groupings of elements into useful units than we see in the HTML version (Figure 4).

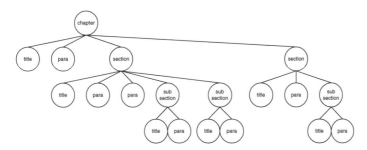

Figure 3 Tree graph of sample structured document.

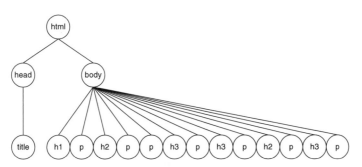

Figure 4 Tree graph of HTML version of Figure 3's structured document.

Why are these groupings valuable? Let's say I want to pull out the structured version's first section for use in another document. It would be easy to write a program that finds the first <section> tag in that chapter and then copies everything from there up to its corresponding </section> end-tag. With the HTML version, the first section begins at the chapter's first <h2> tag (line 5), but the corresponding </h2> end-tag on the same line only shows the end of the section's title. Our program must look for the next <h2> start tag (line 12) to know where the target section ends: just before that <h2> tag at the end of line 11.

If the program was pulling out that section's first subsection, it would have to look from that subsection title's <h3> start-tag (line 8) to just before the next <h3> start-tag (line 10), but what if we want to pull out that second subsection? If we grab everything from its <h3> tag (line 10) to just before the next <h3> tag (line 14) the way we did when we extracted the first subsection, we'd get the following section's title and introductory paragraph as well (lines 12 and 13)—lines that are outside of the subsection we want. Our program that extracts subsections from the HTML file needs extra rules and logic to figure out what lines it needs, but when extracting from the non-HTML file, it only needs one simple rule: to extract a subsection, get everything from its <subsection> start-tag to that tag's corresponding </subsection> end-tag.

In terms of the tree pictures, a document processing program can extract a useful subset of the document by simply clipping a particular branch and taking all of its descendants. This is much simpler than hunting through a series of HTML sibling elements and looking for the ones that meet certain complicated conditions. (This branch clipping approach is less abstract than it sounds—many software development kits for XML, SGML, and other kinds of applications read the data into the equivalent of a tree so that you can manipulate that tree to get what you want.)

Why would you want to extract anything? What's the advantage of moving through a document and pulling out pieces? Because information is an asset, and information that can be reused for multiple purposes has more value than information that is only available for one purpose. In business terms, the ability to make multiple products from the same body of information means more revenue from the same assets. For example, if you have all the details about a car's engine stored in a format that be easily searched and manipulated, you can write programs that pull out

- A complete reference work on the engine.
- A tutorial on fixing it.
- A quick reference card on troubleshooting engine problems.

And that's just paper publications. Each of these three could be published on other media:

- CD-ROM versions of the complete reference, the tutorial, and the quick reference card, giving you three more products.
- Hand-held computer versions of all three for mechanics crawling under the car.
- Web versions of all three.

This makes a total of twelve products from the same information. When the engine is upgraded, instead of undertaking twelve revisions, you update the main body of information once and then kick off the automated processes that create updated versions of the twelve publications.

Because HTML lacks the ability to represent such structure, it's not the best way to store a huge amount of information that you're going to put to multiple purposes. It became popular because of its simplicity and one particular application that used HTML files. This application—a free product—became the "killer app" for the Internet. "Killer app" is a computer industry term for an application that convinces huge amounts of people that they need a certain new technology. The killer app Long Playing record for hi-fi record players in the late nineteen-fifties was the soundtrack to the Broadway show "South Pacific"; the killer app that got millions of people to buy IBM's first personal computer in the early nineteen-eighties was the Lotus 1-2-3 spreadsheet; the killer app for the Internet was Mosaic.

Mosaic

From 1990 on, various experimental Web browsers were developed and released for public use. In February of 1993, the National Center for Supercomputing Applications (NCSA) released the first alpha, or early test version, of Marc Andreessen's Mosaic browser for UNIX machines. By running in a graphical interface environment (at first, UNIX XWindows), this program could display different elements in different fonts and even display pictures—color pictures! It wasn't necessarily the first program to do this, but once the NCSA released Windows and Macintosh versions, nearly everyone with access to a computer that was connected to the Internet could download Mosaic for free, view Web pages graphically, and follow the hypertext links to other Web sites around world. Anyone with an account on a UNIX machine that was running a Web server (a program that could send Web pages in response to requests made by browsers via the Internet) could create personal Web pages that were accessible by all these browsers. Familiarity with HTML was not required for this; plain text files also worked, but Mosaic displayed these in a boring, typewriter Courier font, and HTML wasn't that hard to learn, so soon everyone was cranking out HTML markup for their Web pages. Although the name "World Wide Web" had been around since 1991, it had finally become world-wide.

In March of 1994, Andreessen and some of his colleagues left the NCSA to form their own company: Mosaic Communications Corporation. Their new company, which later changed its name to Netscape Communications Corporation, made its browser available over the Internet for people to download for free. Another company known as

Spyglass used much of Mosaic's code to develop its own browser, which Microsoft snapped up and turned into its Internet Explorer product after it realized in 1995 that it should take the Internet seriously after all. While the Web's growth didn't really explode until after the name Mosaic had faded away to a trivia question for old computer hackers, the two dominant Web browsers as we finish up the century started off as spinoffs of this historic application that made millions of people aware of the power of HTML and hypertext documents.

For many people, however, Mosaic wasn't an example of what you could do with HTML; Mosaic, HTML, the Web, and even the Internet were a seamless whole. For these people, h1 went from meaning "first level header" to "24 point bold Times Roman, suitable for first level headers". If they wanted slightly smaller bold Times Roman text to appear on their Web page, they tagged it with h2 tags. If they wanted a word in the middle of a sentence bolded, they put b tags around it, and if they wanted it italicized, they put i tags around it. The possibility that someone might read their Web page using a Braille Web browser, or listen to an automated voice system read it, never occurred to them; they were creating pages to be read using Mosaic (and eventually Netscape and Internet Explorer), so whether they italicized a word because it was a foreign term or a C++ keyword was irrelevant. Since the blockquote tag added a wider left and right margin to text tagged as a blockquote, it became common practice to put a <blockquote> start-tag at the beginning of a document and the </blockquote> end-tag at the end to give the whole thing a more professional-looking margin. This element's original purpose—identifying a quotation that was more than one or two lines long—became as irrelevant as the effect of b and i tags on Braille browsers.

People were confusing structure and appearance. Document designers who thought "h1 is how you make text appear in 24-point bold Times Roman" misunderstood the distinction between structure and appearance—a misunderstanding that made it difficult to fully exploit either. Even the img element type showed at least one symptom of this confusion: its align attribute did not provide information about the image specified by the element's `src` attribute, but instead described how the image should appear visually on the screen.

This emphasis on using HTML tags to control visual design led to a wish for even greater control over document appearance. (While you could reset typefaces and fonts for your own copy of the browser, so that all `h1` elements sent to your browser displayed on your screen using a font of your choice, this wasn't good enough; people wanted control over how their documents appeared to other people on the Internet.)

Eventually, the `font` tag was added, which let you specify the typeface and size of the text outright. (For example, the word "hello" after the `font` start-tag `<font face="arial" size="4">` will be displayed in the Arial font a little larger than normal body text. Don't ask about the details of specifying font size this way; it's one of HTML's messier details, and the Cascading Style Sheets described below let you describe font size in points, a much more natural way to do it.)

Using this element let you design an attractive Web page if you had a knack for selecting appropriate fonts, but for applications that treated Web pages as structured data, it was useless. A program that extracts particular sections or subsections of a chapter can't possibly know their boundaries based on markup for font sizes and typeface names used in place of more structural elements such as `h1`, `h2`, and `p`.

I mentioned earlier that markup indicates the structure *or* appearance of documents. A collection of markup tags that indicate some structure and some appearance, which is how HTML came to be used by 1997, is like jazz-rock fusion: in trying to be two things at once, it does both badly. People needed a way to indicate structure and appearance separately so that they would have greater control over both.

Cascading Style Sheets

One approach that gained popularity around this time was Cascading Style Sheets (CSS). At its simplest level CSS lets you define, at the beginning of your document, how you want each of your element types to look. As an alternative to scattering font tags throughout your document, a Cascading Style Sheet lets you use the HTML structural tags and be confident that the document's elements will look the way you want with a minimum of markup.

For example, after you include the style element shown in Example 9 inside of a Web page's head element, a browser will display the body, h1, h2, and pre elements according to these instructions instead of using the default font faces and sizes.

Example 9: An HTML document's Cascading Style Sheet

```
<style><!--
body { background: whitesmoke; margin: 20px 50px 20px 50px }
h1   { font-family: arial,helvetica; font-size:140% }
h2   { font-family: arial,helvetica; font-size:110% }
pre  { font-family: system; font-size:75% }
--></style>
```

This approach gives you easier control over a document's appearance by isolating presentation information at the document's beginning. This way, you can rely on structural tags for the remainder of the document. This makes the document more valuable to applications that use it for other purposes, because these applications won't need to scan through font, b, and i tags to find the content they want. (Identifying the ending of hierarchical sections, however, will still be the same problem it always was in HTML.)

HTML and Standards

HTML had another problem: while an official standard defining HTML existed, it had competition. Since 1994, the standard has been maintained by the World Wide Web Consortium (or "W3C"), a collection of companies and universities around the world interested in developing and promoting common protocols for the Web's evolution. Before then, Web development activity was centered in the European Laboratory for Particle Physics (CERN) in Geneva, Switzerland, where the Web was first developed around the ideas of CERN's Tim Berners-Lee. Being more concerned with particle physics than the Web, CERN (with MIT's Laboratory for Computer Science) helped to found the W3C to oversee standards development.

Mosaic's derivatives supported the W3C's HTML standard, but they had big ideas about going beyond that standard. Any software vendor tries to outdo its competition by adding new features to its applications that are unavailable in competing products, and browser vendors often did this by inventing flashy new HTML element types that your documents could use if people viewed them with the vendor's latest browser. Sometimes these features would eventually be incorporated into the W3C standard, but the vendors' attempts to outpace each other have always sent them along paths that differed slightly from each other and from the standard.

SGML Web Pages?

Cascading Style Sheets encouraged a return to the use of HTML's structural tags, which was great for programs creating a table of contents from Web pages with properly arranged h1 and h2 elements. SGML people, however, knew that designing their own classes of elements, or "element types", let them create documents that were useful to a wider variety of applications.

For example, plenty of Web sites offered HTML pages of recipes; if ingredients were tagged as `ingredient` elements instead of HTML `li` list items, and the total preparation time was tagged as a `totpreptime` element instead of as an italicized paragraph, an application could easily search a cookbook Web site for a recipe that used chicken and lemon grass but took less than 40 minutes to cook. (Web sites that did offer this kind of capability didn't search through HTML pages of recipes—they searched SGML documents or relational databases and then temporarily converted any found recipes to HTML for retrieval by the browser that sent the query.)

So why not put SGML pages on the Web instead of HTML pages? SGML was designed—a decade before the Web even reached the experimental stage—to be very flexible so as to accommodate the widest possible range of uses. A proper SGML application must account for all of this flexibility, which makes for a difficult, complicated program to write.

For example, SGML lets you redefine the tag opening and closing characters so that you can write an `ingredient` start-tag as `(ingredient)` instead of `<ingredient>` and its end-tag as `(!ingredient)` instead of `</ingredient>`. You can redefine the characters that delimit an entity reference, so that instead of entering `&lt;` when you want the processor to output a "<" you could use `{lt}` instead.

Although a negligible number of SGML documents actually redefine tag and entity reference delimiters, proper conforming SGML software must be prepared to handle these redefinitions, and that makes for bigger, more complex programs.

SGML also allows the omission of start- and end-tags when a system can figure out the omitted tags from the included markup. HTML uses this often; for example, while the end of an ordered list must almost always be clearly specified with an `ol` end-tag (`</ol>`), HTML paragraph start-tags (`<p>`) rarely need a matching `</p>` end-tag because a paragraph's end is usually obvious. If a `<p>` start-tag is followed by text and then another `<p>` start-tag, it wouldn't make sense to consider the second p element as being inside the first one. A browser can therefore assume that the first p element ends just before the second one begins.

For example, if line 6 of Example 8 (lines 5 through 8 are reproduced in Example 10) had no </p> end-tag, a browser wouldn't treat line 7's p element as being inside of the p element begun on line 6; it would assume that line 6's p element was finished.

Example 10: Excerpt from Example 8

```
5. <h2>Section 1</h2>
6. <p>Here is the first section's first paragraph.</p>
7. <p>It has two paragraphs.</p>
8. <h3>Section 1's First Subsection</h3>
```

(An ordered list usually needs its </ol> end-tag because many element types are legal inside of a list item. Therefore, the beginning of a particular new element after the start of the last item of the ordered list may not indicate the end of the list.)

Deducing the location of missing end-tags is not difficult for HTML Web browsers because they always deal with the same limited set of element types and assumptions. SGML software must calculate a new set of assumptions each time it comes across a new set of element types and element ordering rules, and writing software to do this is no trivial task.

SGML also offers many markup abbreviation techniques that may not be widely used but must still be supported by SGML applications. SGML's designers included these features to reduce the amount of typing required when entering SGML markup into text editing programs. Tag omission is one such technique; others have been forgotten or never learned by those SGML users who create SGML documents using editing tools that automate much of this markup entry for them.

For example, with the right setup of your SGML environment, entering an ingredient start-tag as <ingredient/ lets you enter its end-tag as a simple slash. Instead of marking up the word "carrots" as

`<ingredient>carrots</ingredient>` you could just enter `<ingredient/carrots/`. People rarely need such a trick when using an SGML editing program that lets you pick "ingredient" from an element type menu and then enters the complete `ingredient` start- and end-tag for you. You only need to type the element's content: the word "carrot".

An SGML Web browser needs one more thing, a requirement unrelated to the SGML standard: instructions for displaying the various elements. Any HTML browser knows that `h2` is a second level heading, and should look similar to a first level heading but a little smaller, and that text between `b` tags should be bolded and text between `i` tags should be italicized.

When an SGML browser receives a document using a customized set of element types called `recipe`, `ingredient`, `totpreptime`, and `step`, how does it know the font to use for each of these? Which elements does the browser display on their own line, and which get displayed on the same line as their parent element? If any elements are hypertext links, how does the browser know this, and where does it look for information about their link destinations?

All this information must be supplied as a stylesheet. There was no real standard for stylesheet syntax until ten years after SGML became a standard, and when DSSSL (the Document Style Semantics and Specification Language) did come along, it was powerful enough to present many of its own intimidating requirements to developers who wanted to create software for it.

For an SGML browser to be prepared for all of this, it had to be a large, complex program. Gloomy as this sounds, some SGML Web browsers were developed. They each had a unique syntax for specifying document appearance, they were often difficult to set up and use, and any free versions had limited features and availability. (After all the work that went into developing them, asking their developers to give away the product of this labor would be a bit much.)

The Solution: XML

To summarize (and perhaps oversimplify), full SGML was too much for what many needed, and HTML wasn't enough. Some tried to remedy the latter by adding features to HTML such as new tags, embedded programming languages to manipulate data, and new ways to specify element appearance. All these expanded the range of an HTML Web page's possibilities; unfortunately, the lack of coordination of these efforts and their accumulation on a foundation that was unprepared for so much all added up to a mess.

If full SGML was too much, and HTML wasn't enough, and adding on to HTML didn't work well, how about a version of SGML that stripped away the fancier, little-used parts to leave something easier to implement? In 1986, SGML offered many, many features to account for the wide variety of directions that publishing technologies might take and to accommodate the specialized needs of users with enormous document collections. Ten years later, the World Wide Web had emerged as a unique user environment, well-defined enough to make it easier to decide which SGML features were superfluous to its needs.

In the summer of 1996, Jon Bosak of Sun Microsystems recruited a group of SGML experts and formed the XML Working Group. Working under the auspices of the W3C (with Dan Connolly, a key figure in HTML's early history, serving as the Working Group's contact with the W3C), they hammered out a version of SGML that was simpler to implement, especially for delivering documents over the Web.

In the course of numerous meetings, conference calls, and over three megabytes of e-mailed discussion and proposals among the Working Group and the XML Special Interest Group (an advisory body of SGML experts) they managed to put together release 0.01 of the specification's initial working draft by November of that year. They told the world about it at the SGML '96 conference in Boston, the largest group of SGML people ever assembled up to that time.

XML's customization of SGML had several important properties:

- It made specific choices of syntax characters which must be used in all documents. For example, all XML tags must begin with the less-than (<) character and end with the greater-than (>) character, and all entity references must begin with an ampersand (&) and end with a semicolon (;).

- Empty XML elements can either have a normal start- and end-tag with no content between them or an empty-element tag, which looks like a start-tag with a slash character just before the closing bracket, like this:

```
<img src="largeglass.jpg"/>
```

- Tag omission is not optional.

- The Document Type Definition (DTD) that spells out the structure of a particular class of SGML documents need not be present, or even identified. Because no tags or attribute names can be omitted from an XML document, applications can accomplish plenty with a document that has no DTD. (They can do even more using the DTD, which plays an important role in the more powerful XML applications.)

These simplifications mean less work for programs that have to parse (that is, determine the structure of) XML documents, which means that software should be much easier to develop.

Although XML is essentially a stripped-down version of SGML, and an understanding of full SGML provides interesting perspectives on XML's heritage, no knowledge of full SGML is required to use XML. The XML specification (far, far briefer than the SGML specification) stands on its own as a self-contained document. Along with the XLink, XPointer, and XSL specifications, it provides you with the power to create rich, valuable documents that will someday make

HTML Web pages look like primitive early attempts at Internet publishing.

XML, XLink, XPointer, and XSL

We've seen that XML provides a way to define your own structure for documents, and we've seen the advantage of keeping structure and presentation information separate. Pushing presentation out of the picture gives us more flexible and therefore more valuable documents, but what happens when we want to present our documents? If XML is supposed to provide a superior alternative to HTML, it better look as least as good as HTML looks with Cascading Style Sheets. The documents should let you *do* more with them, too, if XML is more sophisticated than HTML.

This is where XLink, XPointer, and XSL come in. The Extensible Linking Language (XLink) does much more than define ways to offer hypertext links—it provides a mechanism for defining relationships between elements and offers multiple ways to represent those relationships. Underlined text that jumps you to some point in the current document or another document, the way HTML's anchor (a) element does, is only one way to represent such a relationship. Its companion, the XML Pointer Language (XPointer) provides ways to point to specific elements, character strings, or even individual characters of an XML document, even if that target has nothing identifying it as part of a link.

The Extensible Stylesheet Language (XSL) lets you define the appearance of your XML elements: fonts, text size, bolding, italicizing, line spacing, and other aspects of a document's visual design. It goes beyond this (and Cascading Style Sheets) by offering a scripting language that allows you to rearrange document content and to conditionally execute instructions based on evaluation of the document's data, structure, or other properties—for example, to format a report one way if the `report` element's `stage` attribute has a value of "draft" and another way if it is "final".

XML, Hypertext, XLink, and XPointer

Hypertext has a long, distinguished history of investigation into different ways to represent and follow relationships among electronic document content. HTML implemented a simple way to indicate that a word or phrase was related to either another element in the same document, an element in a different document, or to an entire separate document: you enclose the word or phrase with start- and end-tags for the a element and use this element type's `href` attribute to indicate where to jump when the user clicks the tagged text.

For example, the code in Example 11 tells an HTML Web browser to display the phrase "World Wide Web Consortium" differently from the other text and to jump to the W3C's home page when that text is clicked.

Example 11: Coding an HTML hypertext link

```
The <a href="http://www.w3c.org">World Wide Web
Consortium</a> was founded in 1994.
```

Six years after SGML became a standard, the Hypermedia/Time-based Structuring Language, or "HyTime", became an ISO standard: ISO/IEC 10744. As a hypermedia structuring language, it offers ways to define relationships (whether implemented as links or not) between components of document content. As a time-based structuring language, it lets you describe relationships between more than just elements of text and static pictures; you can specify a link between the fourth second of an audio clip and a particular point on an image ten seconds into a video clip. HyTime was designed as a set of standardized constructs for using SGML to represent hypermedia and multimedia information.

Like SGML, HyTime gained a reputation for being powerful but difficult to implement; the many features in its broad scope have given the XML Working Group a lot of good ideas about ways to represent relationships between elements. They were also influenced by the Text Encoding Initiative (TEI), an international organization developing a set of standards for representing classic works of literature for scholarly study (in particular, developing DTDs for the SGML markup of this literature).

The TEI's concept of extended pointers provided the XML Working group with the model for the XML Pointer Language, or XPointer. XPointer offers ways to define link targets that are much more flexible than HTML's a href links, and the TEI's use and refinement of extended pointers over several years gave XPointer the advantage of being based on a practical reality instead of mere theory.

XLink describes syntax for defining relationships between objects, or the "participating resources" of a link. According to the XLink specification, XLink "uses XML syntax to create structures that can describe the simple unidirectional hyperlinks of today's HTML as well as more sophisticated multi-ended and typed links". More sophisticated links allow greater descriptive possibilities for describing a linking element and its anchor resources than the HTML anchor (a) element offers when describing a link's source and target.

More information in a linking element means that a processing application can determine an appropriate way to represent it. A link resource might be implemented as:

- A pop-up window.

- Highlighted text in a secondary "References" browser window.

- An e-mail message to your mailbox.

- One of the HTML ways: by replacing a linking element that is also a participating resource with another resource—either a document or an a element with a `name` attribute.

XLink takes from HyTime the ability to describe different links by their purpose (for example, a footnote reference, a citation, or a glossary reference) and to then keep the implementation details of each link type separate from its meaning, much as XML and SGML keep an element's purpose separate from its presentation details.

As a companion to XLink's greater flexibility in describing the nature of a link, XPointer offers many powerful new capabilities to describe participating link resources such as link targets. (Well, they're new to the HTML user—researchers involved in serious hypertext have known about them for a while.)

While an HTML a `href` element links either to an entire document or to a specific a element with a `name` attribute specified, XPointer offers ways to point at anything you want in a target document without requiring the target document to have predefined link anchor elements. XPointer offers syntax that lets you say "link to the third bulleted item in the second bulleted list in the fourth chapter", or even to the third letter in that bulleted item. Instead of forcing you to link to either an entire document or to a single element in that document, you can specify two points anywhere within a target document as the beginning and end of a link resource. This lets you link to a particular quotation, description, single word, or any range of text you like.

XLink's extended links (not to be confused with the TEI extended pointers that influenced the XPointer language) let you link one piece of information to several others. Such links might pop up a list of the choices, or send you to all the resources in some order of your choosing, or let you search the set of participating resources for something—the possibilities are up to the imaginations of developers creating XML applications.

Once browsers are available that support these new ways of linking information, XLink's features will provide many of the most exciting aspects of XML systems. Why? Because while XML and XSL offer sensible ways to do things that proprietary publishing systems have already done for years, XLink gives us ways to do entirely new things, creating Web pages that are a huge step beyond HTML's capabilities.

XML, Stylesheets, Scripting, and XSL

The Extensible Stylesheet Language (XSL) lets you define the visual appearance of the elements in your XML documents. Formatting may be based, among other criteria, on

- An element's position: for example, assigning one style to the first element of a bulleted list and a different style to the list's remaining elements.

- An element's ancestors: for example, assigning one style to a `title` element inside of a `chapter` element and another to a `title` in a `section` element.

- An element's attribute values: for example, assigning one style if an element's `status` attribute has a value of "overdue" and another if it equals "pending".

It also provides for generated text, the use of a scripting language for more sophisticated tasks, the definition of reusable macros, and many other powerful features.

XSL is also based on a standard designed to work in conjunction with SGML: the Document Style Semantics and Specification Language, or DSSSL. DSSSL (another ISO standard—ISO/IEC 10179), defines processing of SGML documents. By "processing", this certainly means the specification of fonts, type sizes, text spacing and colors, but it also means any useful manipulation of SGML documents.

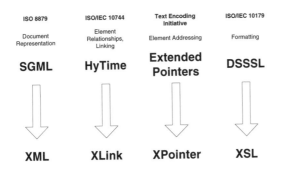

Figure 5 Standards on which XML and its family are based.

DSSSL, like HyTime, is considered too much to implement in a browser receiving documents over the Web. Early efforts to create a simpler version called "DSSSL-O" (for "DSSSL-online") involved several of the same people working on XML, and DSSSL-O evolved into XSL.

At first glance, XSL doesn't at all resemble DSSSL, whose roots in the Scheme and LISP programming languages mean that it groups related programming structures by using lots and lots of parentheses. XSL looks like XML, in accordance with its second design goal: "XSL should be expressed in XML syntax".

The fifth design goal is that "XSL will be a subset of DSSSL with the proposed amendment" (that is, once the DSSSL specification is amended to make it a proper superset of XSL). Although XSL and DSSSL look different, they're semantically similar enough that one of the first pieces of XSL software available was Henry Thompson's xslj program, which converts an XSL stylesheet to a DSSSL specification.

While XSL addresses many of the same problems as Cascading Style Sheets, it doesn't compete with CSS, a W3C standard you can use with XML documents as well as with HTML documents. XSL design goal six states that "A mechanical mapping of a CSS stylesheet into an XSL stylesheet should be possible". In other words, programs that convert a CSS stylesheet to an XSL one should be easy to write.

Why convert a CSS stylesheet to XSL? CSS stylesheets can do quick formatting with very little code and often make an ideal starting point for formatting a particular class of documents for Web delivery. However, as an online publishing system grows more complex, a developer trying to squeeze too much out of CSS will eventually hit a wall. For example, CSS offers no way to reorder elements, an essential capability when creating customized publications from subsets of a large document collection.

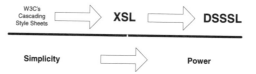

Figure 6 XSL's relationship to other formatting languages. When necessary, converting a stylesheet from CSS to XSL to DSSSL is mechanical enough that simple utilities can do it for you.

Converting an XSL stylesheet to a CSS one isn't so easy, because XSL can do so much more than CSS. In addition to macros and element reordering it offers ECMAScript, a nonproprietary specification of Netscape's JavaScript programming language developed by the European Computer Manufacturer's Association. ECMAScript is the key to going beyond the specification of element appearance to real application development, because it lets you evaluate document content and then conditionally execute different script instructions based on the results.

The Annotations

The W3C's Web site (http://www.w3.org) has special sections that are only accessible to members and invited experts taking part in W3C work. However, the Notes, Working Drafts, Proposed Recommendations, and Recommendations are available for the world to see and read at `http://www.w3.org/TR`. This includes the XML specification, so why publish a book of them?

Design goal 8 of the XML specification (1.1, "Origin and Goals") tells us that "the design of XML shall be formal and concise". *Webster's New World College Dictionary* has over ten definitions of "formal" as an adjective; the most common uses of the word are defined by definitions 4b ("stiff in manner; not warm or relaxed") and 5a ("designed for use or wear at ceremonies, elaborate parties, etc. [formal dress]"). XML design goal 8 uses the word in the sense of Webster's definition 8, a less commonly used meaning: "done or made according to the forms that make explicit, definite, valid. etc. [a formal contract]".

Specifying XML according to forms that make it explicit and definite mean using the concise language of computer science, which often means using well-known English words in a sense very different from their commonly understood meanings. "Formal" is one example; others include "grammar", "production", "token", "deterministic", and "terminal". Someone with a computer science background knows that "production" is unrelated to show business and that "terminal" doesn't describe a place where one can use public transportation, or even a keyboard and monitor hooked up to a computer somewhere. They'll also understand terms such as "nonterminal", "big-endian", and "Extended Backus-Naur Form", which mean little outside of the world of computer science.

Why doesn't the specification explain these terms? Because of the other part of design goal 8: the specification should be concise. The background and definitions necessary to understand these terms are out there, available for looking up. That's still a lot of work to ask of your average Web page designer who's interested in new technology but lacks a computer science degree. The goal of this book is to save that designer all that work by adding all the necessary explanations to the specs themselves.

But this book adds more than that: in addition to background on the "what", this book explains the "why" of much of the XML specification. After the XML Working Group debated a point and then decided how XML would handle a certain issue, they just laid it out in the spec: "here's how to do this part". They didn't need to justify themselves, explaining the alternatives they considered and the relative merits and deficiencies of each approach; they wanted to be concise, and we trust that this group of some of the most expert people in the SGML world carefully reasoned out their decisions.

Well, sure, trust is great, but besides satisfying our curiosity, knowing the "why" of various decisions helps us to better understand XML's strengths. If SGML offered four ways to accomplish some task and the XML Working Group picked one and threw out the other three, knowing the reasoning that led to this decision helps you to make better use of that feature of XML.

To learn this reasoning, I read through many megabytes of the debates and discussions that led to the XML specification. It was a tremendous learning experience for me and I've done my best to assure that what I learned is reflected in this book's annotations.

A Note on the Punctuation

I chose to show commas and periods outside of quotation marks, according to the British style, "like this", instead of putting them inside as is usually done in American publishing, "like this." The main reason was to stay consistent with the style used in the specification itself. The British style makes more sense anyway when writing about computers and software; if I use the American style to tell you that your password is "swordfish," it is ambiguous whether the comma is part of the password. If I use the British style to tell you that it's "swordfish", it's much clearer exactly which characters make up your password.

In keeping with this theme of American work in a British style, most example text that I didn't make up myself is from T.S. Eliot's "The Waste Land", a work whose recent seventy-fifth birthday has put it into the public domain.

Specification
Preface

In this book, official W3C XML specification material is shown in a sans-serif font with a gray background. For example, in the gray boxes beginning on page 36, the headers "This version", "Latest version", "Previous version", "Editors", and "Abstract" are headers in the official specification.

The paragraph after the "Abstract" header that begins "The Extensible Markup Language (XML) is a subset of SGML…" is typical of specification body text. Text representing file names, XML keywords, element type names, and Web addresses (like those under the headings "This version", "Latest version", and "Previous version") are shown in a typewriter font to distinguish them, but most body text is in a sans-serif font.

My annotations that are not part of the specification use a serif font for their body text (as in this paragraph).

Tip   Note that the specification itself is copyrighted by the World Wide Web Consortium; see the Supplementary Annotations appendix of this book for their full "Document Notice" detailing the copyright conditions. The annotations, however, are a separately copyrighted part of this book and may not be reproduced without permission of the publisher, Prentice Hall PTR.

REC-xml-19980210

Extensible Markup Language (XML) 1.0

W3C Recommendation 10-February-1998

This version

```
http://www.w3.org/TR/1998/REC-xml-19980210
http://www.w3.org/TR/1998/REC-xml-19980210.xml
http://www.w3.org/TR/1998/REC-xml-19980210.html
http://www.w3.org/TR/1998/REC-xml-19980210.pdf
http://www.w3.org/TR/1998/REC-xml-19980210.ps
```

In the Web version of the specification, the URLs above are links to copies of the specs in other formats, including Acrobat (pdf) and PostScript (ps).

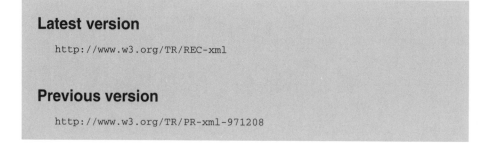

Latest version

```
http://www.w3.org/TR/REC-xml
```

Previous version

```
http://www.w3.org/TR/PR-xml-971208
```

Each version has a link to one or more preceding versions. Tracing the evolution of certain parts of the spec can make it easier to understand how they arrived at their final form.

Editors

Tim Bray, Textuality and Netscape *(tbray@textuality.com)*
Jean Paoli, Microsoft *(jeanpa@microsoft.com)*
C. M. Sperberg-McQueen, University of Illinois at Chicago
(cmsmcq@uic.edu)

Abstract

The Extensible Markup Language (XML) is a subset of SGML that is completely described in this document. Its goal is to enable generic SGML to be served, received, and processed on the Web in the way that is now possible with HTML. XML has been designed for ease of implementation and for interoperability with both SGML and HTML.

As a simplified version of SGML, XML leaves out many of SGML's optional features; as a subset of it, all XML documents still qualify as SGML documents. Because it's "completely described" in this specification, everything about XML syntax that you need to know to create conforming XML documents (or, if you're more ambitious, software that can parse conforming XML documents) is all here.

Since HTML is an SGML application, one could say that SGML has been delivered over the Web before, so the spec's abstract uses the term "generic SGML" to show what XML offers that nothing has before. The Merriam Webster dictionary's third definition of "generic" elaborates on this nicely: "having no particularly distinctive quality or application". HTML is an application, or a particular flavor of SGML; XML, although a subset of SGML, is not a specific application, and lets you create your own document types and applications the same way SGML does.

While people use XML for purposes ranging from permanent storage of archival documents to passing a few numbers between two programs, the goal that inspired XML's creation was the delivery of "generic" documents over the Web the same way that Web servers send HTML documents.

Tip   Keep this "ease of Web delivery" design goal in mind when putting XML to some other use—XML is well-suited to many tasks, but some applications, such as archival storage, have many requirements not addressed by a system designed to ease quick document delivery.

"Ease of implementation" was important for encouraging the development of XML software. The specification's authors wanted to help software vendors make XML tools available quickly, but more importantly, they wanted to encourage XML software development by people who are not professional programmers. This lets publishing professionals, entrepreneurs excited about the new opportunities available, hobbyists, and academics from outside of computer science create their own tools instead of waiting for software companies to do it for them.

Being compatible with SGML also speeds tool availability, because software companies who already offer SGML tools can create versions that accommodate this simpler dialect of SGML more quickly. Interoperability with HTML was a selling point for end-users: instead of being an alternative to HTML, this positions XML as an upgrade path that does everything that HTML users are used to and more.

Status of this document

This document has been reviewed by W3C Members and other interested parties and has been endorsed by the Director as a W3C Recommendation. It is a stable document and may be used as reference material or cited as a normative reference from another document. W3C's role in making the Recommendation is to draw attention to the specification and to promote its widespread deployment. This enhances the functionality and interoperability of the Web.

This document specifies a syntax created by subsetting an existing, widely used international text processing standard (Standard Generalized Markup Language, ISO 8879:1986(E) as amended and corrected) for use on the World Wide Web. It is a product of the W3C XML Activity, details of which can be found at `http://www.w3.org/XML`. A list of current W3C Recommendations and other technical documents can be found at `http://www.w3.org/TR`.

A Recommendation is the highest level that a W3C specification can reach. (For more on the W3C and the road to achieving Recommendation status, see the section "Becoming a W3C Recommendation" on page 291.) Before reaching this point on February 10, 1998, there was enough buzz about XML that people started writing books and software based on the evolving working draft of the specification, possibly without realizing that the XML Working Group was still working on it. (With titles like "Working Draft" and "Working Group", this should have been obvious.) All of the Recommendations, Proposed Recommendations, Working Drafts, and Notes available from the `http://www.w3.org/TR` Web address listed by the spec have this "Status of this document" section to make their roles clear.

SGML and its relationship to XML are described further in "HTML, SGML, and XML: History and Influences" on page 3. The ISO (International Organization for Standardization)[†] creates stan-

---

[†] ISO isn't an acronym, but a coinage derived from the Greek "isos", for "equal".

dards for everything from the aluminum used in aerospace construction (ISO 8591-1) to computer languages.

SGML is ISO standard 8879, formally approved in 1986. The phrase "as amended and corrected" is technically unnecessary; however, it emphasizes XML's dependence on revisions made in 1988 and 1998.

> This specification uses the term URI, which is defined by [Berners-Lee et al.], a work in progress expected to update [IETF RFC1738] and [IETF RFC1808].

(Terms in square braces refer to bibliography entries.) "URI" stands for "Uniform Resource Identifier", the system for naming resources on the Web. This includes URLs (Uniform Resource Locators, or Web addresses such as `http://www.w3.org`) and more. The group that develops and propagates Internet standards for URIs and URLs is the Internet Engineering Task Force, or IETF; their specifications are published as part of their "Request for Comment" (RFC) document collection on Internet issues that they have accumulated since 1969.

IETF RFC 1738, written in 1994 by Larry Masinter of Xerox and Tim Berners-Lee of the European Laboratory for Particle Physics (CERN) in Geneva, Switzerland, specifies how URLs work. That includes, for example, the role of each part of a URL, and why starting one with `http://` or `ftp://` is OK but `xxx://` is not.

IETF RFC 1808 by Roy Fielding of the University of California lays down the ground rules for using Relative Uniform Resource Locators, or partial URLs whose missing pieces must be inferred from the last complete one read. (For example, if you're reading `http://www.snee.com/pubs/toc.html` and link to the partial URL `cheese.html`, this RFC's rules tell the server to look for `http://www.snee.com/pubs/cheese.html`.)

As of XML 1.0's publication, Berners-Lee, Masinter, and Fielding were working on a new specification that would combine RFCs 1738 and 1808 to define URIs as something broader than URLs. This is important for XML documents, which must often refer to other resources on the Web such as images, DTDs, XSL stylesheets, or any of the wide range of link destinations made possible by the XPointer specification. While earlier drafts of the XML specification used the term "URL" exclusively, the Proposed Recommendation and final Recommendation versions use the new term to take advantage of the wider possibilities defined by Berners-Lee and his co-authors as they work out a new system.

See 4.2.2, "External Entities", which includes more on the use of URIs.

> The list of known errors in this specification is available at `http://www.w3.org/XML/xml-19980210-errata.`
>
> Please report errors in this document to `xml-editor@w3.org.`

The error list was available as soon as the spec was, starting off with "None yet" as its single entry.

The specification is divided up into six main sections, which each have their own chapter in this book:

- Chapter 1, "Introduction", lists the design goals that were laid out before the spec's development and clarifies potentially confusing terminology used in the spec's language.

- Chapter 2, "Documents", describes issues that apply to an XML document as a unit. It also covers the smallest possible units that can be combined to eventually form a document: the characters that a document can use, what we mean by "space", and various declarations and constructs such as comments and processing instructions that don't take an active part in defining a document's logical or physical structure.

- Chapter 3, "Logical Structures", describes the markup used to indicate the kinds of information stored in a document. For example, to describe a book as being composed of a title followed by chapters, with each chapter being a title followed by paragraphs with optional illustrations, is to describe the "book" document type's logical structure.

- Chapter 4, "Physical Structures", covers issues related to a document's relationship with the system on which it resides. If the host operating system stores groups of information in files, the markup for a document's physical structure will identify the files and their location. If certain files are encoded for non-Western alphabets, markup must be included to identify the encoding. Markup for defining a document's physical structure also lets you identify pieces of documents for re-use in defining a document's content and physical and logical structure.

- Chapter 5, "Conformance", lays down the law about what constitutes a legal, working XML document. Because the specification's distinction between well-formed and valid documents may cause confusion, this section spells out their relationship.

- Chapter 6, "Notation", gives a little background on the formal notation used in the specification's productions.

The XML specification has more appendixes than main sections:

- Appendix A, "References" is a bibliography of specs and computer science works that inform many of the decisions made in developing the XML spec.

- Appendix B, "Character Classes" lists the codes for all the alphabetic and ideographic characters considered to be letters, numbers, punctuation, and so forth. When you get away from your own alphabet, it's an imposing problem.

■ Appendix C, "XML and SGML (Non-Normative)" tells where to find a precise definition of XML's restrictions in terms of full SGML.

■ Appendix D, "Expansion of Entity and Character References (Non-Normative)" steps through two complex examples to show how an XML processor approaches a combination of different categories of entity references.

■ Appendix E, "Deterministic Content Models (Non-Normative)" gives a little background on the concept of deterministic content models.

■ Appendix F, "Autodetection of Character Encodings (Non-Normative)" explains in detail how an XML processor should go about determining an external entity's encoding.

■ Appendix G, "W3C XML Working Group (Non-Normative)" lists the members of the XML Working Group and their affiliations.

Introduction

This chapter lists the design goals that were laid out before the spec's development and clarifies potentially confusing terminology used in the spec's language.

Extensible Markup Language, abbreviated XML, describes a class of data objects called XML documents and partially describes the behavior of computer programs which process them. XML is an application profile or restricted form of SGML, the Standard Generalized Markup Language [ISO 8879]. By construction, XML documents are conforming SGML documents.

Since the nineteen-eighties, object-oriented approaches to software engineering have contributed much to data modeling and system development. New tools and design techniques have provided ways to represent both real-world objects and abstract concepts as software objects instead of as tables of rows and columns, which is how relational databases and their predecessors since the nineteen-sixties have stored inventory records, personnel records, and everything else.

45

XML documents are a class, or family, of data objects. While "document" may have once referred to one or more pieces of paper with an organized set of information on that paper, computers have broadened our concept of the term, and XML may broaden it further. Although the XML specification doesn't actually define "document", we see here that "XML documents are conforming SGML documents", and the SGML definition of the term seems fitting: "a collection of information that is processed as a unit" (ISO 8879 4.96).

 ***Tip*** *The collection is processed as a logical unit, but not necessarily stored as a physical unit; storage arrangements depend on a document's entity structure.*

XML describes this class of data objects "and partially describes the behavior of computer programs which process them". The parts of the behavior described are the responsibilities of a parser: what it looks for, when it should report an error and keep going, and what kinds of errors are bad enough to give up on a document. The spec doesn't completely describe what the program does after it successfully reads in an XML document; this is left up to the imagination of the application developer.

An application profile of SGML is, as it says, a restricted form of it: SGML with certain limitations chosen to suit a particular class of applications. The last sentence of the above specification paragraph has proven too easy to forget by some people, as they attempt to compare XML with SGML or discuss XML's potential for replacing SGML: XML *is* SGML.

> XML documents are made up of storage units called entities, which contain either parsed or unparsed data. Parsed data is made up of characters, some of which form character data, and some of which form markup. Markup encodes a description of the document's storage layout and logical structure. XML provides a mechanism to impose constraints on the storage layout and logical structure.

Entities are defined in Chapter 4, "Physical Structures", as "storage units". This is often a file (an external entity) or a character string delimited by quotes and included as part of the entity's declaration (an internal entity). The specification uses the term "external entity" instead of "file" for two reasons:

- Some existing operating systems (for example, OS/400 and MVS) and undoubtedly many future ones use a term other than "file" to describe a single stored collection of information.

- Some publishing systems may generate document components on the fly, or extract pieces of them from a database or archiving system, or get them from some other source besides a collection of information sitting as a unit on a disk. XML can still treat these components as entities, even though they don't exist as files or the host operating system's equivalent.

Parsed data is not data that has been parsed, but data for the XML processor (defined in the specification's next paragraph) to parse. Earlier drafts of the spec, instead of of the terms "parsed" and "unparsed", used the terms "text" and "binary" to distinguish between entities that contained marked-up XML data and those that stored non-XML data such as picture or audio files. Non-XML entities aren't always binary, however; an RTF file exported from a word processor and a LaTeX file (a format popular with mathematicians and scientists) are not binary files, but an XML processor shouldn't look for XML markup in them. Because of this potential confusion, the spec now uses the term "parsed" for entities to be parsed as XML text and "unparsed" for non-XML data.

Character data is the actual information content of your document, while markup is the tags, entity references, and other delimited text that identifies the structure and other properties of your document. In the snee element shown in Example 1.1, "Unshaven, with a pocketful of currants" is the character data and everything else is markup.

Example 1.1: XML element with character data content

```
<snee line="210">Unshaven, with a pocketful of currants</snee>
```

Chapter 2, "Documents", compares the concepts of storage layout, or "physical structure", and "logical structure". The third sentence in the specification paragraph above tells us that "XML provides a mechanism to impose constraints on the storage layout and logical structure" of a document. When these constraints are imposed, and the document is stored in a form that can be read by a processing program, application developers can devote their energy to writing programs that use that document's information instead of programs that perform all kinds of checks to make sure that the information is stored in the appropriate format.

As a "mechanism to impose constraints" on logical and physical structures, XML provides a way to define rules, called a "DTD", to ensure consistency for a particular class of documents. For example, a DTD for a "cookbook" document type might specify that a recipe must have a title followed by a list of ingredients and then the preparation steps. Authors who are writing recipes using XML-compliant software with that DTD can't put the first step in preparation right after the title—they must put the list of ingredients there.

A software module called an *XML processor* is used to read XML documents and provide access to their content and structure. It is assumed that an XML processor is doing its work on behalf of another module, called the *application*. This specification describes the required behavior of an XML processor in terms of how it must read XML data and the information it must provide to the application.

Tip *A term in the specification shown in italic text, like "XML processor" above, is defined at that point.*

To someone running an XML application, the XML processor and application are probably all the same program. If you're developing such a program, however, this separation makes life easier, because you can select one of the XML processors out there to do the mundane tasks of parsing out the pieces of an XML entity and reading them into the appropriate data structures. You can then concentrate your energy on the interesting part of application development: what you do with that data. The last sentence of that specification paragraph shows why the spec is so important to developers, because it spells out what they can expect from the XML processor as they build applications that work with it.

1.1. Origin and Goals

XML was developed by an XML Working Group (originally known as the SGML Editorial Review Board) formed under the auspices of the World Wide Web Consortium (W3C) in 1996. It was chaired by Jon Bosak of Sun Microsystems with the active participation of an XML Special Interest Group (previously known as the SGML Working Group) also organized by the W3C. The membership of the XML Working Group is given in an appendix. Dan Connolly served as the WG's contact with the W3C.

The "HTML, SGML, and XML: History and Influences" section of this book's "Annotation Introduction" chapter gives more detail on how the XML specification was developed.

Design goals play an important role as a starting point in any specification, because as various potential features and implementation restrictions are hammered out the design goals provide an anchor that helps participants get back on track when necessary. For example, when debate over a particular XML issue came down to a classic software development choice, like the relative merits of something that is easy to write versus something that is easy for programs to process, the fourth design goal made it easier to prioritize these issues and move on.

The design goals for XML are:

1. XML shall be straightforwardly usable over the Internet.
2. XML shall support a wide variety of applications.

The first design goal sets the priority here, but the second keeps the first from being too limiting. Since XML's conception, everyone looked forward to browsers that would let them view nicely-formatted XML documents the same way they view HTML documents. However, long before XML-capable browsers existed XML was making the news for other kinds of applications in electronic commerce, software distribution, and other areas. There, just the sheer ability to distribute structured information was important enough in its own right to make the presentation of the data irrelevant.

> **3. XML shall be compatible with SGML.**

This goal was achieved with the cooperation of the ISO's SGML committee, who are currently revising the SGML standard. They adjusted the revision schedule to prioritize XML's needs.

Accomplishing this goal had two important benefits:

- It speeded the development of the first set of XML tools by making it easier for those with existing SGML tools to adapt them to XML.

- It made it clear that XML is a special-purpose version of SGML (an "application profile") intended for a specialized—though very large—market, and not a competitor.[†]

> **4. It shall be easy to write programs which process XML documents.**

For any new technology to hold its own, its strategy must provide for easy software development from the beginning. When this technology comes from a software company, it must provide developers with tools to quickly take advantage; if the origin is a non-profit consortium, they must do whatever they can throughout the specification to make software development easier. As we'll see, most of XML's remaining design goals each contribute in their own way to this one.

---

† Several SGML applications actually have document collections larger than the Web.

> 5. The number of optional features in XML is to be kept to the absolute minimum, ideally zero.

Minimizing the number of optional features helps software development because it gives developers a more focused target. It also makes education in the new technology easier by reducing (and hopefully eliminating) the category of "there's some other stuff you can do that people use sometimes" features.

One disadvantage of excess optional features is that some may fall into disuse and may not be supported everywhere they should, blurring the distinctions of what (in practice, as opposed to in fact) is part of that technology. Documents intended for transmission exacerbate the problem, because the use of arcane optional features by a document's sender increases the likelihood that the receiver won't completely understand the document.

> 6. XML documents should be human-legible and reasonably clear.

This prevents a complete dependence on specialized tools to create and use XML documents. If people can read and edit XML documents using text editors that are unaware of XML, there are several important advantages:

- It lets developers who create the first generation of XML tools use existing text-based tools to get started.

- It makes it easier to teach and understand the markup of an XML document.

- It makes it possible to create a valid XML document by hand with no specialized tools.

For example, compare the sample XML document shown in Example 1.2 with its equivalent in RTF (Example 1.3), a text format devel-

oped by Microsoft in the hope of making formatted documents more
portable.

Example 1.2: XML version of Example 1.3's RTF document

```
<?xml version='1.0'?>
<chapter>
  <title>A Sample Document</title>
  <para>Here is a bulleted list:</para>
  <itemizedlist>
    <listitem>
      <para>The list's first item.</para>
    </listitem>
    <listitem>
      <para>The list's second and final item.</para>
    </listitem>
  </itemizedlist>
  <para>This concludes our test.</para>
</chapter>
```

Example 1.3: RTF version of Example 1.2's XML document

```
{\rtf1\ansi\deff0 {\fonttbl{\f1\fnil\fcharset0 Arial;}
{\f0\fnil\fcharset0 Times New Roman;} }{\colortbl;}
{\stylesheet{\s1 Heading 1;}{\s2 Heading 2;}{\s3 Heading 3;}
{\s4 Heading 4;}{\s5 Heading 5;}{\s6 Heading 6;}
{\s7 Heading 7;}{\s8 Heading 8;}{\s9 Heading 9;}}
\deflang1024\notabind\facingp\hyphauto1\widowctrl
\sectd\plain\pgwsxn12240\pghsxn15840\marglsxn720
\margrsxn1440\margtsxn1440\margbsxn1440\headery0\footery0
\pgndec\titlepg{\headerf\pard\sl-240\sb530\sa670\plain
\tqc\tx5040\tqr\tx10080 \tab \tab \par}{\footerf\pard\sl-240
\sb530\sa670\plain\tqc\tx5040\tqr\tx10080 \tab \tab \i\fs20
\chpgn \par}{\header1\pard\sl-240\sb530\sa670\plain\tqc
\tx5040\tqr\tx10080 \tab \tab \i\fs20\f1 A Sample Document
\par}{\footer1\pard\sl-240\sb530\sa670\plain\tqc\tx5040\tqr
\tx10080 \tab \tab \i\fs20 \chpgn \par}{\headerr\pard\sl-240
\sb530\sa670\plain\tqc\tx5040\tqr\tx10080 \tab \tab \i\fs20
\f1 A Sample Document\par}{\footerr\pard\sl-240\sb530\sa670
\plain\tqc\tx5040\tqr\tx10080 \tab \tab \i\fs20 \chpgn \par}
\pard\sb311\sl-456 \b\fs41\f1 A Sample Document\keepn
\hyphpar0\par\pard\li960\sl-240 \b0\fs20\f0 \hyphpar0\par
\pard\sb207\li960\sl-220 \f1 Here is a bulleted list:
\hyphpar0 \par\pard\sb100\li1160\sl-220\fi-200 \tx1160
```

```
\fs16 \'95\tab \fs20 The list's first item.\hyphpar0\par
\pard \sb100\li1160\sl-220\fi-200 \tx1160 \fs16 \'95\tab
\fs20 The list's second and final item.\hyphpar0\par\pard
\sb100 \li960\sl-220 This concludes our test.\hyphpar0\par}
```

(Keep in mind that I added many carriage-returns to force some of the RTF lines to fit on this page—before I did that, it was even more illegible.)

Some complain that XML markup makes documents difficult to read, but for those who have wrestled with RTF, documents with XML markup are a vast improvement. Also, while "human-legible" implies "you don't need a special program to read it", writing software to read something with such a clear layout is much easier than writing code that understands a mess like RTF.

> 7. The XML design should be prepared quickly.

Like the encouragement of software development, this encourages the adoption of the new standard. If a specification's authors keep revising and revising for too long, people tire of waiting and forego it for technology that gives them more immediate gratification.

The Working Group spent less than fifteen months from the first publicly available draft of the XML specification to approval of the final Recommendation version by the W3C. Despite this Herculean effort, many still got impatient waiting for the official 1.0 spec!

> 8. The design of XML shall be formal and concise.

In this book's "Annotation Introduction", the section titled "The Annotations" explains the use of the term "formal" here: the spec uses software engineering language in order to make its meaning absolutely clear to software developers.

Instead of hundreds and hundreds of interdependent rules, the XML Working Group wanted to specify XML with the kind of minimal, straightforward rule set that could be expressed in as few pages as possible. With the Acrobat version of the spec weighing in at 32 pages, it certainly succeeded at this.

> 9. XML documents shall be easy to create.

The reasoning here is pretty obvious: if they're difficult to create, people won't want to create them. People might wait for the tools that do the difficult part, but if documents are difficult to create, it will increase the wait: the programs will be more difficult to create, violating the fourth design goal. Keeping document creation simple makes things easier for everyone.

> 10. Terseness in XML markup is of minimal importance.

Many points of software design debate boil down to comparing the shortest, most compact approach with a more verbose way. The terse approach may mean smaller programs or quicker data transmission times, but it can also make markup more difficult to read by a human or by a program. Design goal 10 tells us that when a point of XML design comes down to such a debate, terseness has a lower priority.

> This specification, together with associated standards (Unicode and ISO/IEC 10646 for characters, Internet RFC 1766 for language identification tags, ISO 639 for language name codes, and ISO 3166 for country name codes), provides all the information necessary to understand XML Version 1.0 and construct computer programs to process it.

ISO/IEC 10646, which specifies the Universal Multiple-Octet Coded Character Set, is described further in 2.2, "Characters". The

IETF's RFC 1766 ("Tags for the Identification of Languages") along with ISO 639 ("Codes for the representation of names of languages") and ISO 3166 ("Codes for the representation of names of countries") are described more in 2.12, "Language Identification" and its annotations. By saying that XML "together with [these] associated standards...provides all the information necessary to understand XML", it tells us that for a complete understanding of XML, you don't need to look anywhere else. For example, while knowing SGML makes it easier to learn XML faster, it is not, unlike these other standards, something you *must* know in order to use XML.

> This version of the XML specification may be distributed freely, as long as all text and legal notices remain intact.

It's OK to make copies of the spec, as long as you copy the whole thing, including the legal notices that provide details on these rights (see the W3C Copyright Notice in the "Supplementary Annotations" appendix of this book.) Requiring that you copy the whole thing prevents people from taking parts of it out of context—for example, to create an "alternative" XML by adding their own ideas to portions of the W3C spec.[†]

1.2. Terminology

The terminology used to describe XML documents is defined in the body of this specification. The terms defined in the following list are used in building those definitions and in describing the actions of an XML processor:

---

† This book was produced with the express permission of the W3C. In keeping with the spirit of this rule, the official spec is carefully distinguished typographically from the other content.

Sometimes a specification looks a lot like a contract, because it spells out obligations and responsibilities. For example, if there's something that XML won't allow, it's not always enough to say "this is forbidden", so the spec often describes how an XML processor must react to a violation of the rule.

As we saw in Chapter 1, "Introduction", the spec "partially describes the behavior of programs which process" XML documents. When software developers know that they can expect certain behavior from a conforming parser, it's easier to build a system around that parser without worrying about the features offered by competing vendors' products, because the spec establishes a baseline that they must all follow.

As the following shows, common words like "may", "must", and "error" have very specific meanings in the specification. By defining even these everyday terms, the spec narrows the possibility of varying interpretations of it, strengthening the very purpose of a specification: giving everyone a common set of rules to work with so that their products work better together.

> **may**
>
> Conforming documents and XML processors are permitted to but need not behave as described.
>
> **must**
>
> Conforming documents and XML processors are required to behave as described; otherwise they are in error.
>
> **error**
>
> A violation of the rules of this specification; results are undefined. Conforming software may detect and report an error and may recover from it.

One example of an error is in 2.8, "Prolog and Document Type Declaration", which tells us that it is an error for a document to have "1.0" in the XML declaration if the document does not conform to this version of the specification.

"Undefined" in the mathematical sense means "if this happens, there's no point in describing the result". For example, division by zero is undefined—if you divide six into zero parts, how big is each part? It doesn't matter, because dividing six into zero parts makes no sense.

Whether the parsing process is in a program completely separate from the application using the parsed data, or in a separate module of the same program, the parser and application parts must communicate if the application is going to do anything useful. "Reporting" of an error refers to a message from the parsing process to the application about what happened.

"May recover" tells us that a program is given the option of either aborting, ideally with a message about the cause of the premature termination, or continuing to run after detecting the error.

fatal error

An error which a conforming XML processor must detect and report to the application. After encountering a fatal error, the processor may continue processing the data to search for further errors and may report such errors to the application. In order to support correction of errors, the processor may make unprocessed data from the document (with intermingled character data and markup) available to the application. Once a fatal error is detected, however, the processor must not continue normal processing (i.e., it must not continue to pass character data and information about the document's logical structure to the application in the normal way).

For example, according to 4.4.4, "Forbidden", if an attribute value has a reference to an external entity (such as an entity stored in a separate file), it's a fatal error. Reporting the error is not optional, as it is with a nonfatal error. Moreover, continuing normal processing of a document with a fatal error is prohibited.

An error report should say more than "something's wrong, sorry". The above specification paragraph tells us that if the parser couldn't process part of the document, it may pass the application the unprocessed part that it choked on and anything else that may "support correction of errors"—for example, the problem area's line number and the text surrounding that line. Unlike the processing of a non-fatal error, however, the processor must not try to finish processing the document in an attempt to work around the error.

> **at user option**
> Conforming software may or must (depending on the modal verb in the sentence) behave as described; if it does, it must provide users a means to enable or disable the behavior described.

By "modal verb", this means "the verb in the specification plus the modal auxiliary 'may' or 'must' used with it". More simply, the sentence means "Conforming software may or must, depending on whether the specification language in question uses the term 'may' or 'must', behave as described". More importantly, it must offer a way to turn off the behavior.

For example, 3.2, "Element Type Declarations", tells us that if an element type declaration's content model refers to a nonexistent element type, the processor may warn the user, but "at user option". This means that the user must have a way to turn these warnings off.

> **validity constraint**
> A rule which applies to all valid XML documents. Violations of validity constraints are errors; they must, at user option, be reported by validating XML processors.

The term "valid" applied to an XML document has a very specific meaning, and a document that isn't valid isn't necessarily worthless the way an invalid C++ program or an invalid PostScript file might be. It may still be well-formed, which makes it useful to many applications.

For a well-formed document to also be considered valid, it must meet a certain set of additional conditions called "validity constraints" that you'll find after many of the specification's productions. See 2.1, "Well-Formed XML Documents", for more on well-formed documents, 2.8, "Prolog and Document Type Declaration", for more on valid documents, and "" in the "Supplementary Annotations" appendix for an introduction to productions.

> **well-formedness constraint**
>
> A rule which applies to all well-formed XML documents. Violations of well-formedness constraints are fatal errors.

These are the rules that a character string must conform to in order to qualify as a well-formed document. Like the validity constraints described above, you'll find these after the relevant productions in the specification. Unlike a document that violates validity constraints, a document that violates a well-formedness constraint is no good to any processing program and is not considered to be an XML document.

> **match**
>
> (Of strings or names:) Two strings or names being compared must be identical. Characters with multiple possible representations in ISO/IEC 10646 (e.g. characters with both precomposed and base+diacritic forms) match only if they have the same representation in both strings. At user option, processors may normalize such characters to some canonical form. No case folding is performed. (Of strings and rules in the grammar:) A string matches a grammatical production if it belongs to the language generated by that production. (Of content and content models:) An element matches its declaration when it conforms in the fashion described in the constraint "Element Valid".

"String" is computer science talk for a sequence of characters. Comparing two strings for equality is the most fundamental task of a text processing program, which performs its more complex tasks based on the results of these comparisons. For example, when an XML parser sees an <xyz> start-tag in a document, it tries to match this "xyz" with the names of any element types declared for the document. Success or failure at this makes a big difference in what it does next.

A notation that allows characters to be represented more than one way complicates string matching issues. For example, in an SGML document using the default (reference) concrete syntax, if a parser sees an <xyz> start-tag in a document for which an Xyz element type was declared (note the upper-case "X" in the latter), it would consider it to be the same thing. However, if an lt entity was declared and an Lt entity wasn't declared, the parser won't recognize an ≪ entity reference.

Characters composed of a base character plus a diacritic character (an accent mark that combines with a character or characters to indicate a different pronunciation, like the "`" in "è") present other problems, because some systems offer a choice for representing certain characters. For example, "ñ" may have its own character, which the above specification paragraph describes as "precomposed" because the pieces are already combined. In addition, there may be some way to indicate that you want a tilde character ("~") to appear over an "n" character. If the Spanish word for "Spain" ("España") has the fifth character coded one way in one place and another way somewhere else, what does a processor do when comparing them?

The definition of "match" here lays out the ground rules for dealing with these problems:

- If the same character is represented two different ways, XML won't treat them as the same character.

- If some "canonical form", or simplest possible form for each character has been specified, the processor may "normalize" the characters, or convert various representations of each character to the simplest form, before comparing strings. For example, if you knew that the processor was going to convert the codes for "~ over n" to the single "ñ" character every time it found those codes (and whether it performs this conversion is "at user option") then you wouldn't have to worry about not matching one version of "España" with another.

- Case folding, or case conversion, is not done in XML. The Latin alphabet has two versions of each letter ("A" and "a", "B" and "b", etc.) and we sometimes treat them as equivalent and sometimes don't. XML simplifies processing by never assuming conversion. (Conversion isn't always as simple as you'd think—in Paris, an upper-case "è" is "È", while in Montreal it's "E".) This means, in XML's most dramatic change from the SGML reference concrete syntax *and* from HTML, that XML markup is always case-sensitive. If an element type is declared with the name List, an XML processor won't recognize the start-tags <list> or <LIST> as starting one of these elements. (Note that all of XML's keywords, such as DOCTYPE and DTD declaration keywords, are in upper-case.)

A "language" in the computer science sense is the collection of patterns that fit a given production (see "" in the "Supplementary Annotations" appendix for more on productions). Therefore, a string that matches a grammatical production is part of its language. The last sentence of the specification paragraph above tells us that an element matches its declaration when it conforms to the rules described in the "Element Valid" validity constraint on page 129.

for compatibility

A feature of XML included solely to ensure that XML remains compatible with SGML.

for interoperability

A non-binding recommendation included to increase the chances that XML documents can be processed by the existing installed base of SGML processors which predate the WebSGML Adaptations Annex to ISO 8879.

The "WebSGML Adaptations Annex to ISO 8879" is annex K of the SGML standard. These tweaks to the SGML standard allowed XML to include many desirable new features and remain an SGML application profile. Something added to XML "for interoperability" refers to something added to make it more compatible with SGML software created before WebSGML.

Documents

T his chapter describes issues that apply to an XML document as a unit. It also covers the smallest possible units that can be combined to eventually form a document: the characters that a document can use, what we mean by "space", and various declarations and constructs such as comments and processing instructions that don't take an active part in defining a document's logical or physical structure.

A data object is an *XML document* if it is well-formed, as defined in this specification. A well-formed XML document may in addition be valid if it meets certain further constraints.

Splitting XML documents into these two tiers made it easier to achieve design goal five of the spec: that the "number of optional features in XML is to be kept to the absolute minimum, ideally zero". The two-tier system offers flexibility in the ease of document creation and strictness of conformance without requiring sending and receiving systems to run down a checklist of "optional" features that each may or may not support.

In 1.2, "Terminology", entries for "well-formedness constraint" and "validity constraint" tell more about the form these "further constraints" take.

> Each XML document has both a logical and a physical structure. Physically, the document is composed of units called entities. An entity may refer to other entities to cause their inclusion in the document. A document begins in a "root" or document entity. Logically, the document is composed of declarations, elements, comments, character references, and processing instructions, all of which are indicated in the document by explicit markup. The logical and physical structures must nest properly, as described in **Section 4.3.2: Well-Formed Parsed Entities**.

A document's physical structure is the relationship of the entities (usually, the files) that make up the document. Within a collection of entities, the main one is the "document entity". A program reading the collection reads that one and, for each reference to another entity it finds in the document entity, it proceeds as if the entity itself had replaced the reference to it (that is, "to cause their inclusion in the document"). These entities can in turn refer to other entities; a diagram of their relationships would show branches fanning out from the central entity to form a tree, which is why we call the document entity the "root".

Logical structure is the schematic structure of the information. Just as a database specialist usually designs a relational database's tables and columns before considering the number and organization of files to use in storing the database, a document designer typically plans out the structure of an XML document's elements before worrying about its physical entity structure.

To be as efficient as possible, a document's physical structure is often customized for the host operating system. This separation of physical from logical design issues allows document collections to have a consistent logical design on different operating systems, allowing the development of more portable documents.

For example, a collection of documents conforming to a single document type might be stored on two different computers, each running a different operating system. The documents would all have the same logical structure, but could have different physical structures on each computer, optimized for the characteristics of that computer's operating system.

For more on declarations, see 2.8, "Prolog and Document Type Declaration"; 2.9, "Standalone Document Declaration"; 3.2, "Element Type Declarations"; 3.3, "Attribute-List Declarations"; 4.2, "Entity Declarations"; 4.3.1, "The Text Declaration"; and 4.7, "Notation Declarations". For more on the other document components listed, see 2.5, "Comments"; 4.1, "Character and Entity References"; and 2.6, "Processing Instructions".

"Nesting" is the containment of one entity or logical structure (usually an element) within another. 4.3.2, "Well-Formed Parsed Entities", further describes the requirements of proper nesting.

2.1. Well-Formed XML Documents

A textual object is a well-formed XML document if:

1. Taken as a whole, it matches the production labeled `document`.
2. It meets all the well-formedness constraints given in this specification.
3. Each of the parsed entities which is referenced directly or indirectly within the document is *well-formed*.

Production 1 below, for a **document**[†], is number one for a reason: as a parser figures out the structure of your XML document, it recognizes combinations of bigger and bigger pieces (or, in computer sci-

---

[†] Throughout these annotations, symbols defined by productions are shown in a bold Courier font.

ence parlance, "nonterminals") that ultimately result in a prolog, document element, and optional miscellaneous markup (processing instructions, white space, and comments). As this production shows, these are combined into the document itself.

Document

[1] document	::= prolog element Misc*

"Well-formedness constraints" are rules attached to certain productions. These specify that, for the nonterminal defined by the production to be considered well-formed, it must also meet any constraints described under the production. For example, production 39 has the constraint `wfc: Element Type Match` listed on its right and described underneath it. Similarly, "validity constraints" are additional rules that a nonterminal must meet if the document containing it is to qualify as valid.

For a computer, parsing is the process of analyzing text notated in some programming or data description language and determining its components in accordance with the grammar of that language. For an XML processor, this means reading text in "parsed" entities, distinguishing the data content from the markup, and analyzing the markup.

4.3.2, "Well-Formed Parsed Entities", further describes the concept of a well-formed parsed entity. To summarize, it says that all the elements and entities must nest properly (that is, if one is enclosed by another, the enclosed one ends before the enclosing one) and that elements (and other structures listed in 4.3.2, "Well-Formed Parsed Entities") can't begin in one entity and end in another.

Tip   Parsing is the first step in validating, or deciding whether a document meets the rules specified by XML and the document's DTD, so the terms "parsing" and "validating" are often confused. Part of the confusion results from people using the expression "the document doesn't parse" to mean "it's not valid" and "it parses" to mean "it's valid".

Matching the `document` production implies that:

1. It contains one or more elements.
2. There is exactly one element, called the *root*, or document element, no part of which appears in the content of any other element. For all other elements, if the start-tag is in the content of another element, the end-tag is in the content of the same element. More simply stated, the elements, delimited by start- and end-tags, nest properly within each other.

Elements, described further in Chapter 3, "Logical Structures", are the building blocks of an XML document. Elements have start- and end-tags, and may have character data, other elements, or both between these tags. (Empty elements may use an empty-element tag instead of a start- and end-tag pair.) In an HTML document, an `h2` element usually has only character data between the tags (for example, "`<h2>The Fire Sermon</h2>`"), while the start- and end-tags for the HTML `body` element have other elements between them.

XML elements can also be empty. These can be represented as a start-tag immediately followed by an end-tag or as a shorter alternative known as an empty-element tag, which has a slash before its closing ">". For example, an empty HTML `img` element such as `<img src='whale.gif' align='right'>` could be written as `<img src='whale.gif' align='right'/>` in XML.

Just as a document's entities have a root, so do its elements. If you draw a graph of a document's elements that shows each element branching off into its children (that is, the sub-elements, or elements contained within it) there will be one element containing them all.

This element is the root of the tree picture created by your graph, so we call it the root element of the document. (The term is interchangeable with "document element".) It's not enclosed by any other element, and all the other elements of a document are enclosed within it.

> As a consequence of this, for each non-root element C in the document, there is one other element P in the document such that C is in the content of P, but is not in the content of any other element that is in the content of P. P is referred to as the *parent* of C, and C as a *child* of P.

In other words, an element anywhere inside the root element has one and only one parent element. (The C and P in the spec's example stand for "child" and "parent".) A child element is inside its parent and not inside any of the parent's other child elements.

2.2. Characters

A parsed entity contains *text*, a sequence of characters, which may represent markup or character data. A *character* is an atomic unit of text as specified by ISO/IEC 10646 [ISO/IEC 10646]. Legal characters are tab, carriage return, line feed, and the legal graphic characters of Unicode and ISO/IEC 10646. The use of "compatibility characters", as defined in section 6.8 of [Unicode], is discouraged.

The ISO/IEC 10646 standard created by a joint commission of the ISO and the International Electrotechnical Commission in 1993 specifies the Universal Multiple-Octet Coded Character Set (UCS).

Let's break down this phrase "Universal Multiple-Octet Coded Character Set". The Universal Character Set is a collection of characters (usually, elements of alphabets, numeric digits, and other characters such as punctuation) that aims to represent all the written languages of the world.

What does it mean to do this with multiple octets? An octet is a grouping of eight bits of information. (On PCs and Macintoshes, a byte is eight bits, but not on all other machines, so it's incorrect to always refer to eight bits as a byte.) An octet can represent 256 different values. This is enough for all the characters on an English-language keyboard and some other miscellaneous ones, but certainly not enough to cover all the characters in all the languages that people want to use when storing documents on computers. Doing this requires multiple octets for each character.

Using two octets per character, you can represent 65,536 different characters; the ISO 10646 version of this is known as UCS-2. Four octets, UCS-4, can represent over two billion different characters (of the 32 bits in the four octets of a UCS-4 character, the first must be "0", leaving over two billion possible combinations of the remaining thirty-one bits).

Unicode is a standard developed by the Unicode Consortium for representing characters with 16 bits. This group of mostly American computer manufacturers is a separate organization from the ISO that has worked closely with them to keep their standard aligned with the UCS-2 subset of ISO 10646. These two standards, in order to remain backward-compatible with existing text files, have the same first 128 characters as the 128 characters in the ASCII character set used by PCs, Macintoshes, and UNIX computers. Therefore, an upper-case "A" is still represented by character 65 and a lower-case "a" by character 97. The XML specification cites both standards because citing only one would imply that XML would follow that one's lead if it ever diverged from the other standard, so identifying the two together encourages them to stay in synch.

Unicode represents some characters more than once, with the extra versions known as "compatibility characters". These are added to ease "round-trip" conversions with (that is, conversions into and then back from) other character set standards. The XML spec doesn't look kindly on these because multiple ways to represent the same character—especially when one way is more efficient and the other is only there as a compromise with other standards—leaves more room for error in a text processing system.

Character Range

```
[2]  Char  ::=  #x9  |  #xA  |  #xD  |  [#x20-#xD7FF]  |     /* any Unicode character,
                [#xE000-#xFFFD]  |  [#x10000-#x10FFFF]      excluding the surrogate
                                                            blocks, FFFE, and FFFF. */
```

"#x" at the beginning of a number shows that it's written in hexadecimal, or base 16 notation, as opposed to the decimal, "base 10" notation that non-programmers are accustomed to. Hexadecimal notation represents the decimal notation numbers 10 through 15 using the letters A through F, so the decimal numbers 8, 9 10, and 11 would be "#x8", "#x9", "#xA", and "#xB" in hexadecimal. "#x10" represents the decimal number 16, "#x11" is 17, "#x12" is 18, "#xA0" is 160 (as is "#xa0"—the case of alphabetic digits in hexadecimal numbers doesn't matter), "#xA1" is 161, and so on. Production 2 shows that the decimal values 9, 10, 13, 32 – 55295, 57344 – 65533, and 65536 – 1114111 can be used to represent XML characters.

Why use hexadecimal, or in programmer slang, "hex"? Translated to binary, a single hex digit requires four bits, so the eight bits represented by two hex digits will fit into, and completely occupy, a single octet. The use of hexadecimal digits is an efficient compromise between the decimal representation so familiar to humans and the binary representation used by computers. It's also important in the XML world because Unicode refers to each character by its hexadecimal, not decimal value.

The mechanism for encoding character code points into bit patterns may vary from entity to entity. All XML processors must accept the UTF-8 and UTF-16 encodings of 10646; the mechanisms for signaling which of the two is in use, or for bringing other encodings into play, are discussed later, in **Section 4.3.3: Character Encoding in Entities**.

Two different entities may use different encodings, or sets of associations between characters and the bit patterns that represent them in computer storage. All programs that process XML documents must accept the ISO 10646 UTF-8 and UTF-16 encodings. UCS Transformation Format (UTF) 8 and UTF-16 are specific encodings of ISO 10646 characters as sequences of octets.

The "discussion of character encodings" alluded to is 4.3.3, "Character Encoding in Entities", on page 210.

2.3. Common Syntactic Constructs

This section defines some symbols used widely in the grammar.

S (white space) consists of one or more space (#x20) characters, carriage returns, line feeds, or tabs.

By "space (#x20) characters", it means ASCII character 32—the character you type by pressing your keyboard's space bar. ("x20" is the hexadecimal equivalent of 32.)

White Space

| [3] | S | ::= | (#x20 | #x9 | #xD | #xA)+ |

#x9 is the character that you type with your Tab key. Carriage returns and line feeds are two different characters (numbers 13 and 10, or in hex, #xD and #xA) used by different operating systems to represent the end of a line of text; see 2.11, "End-of-Line Handling" for more on these.

Characters are classified for convenience as letters, digits, or other characters. Letters consist of an alphabetic or syllabic base character possibly followed by one or more combining characters, or of an ideographic character. Full definitions of the specific characters in each class are given in **Appendix B: Character Classes.**

"España", the Spanish word for "Spain", has a good example of a letter (n-tilde, or "ñ") that could be coded as the alphabetic base character "n" with the combining character "~".

An ideographic character, unlike the characters of most Western alphabets, represents an object or idea instead of a particular sound. Appendix B, "Character Classes", lists which characters are considered letters, which are digits, and so forth.

> A *Name* is a token beginning with a letter or one of a few punctuation characters, and continuing with letters, digits, hyphens, underscores, colons, or full stops, together known as name characters. Names beginning with the string "xml", or any string which would match (('X' | 'x') ('M' | 'm') ('L' | 'l')), are reserved for standardization in this or future versions of this specification.

The concept of a name is important in XML because it's used so often in defining other XML constructs. A token, or terminal, is one of the indivisible units of a document. Tokens are combined according to production rules into nonterminals which are combined into larger nonterminals. These eventually form the most important nonterminal of them all: the XML document, a nonterminal defined by production 1. Element type names, "DOCTYPE", and many other strings of characters used in markup are name tokens. (A "full stop", by the way, is the punctuation character also known as a "period".)

When you make up names to use, such as element type or entity names, don't begin them with the letters "XML" in any combination of upper- and lower-case. (The part in the specification paragraph above with all the parentheses is the regular expression way of saying "XML in any combination of upper- and lower-case". See Chapter 6, "Notation", for more on regular expression syntax.)

The spec prohibits names beginning with "XML" so that when the specification designates names with particular meanings for use in XML (for example, the xml:space attribute described in 2.10, "White Space Handling"), there will be no conflict. If your document has an element type named `xmlelement` and some future version of XML creates an `xmlelement` keyword for some special purpose that hadn't been invented when you decided on your element type name, you could have a problem with your document.

> **NOTE:** The colon character within XML names is reserved for experimentation with name spaces. Its meaning is expected to be standardized at some future point, at which point those documents using the colon for experimental purposes may need to be updated. (There is no guarantee that any name-space mechanism adopted for XML will in fact use the colon as a name-space delimiter.) In practice, this means that authors should not use the colon in XML names except as part of name-space experiments, but that XML processors should accept the colon as a name character.

The preceding specification paragraph told us that it was OK to use the colon character (":") in names; this one tells us to avoid it. It's being set aside here for eventual use in solving the namespace problem.

A namespace is a set of unique names. Consider a document type that uses element types and entities declared in two other DTDs.[†] For example, if you're doing a business plan for a restaurant, perhaps `finance.dtd` and `kitchen.dtd` both have element types that you need in your document. What if these two DTDs each declare an element type named `instrument`, and the two declarations for this `instrument` element type are different? Which declaration applies when you want to create a new `instrument` element for your document?

One proposal suggests that you assign a name to each of the two DTDs—for example, "kitchen" and "finance"—and then you could refer to the `<kitchen:instrument>` and `<finance:instrument>`

[†] For more on the use of external subsets for markup declarations, see 2.8, "Prolog and Document Type Declaration".

element types to avoid confusion. Whether the namespace problem is resolved with this syntax or some variation of it, the general plan is to somehow use the colon, so don't use it for something else.

> An *Nmtoken* (name token) is any mixture of name characters.

A name token is a slightly relaxed version of a name; as production 7 shows, it's a string of **NameChar** characters. (As production 4 shows, these are letters, numeric digits, the period, hyphen, underscore and colon, plus the **CombiningChar** and **Extender** characters listed in Appendix B, "Character Classes".) Unlike a name (see production 5) a name token doesn't have to begin with a letter, underscore, or colon.

The specification doesn't use name tokens in all the different contexts that it uses names. They're only used for one type of attribute that limits the format of the attribute's values.

For example, declaring an employee element type's phone attribute with the declaration shown in Example 2.1 would give a document's author a very broad leeway in the allowable phone number values (for example, "(4 0 8) 5 5 5 1 2 1 2" with spaces between the numbers would be legal). However, a declaration like that shown in Example 2.2 would tell a validating XML editor to only allow phone numbers that conformed to production 7, thus preventing spaces and various odd punctuation that you wouldn't want in a phone number. (Note that parentheses are also excluded, so NMTOKEN may not be the most ideal choice for a phone number attribute type.)

Example 2.1: Declaring employee element type's phone attribute as type CDATA

```
<!ATTLIST employee phone CDATA #REQUIRED>
```

Example 2.2: Declaring employee element type's phone attribute as type NMTOKEN

```
<!ATTLIST employee phone NMTOKEN #REQUIRED>
```

3.3.1, "Attribute Types", describes the full choice of types available when declaring attributes.

Names and Tokens

[4]	NameChar	::=	Letter | Digit | '.' | '-' | '_' | ':' | CombiningChar | Extender
[5]	Name	::=	(Letter | '_' | ':') (NameChar)*
[6]	Names	::=	Name (S Name)*
[7]	Nmtoken	::=	(NameChar)+
[8]	Nmtokens	::=	Nmtoken (S Nmtoken)*

Literal data is any quoted string not containing the quotation mark used as a delimiter for that string. Literals are used for specifying the content of internal entities (`EntityValue`), the values of attributes (`AttValue`), and external identifiers (`SystemLiteral`). Note that a `SystemLiteral` can be parsed without scanning for markup.

"Any quoted string not containing the quotation mark used as a delimiter" means one of two things:

- A string of characters surrounded by but not containing quotation mark characters (or in programmer slang, double quotes, "like those surrounding this phrase").

- A string of characters surrounded by but not containing apostrophes (programmer slang: single quotes, 'like those surrounding this phrase').

An internal entity consisting of the string "Shantih shantih shantih" could be declared as shown in Examples 2.3 or 2.4.

Example 2.3: Entity replacement text surrounded by double quotes in declaration

```
<!ENTITY sss "Shantih shantih shantih">
```

Example 2.4: Entity replacement text surrounded by single quotes in declaration

```
<!ENTITY sss 'Shantih shantih shantih'>
```

Similarly, either double or single quotes could be used to identify the author's initials in the `chapter` element's attribute specification shown in Example 2.5, or in the DTD file name in the DOCTYPE declaration's external identifier shown in Example 2.6.

Example 2.5: Double quotes used to delimit attribute value

```
<chapter author="TSE">
```

Example 2.6: Single quotes used to delimit system literal in a DOCTYPE declaration

```
<!DOCTYPE harangue SYSTEM 'rant.dtd'>
```

The fact that "a **SystemLiteral** can be parsed without scanning for markup" means that a parser will treat as data anything that looks like markup in the system literal. For example, the parser will not treat the second, third, and fourth characters of the system literal in Example 2.7 as a reference to an a entity even though the "a" is enclosed by the "&" and ";" characters used to delimit an entity reference.

Example 2.7: Markup characters (& and ;) that won't be treated as markup because they're in a system literal

```
<!DOCTYPE harangue SYSTEM "r&a;nt.dtd">
```

(Don't try this at home with important data—using such punctuation in file names is asking for trouble on any operating system, even if the XML application software can handle it.) 4.2.2, "External Entities", has more on using system literals in external entity references.

Literals

[9] `EntityValue`	`::=`	`'"'` `([^%&"]` `|` `PEReference` `|` `Reference)*` `'"'`	
		<code>| "'" ([^%&']</code> `|` `PEReference` `|` `Reference)*` `"'"`	
[10] `AttValue`	`::=`	`'"'` `([^<&"]` `|` `Reference)*` `'"'`	
		<code>| "'" ([^<&']</code> `|` `Reference)*` `"'"`	
[11] `SystemLiteral`	`::=`	`('"' [^"]* '"')` `|` `("'" [^']* "'")`	
[12] `PubidLiteral`	`::=`	`'"' PubidChar* '"'` `|` `"'" (PubidChar - "'")* "'"`	
[13] `PubidChar`	`::=`	`#x20 | #xD | #xA | [a-zA-Z0-9] | [-'()+,./:=?;!*#@$_%]`	

Productions 9 through 13 show delimited strings, or "literals". The first four productions each offer two nearly identical choices that differ only in whether double or single quotes are the delimiters. The square brackets at the beginning of each expression show which characters are prohibited there. The "^" character signifies negation; for example, `[^xyz]` means "any character except x, y, or z". See Chapter 6, "Notation", for more on regular expression syntax.

2.4. Character Data and Markup

Text consists of intermingled character data and markup. *Markup* takes the form of start-tags, end-tags, empty-element tags, entity references, character references, comments, CDATA section delimiters, document type declarations, and processing instructions.

All text that is not markup constitutes the *character data* of the document.

After the first specification paragraph above describes the categories of possible markup, the second defines "character data" as being everything else. To start with a simple case, in Example 2.8 the `<h2>` start-tag and the `</h2>` end-tag are the markup and "The Fire Sermon" is the character data.

Example 2.8: Markup plus character data

```
<h2>The Fire Sermon</h2>
```

Other categories of markup listed in the first paragraph:

- *Empty-element tags* such as `<img src="whale.jpg"/>`.

- *Entity references* such as `&lt;` or `&sss;` and *character references* such as `&#60; &#x3c;`. 4.1, "Character and Entity References", covers both of these in more detail.

- *Comment declarations* such as `<!-- check date -->` that the parser may or may not pass on to the application. See 2.5, "Comments", for more on these.

- *CDATA sections*, which have nothing but character data. If a parser sees "<ingredient>" in a CDATA section, it won't treat it as the start-tag of an `ingredient` element; it just treats it as the data characters "<ingredient>". "<" in a CDATA section is not a reference to an `lt` entity; it's just the data "<". 2.7, "CDATA Sections", describes this further.

- A *document type declaration* at the beginning of a document identifies the document's type and also contains and/or tells where to find its element, attribute, entity, and notation declarations. For example, the document type declaration in Example 2.9, a slightly modified version of the one used by the actual XML specification, tells us that the document type is `spec` and that the declarations are stored in a file called `spec.dtd`.

Example 2.9: Sample document type declaration

```
<!DOCTYPE spec SYSTEM "spec.dtd">
```

See 2.8, "Prolog and Document Type Declaration", for more on these.

- *Processing instructions* are special instructions for the application. See 2.6, "Processing Instructions" for more information.

The remainder of 2.4, "Character Data and Markup", describes five general entities that are so important that you don't have to declare them because they're automatically predeclared for you: &, <, >, ' and ". See 4.6, "Predefined Entities", for more on these.

> The ampersand character (&) and the left angle bracket (<) may appear in their literal form *only* when used as markup delimiters, or within a comment, a processing instruction, or a CDATA section. They are also legal within the literal entity value of an internal entity declaration; see **Section 4.3.2: Well-Formed Parsed Entities**. If they are needed elsewhere, they must be escaped using either numeric character references or the strings "&" and "<" respectively. The right angle bracket (>) may be represented using the string ">", and must, for compatibility, be escaped using ">" or a character reference when it appears in the string "]]>" in content, when that string is not marking the end of a CDATA section.

This lists five situations where you can use the ampersand and left angle bracket characters as they are (that is, the actual "&" and "<" characters instead of their entity references & and <):

- In the markup they were intended for: the ampersand as the beginning of an entity reference, and the left angle bracket as the beginning of a tag, comment, declaration, or processing instruction.

- Within a comment, where they won't be treated as markup, but as their plain old selves. For example, the ampersand and less-than symbol in Example 2.10 won't cause any problems.

Example 2.10: Ampersand and less-than symbol within a comment—no problem

```
<!-- if a = 2 & b = 4, then a < b -->
```

- In a processing instruction, where they're no more trouble than in a comment.

- In a CDATA section, where they won't be treated as markup, because after all, that's the point of CDATA sections.

- Inside an internal entity's replacement text. For example, if an `ltref` entity is defined with the declaration shown in Example 2.11, the entity reference `&ltref;` in a document will actually be replaced by "<" instead of by "<" because the ampersand in the entity declaration's literal entity value (the part between the quotes in the declaration) was treated as a data ampersand and not as the beginning of an entity reference. That's why they call it a "literal entity value": because most characters in it are treated literally.

Example 2.11: An ampersand in an internal entity's replacement text

```
<!ENTITY ltref "&lt;">
```

To include an ampersand or left angle bracket[†] as data in a document it must be "escaped". This term, which has been used in programming languages for years, describes a way of letting markup characters "escape" the parser so that it doesn't treat them as markup.

---

† A "left angle bracket" is also known as a "less-than" symbol, which inspires the `lt` abbreviation used in its entity reference, but the XML specification uses the term "left angle bracket" when referring to the "<" character. Similarly, it prefers the term "right angle bracket" to "greater-than character" for the ">" character, despite the `gt` abbreviation used for its predeclared entity reference.

For the ampersand and left angle bracket, you use the same trick that you would use to put the "ñ" in "España" or the "ä" in "bräu": use each character's entity reference. For ñ, it's `&ntilde;`, for ä, it's `&auml;`, for &, it's `&amp;`, and for <, it's `&lt;`.[†]

The same applies to the right angle bracket, or "greater-than" (">") character, although this is rarely necessary in a document's character data. A parser can't mistakenly treat it as the end of a tag, processing instruction, comment, or declaration because it isn't recognized unless there's an unfinished markup string in progress. You do need the greater-than symbol's entity reference (`&gt;`) after the characters "]]" if your document just happens to need a "]]>" somewhere that isn't ending a CDATA section. See 2.7, "CDATA Sections" for more on these.

> In the content of elements, character data is any string of characters which does not contain the start-delimiter of any markup. In a CDATA section, character data is any string of characters not including the CDATA-section-close delimiter, "]]>".

Now we have a more specific definition of character data, or rather, two definitions, depending on the context:

- Between an element's start- and end-tags (that is, in an element's content), any string where no markup begins. You can't have the end of markup (for example, a > character to represent the end of a tag) unless you recently began some markup, because the parser won't even try to treat > as the end of a tag unless it was looking for one.

[†] One nice feature of the `&amp;` and `&lt;` entity references is that they are among the five special ones that don't need to be declared unless you want to maintain interoperability with pre-WebSGML SGML systems. 4.6, "Predefined Entities", provides further background on this.

- In a CDATA section, every thing is character data except for the string]]>, which means "end of this CDATA section".

> To allow attribute values to contain both single and double quotes, the apostrophe or single-quote character (') may be represented as "'", and the double-quote character (") as """.

The ability to delimit strings with either single- or double-quotes usually means that if you need one of these in your string you delimit that string with the other. What if you need both in the string? Use either to delimit and use the described entity references within the string, as demonstrated in 2.12.

Example 2.12: Using the ' and " entity references to insert quotes in an entity's replacement text

```
<!ENTITY inferno "Dante&apos;s &quot;Inferno&quot;">
```

quot and apos are predefined entities, so there is no need to declare them before referencing them unless you want to maintain interoperability with pre-WebSGML SGML systems.

Character Data

[14]CharData	::=	[^<&]* - ([^<&]* ']]>' [^<&]*)

In the concise language of productions, production 14 tells us what the text preceding it already told us: that character data is any string of characters excluding the ampersand, the less-than symbol, and the "]]>" string.

2.5. Comments

Comments may appear anywhere in a document outside other markup; in addition, they may appear within the document type declaration at places allowed by the grammar. They are not part of the document's character data; an XML processor may, but need not, make it possible for an application to retrieve the text of comments. For compatibility, the string "`--`" (double-hyphen) must not occur within comments.

You can put them in document type declarations "at places allowed by the grammar"—but where does it allow them? Production 28 shows that markup declarations (**markupdecl** in the production) can be part of a document type declaration, and production 29 shows that comments are one type of markup declaration.

As with the comments in computer programs, the processor may just ignore their content. They're often there as notes from the authors to themselves or to others on their writing team, like the one shown in Example 2.13.

Example 2.13: Sample comment within a `par` element

```
<par>The W3C approved XML as an official Recommendation
on February 10, 1998.<!-- double-check that date -->
</par>
```

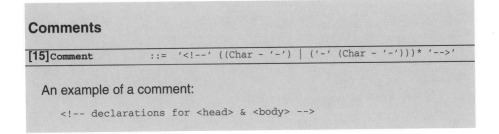

Comments

| [15] Comment | ::= | `'<!--' ((Char - '-') | ('-' (Char - '-')))* '-->'` |

An example of a comment:

```
<!-- declarations for <head> & <body> -->
```

Note how this example demonstrates what 2.4, "Character Data and Markup" said about the < and & characters being allowed within comments.

2.6. Processing Instructions

Processing instructions (PIs) allow documents to contain instructions for applications.

The parser may or may not pass XML comments to the application, but it must pass processing instructions, because that's the purpose of processing instructions: to represent special instructions for the application.

Processing Instructions

[16]PI	::=	'<?' PITarget (S (Char* - (Char* '?>' Char*)))? '?>'
[17]PITarget	::=	Name - (('X' | 'x') ('M' | 'm') ('L' | 'l'))

PIs are not part of the document's character data, but must be passed through to the application. The PI begins with a target (PITarget) used to identify the application to which the instruction is directed. The target names "XML", "xml", and so on are reserved for standardization in this or future versions of this specification. The XML Notation mechanism may be used for formal declaration of PI targets.

The processing instruction in Example 2.14 tells a mythical "stinker" application to generate a particular scent for five seconds.

Example 2.14: A sample processing instruction

```
<?stinker scent="newcar.sml" time="5 secs" ?>
```

A particular document may have processing instructions for several different applications, so the processing instruction target (**PITarget**), right after the opening <?, identifies the target application for this processing instruction.[†]

---

† The XML Working Group considered requiring notation declarations for each processing instruction target, but this would have effectively prohibited the use of processing instructions in well-formed documents, which don't require any declarations. See 4.7, "Notation Declarations", for more information

2.7. CDATA Sections

CDATA sections may occur anywhere character data may occur; they are used to escape blocks of text containing characters which would otherwise be recognized as markup. CDATA sections begin with the string "`<![CDATA[`" and end with the string "`]]>`":

As we saw in 2.4, "Character Data and Markup", to "escape" some text is to identify it as something that should escape parsing. In other words, if there's anything in that text that would normally be considered XML markup, treat it as character data. After an XML parser sees the `<![CDATA[` sequence that indicates the beginning of a CDATA section and before it sees the `]]>` markup that indicates the end, it assumes that all the characters it sees are character data—even any left angle brackets and ampersand characters.

CDATA Sections

[18] CDSect	::=	CDStart CData CDEnd
[19] CDStart	::=	'<![CDATA['
[20] CData	::=	(Char* - (Char* ']]>' Char*))
[21] CDEnd	::=	']]>'

Within a CDATA section, only the CDEnd string is recognized as markup, so that left angle brackets and ampersands may occur in their literal form; they need not (and cannot) be escaped using "`&lt;`" and "`&amp;`". CDATA sections cannot nest.

CDATA sections are popular for showing demonstration XML (or SGML or HTML) markup within an XML document. The markup can be shown as-is with no modifications, but the parser won't confuse the demonstration markup with actual document markup.

For example, in the document fragment in Example 2.15, an XML parser won't consider `<center>`, `<img src="stoppages.jpg">`, or

</center> to be actual markup within the document's par element because that text is inside a CDATA section.

Example 2.15: Use of CDATA section to "escape" img and center tags

```
<par>This HTML code will center the "Standard Stoppages" picture:
<![CDATA[ <center>
<img src="stoppages.jpg">
</center>
]]> </par>
```

The spec tells us that, in CDATA sections, left angle brackets and ampersands "need not (and cannot) be escaped using '<' and '&'". The strings < and & are just character data in a CDATA section, just like everything else other than]]>.

"CDATA sections cannot nest" means that you can't put one CDATA section inside of another. If you think about how CDATA sections work, nesting them doesn't make any sense. For example, in Example 2.16, the CDATA start at line 2 means "this is all character data until the next]]>".

Example 2.16: Attempted nesting of CDATA sections

```
1.  This line isn't in any CDATA section.
2.  <![CDATA[
3.  This is inside of a CDATA section.
4.  <![CDATA[
5.  This is inside of a nested one, which is illegal in XML.
6.  ]]>
7.  This is outside of the inner nested CDATA section, but
8.  still inside the outer one.
9.  ]]>
10. This line isn't in any CDATA section.
```

The next]]> after line 2 is on line 6, so the attempt at starting a new CDATA section on line 4 is just treated by the processor as more character data. The real problem comes when the parser reaches line 9: if line 6 ended the CDATA section begun at line 2, what is line 9 ending? Nothing, so the parser doesn't know what to do—so it's an error.

One more handy thing about CDATA sections: a document with no document type declaration has no information about which elements have carriage returns that really matter. That's because it has no element type declarations to reveal whether an element type has element content (see 3.2.1, "Element Content", for more on this). CDATA sections become even more useful for these documents, because they clearly indicate which parts of a document should have their carriage returns and other white space left alone by the parser.

An example of a CDATA section, in which "`<greeting>`" and "`</greeting>`" are recognized as character data, not markup:

```
<![CDATA[<greeting>Hello, world!</greeting>]]>
```

Tip   *Production 19 is the first production in the XML specification that uses an XML keyword: "CDATA". Note that it's written in upper-case in the production, with no option of writing it in lower-case. This applies to all XML keywords—they have to be written in upper-case.*

2.8. Prolog and Document Type Declaration

XML documents may, and should, begin with an *XML declaration* which specifies the version of XML being used. For example, the following is a complete XML document, well-formed but not valid:

```
<?xml version="1.0"?>
<greeting>Hello, world!</greeting>
```

and so is this:

```
<greeting>Hello, world!</greeting>
```

The second "Hello, world" example's status as a legal XML document demonstrates the potential simplicity (and much of the appeal) of XML. It's well-formed "but not valid" because a valid document's elements all conform to element type declarations in the document's DTD, and this document doesn't even have an associated DTD. See the upcoming specification paragraph beginning "The function of the markup in an XML document…" for more on this.

This section of the XML specification describes markup that can make a document even more useful, because it provides extra information to a processing program about the document and its structure. The first "hello world" example above shows the first thing that you "may, and should" add: an XML declaration, which tells the processor "Hey! This is an XML document! It conforms to version 1.0 of the XML specification!"

The version number "1.0" should be used to indicate conformance to this version of this specification; it is an error for a document to use the value "1.0" if it does not conform to this version of this specification. It is the intent of the XML working group to give later versions of this specification numbers other than "1.0", but this intent does not indicate a commitment to produce any future versions of XML, nor if any are produced, to use any particular numbering scheme. Since future versions are not ruled out, this construct is provided as a means to allow the possibility of automatic version recognition, should it become necessary. Processors may signal an error if they receive documents labeled with versions they do not support.

In case readers are tempted to assume that the next generation of XML documents will begin with `<?xml version="1.1">` or `<?xml version="2.0">`, this rather legalistic paragraph warns them not to make any such assumptions. In fact, it tells them not to assume that there will even *be* another version of XML.

Imagine that you wrote an XML processing application, and now it's three years later and people are still using that program. Perhaps the XML spec has been updated to version 1.2, and these users have some new documents that take advantage of version 1.2's new features. What if they feed the new documents to your program that they have grown to love over the years? How does your program react to the use of these new features? There are two choices:

- It may sputter and choke on the new parts of the document.

- It can first check for the XML declaration's version number and output a warning message if it equals anything other than "1.0".

> The function of the markup in an XML document is to describe its storage and logical structure and to associate attribute-value pairs with its logical structures. XML provides a mechanism, the document type declaration, to define constraints on the logical structure and to support the use of pre-defined storage units. An XML document is *valid* if it has an associated document type declaration and if the document complies with the constraints expressed in it.

This is probably the most important paragraph in the whole specification. Markup identifies storage structure (entity structure) and logical structure (a document's elements and their relationship) and specifies the attribute values that go with each element. By doing this, it makes it easier for software to manipulate a document for different purposes, thereby making the document a more valuable asset.

Software can do even more with documents if it knows their structure—that is, which elements are made up of which other elements and the ordering of the component elements. A document type declaration tells the processing program the definition of a document's structure, or, as database people say, the "schema". By "logical constraints", the specification refers to the definition of an element type's makeup, such as "a chapter element is made of a title element followed by one or more section elements". This is a constraint because in a well-formed XML document that isn't valid, like the first "hello world" example above, you could put any elements you like between a <chapter> start-tag and a </chapter> end-tag. Defined constraints help a processing program know what to expect.

To "support the use of predefined storage units" is to provide a way to reference files and other storage units from within a document. A document can have many reasons for identifying an external file:

- It may be additional marked-up XML content.

- It may store a stylesheet for the document.

- It may store a picture, sound, or audio file that should be made available to anyone viewing the document.

A document type declaration allows this by making it possible to declare entities for use within a document.

A valid XML document declares a document type and conforms to the logical and physical structure (that is, element and entity structure) defined for that document type. For example, the document in Example 2.17 declares a document type of rpt. The document instance comes after the document type declaration, which contains the various element and entity declarations.

Example 2.17: Document with internal declaration subset

```
<?xml version="1.0"?>
<!DOCTYPE rpt [
<!ELEMENT rpt    (title,par+)>
<!ELEMENT title (#PCDATA)>
<!ELEMENT par    (#PCDATA)>
<!ENTITY  auml "[auml  ]">
<!ENTITY  disclaimer SYSTEM "disclaimer.xml">
<!ENTITY  copyright  SYSTEM "copyright.xml">
]>
<rpt><title>Snee: A White Paper</title>
&copyright;
<par>Here is the first paragraph. The German word
for "brew" is "br&auml;u."</par>
<par>Here is the second paragraph.</par>
&disclaimer;
</rpt>
```

The document type declaration must appear before the first element in the document.

In Example 2.17, the document's first element (rpt) doesn't start until after the end of the document type declaration.

Prolog

[22]prolog	::=	XMLDecl? Misc* (doctypedecl Misc*)?
[23]XMLDecl	::=	'<?xml' VersionInfo EncodingDecl? SDDecl? S? '?>'
[24]VersionInfo	::=	S 'version' Eq (' VersionNum ' | " VersionNum ")
[25]Eq	::=	S? '=' S?
[26]VersionNum	::=	([a-zA-Z0-9_.:] | '-')+
[27]Misc	::=	Comment | PI | S

The prolog can provide advance knowledge of the document: the version of XML being used and the structure of the document. It can, but doesn't have to tell us either of these, because as production 22 shows us, the XML declaration and the DOCTYPE declaration are both optional. A prolog is better off including both, because the XML declaration and DOCTYPE declaration both provide valuable information to the XML processor.

In the document in Example 2.18, everything except line 5 is the prolog. In terms of production 22, the first line has the **XMLDecl** followed by a comment, which according to production 27 qualifies as a **Misc**. Next comes a **doctypedecl** at lines 2 through 4, and then another **Misc** after the]> that closes the **doctypedecl** before the brief document element on line 5. Although you can't see anything after line 4's]>, look again at production 27 for **Misc**: the third and last choice is **S**, for white space, and the carriage return at the end of line 4 counts.

Example 2.18: XML document with four-line prolog

```
1. <?xml version="1.0"?><!-- sample XML document -->
2. <!DOCTYPE verse [
3. <!ELEMENT verse (#PCDATA)>
4. ]>
5. <verse>She smoothes her hair with automatic hand</verse>
```

Because single or double quotation marks in a production enclose text that must be included literally, production 24 above tells you that Example 2.19 would be a legal **VersionInfo**, but it wouldn't. The production's author meant (but failed) to show that single or double quotes had to be included around the version number. The two correct versions are shown in Example 2.20.

Example 2.19: Incorrect `VersionInfo` markup

```
version=1.0
```

Example 2.20: Two possible correct versions of `VersionInfo` markup

```
version="1.0"
version='1.0'
```

To show this, the production should have done something like the revision shown in 2.21, essentially quoting the quotes to show that they should be literally included.[†]

Example 2.21: Revised version of production 24

```
VersionInfo ::= S 'version' Eq
                ("'" VersionNum "'" | '"' VersionNum '"')
```

> The XML *document type declaration* contains or points to markup declarations that provide a grammar for a class of documents. This grammar is known as a document type definition, or *DTD*. The document type declaration can point to an external subset (a special kind of external entity) containing markup declarations, or can contain the markup declarations directly in an internal subset, or can do both. The DTD for a document consists of both subsets taken together.

In Example 2.17, the declaration "contains or points to markup declarations"—it *contains* the markup declarations between the square braces (`[]`). In 2.22, it *points to* the `rpt.dtd` file that has the necessary declarations. The DTD file is shown in Example 2.23.

---

† The spec's authors are aware of the error.

Example 2.22: XML document with an external declaration subset

```
<?xml version="1.0"?>
<!DOCTYPE rpt SYSTEM "rpt.dtd">
<rpt><title>Snee: A White Paper</title>
&copyright;
<par>Here is the first paragraph. The German word
for "brew" is "br&auml;u."</par>
<par>Here is the second paragraph.</par>
&disclaimer;
</rpt>
```

Example 2.23: `rpt.dtd` file referenced in Example 2.22

```
<!ELEMENT rpt (title,par+)>
<!ELEMENT title (#PCDATA)>
<!ELEMENT par (#PCDATA)>
<!ENTITY auml "[auml  ]">
<!ENTITY disclaimer SYSTEM "disclaimer.xml">
<!ENTITY copyright  SYSTEM "copyright.xml">
```

These declarations provide a "grammar": a body of rules about the allowable ordering of this document's "vocabulary" of element types. We call this grammar a DTD, or "Document Type Definition". It is also common to refer to the declarations that define the grammar as the DTD, which sometimes causes confusion.

When the rpt DTD is in a separate rpt.dtd file from the "Snee: A White Paper" document, that DTD is an external entity just like the disclaimer.xml and copyright.xml files that the disclaimer and copyright declarations point to. (Compare this with auml, which is an internal entity because its value of [auml] is right in there with the declarations and not in a separate file.)

The rpt.dtd DTD file is described as a "special kind" of external entity because unlike disclaimer.xml or copyright.xml it is an external entity that holds a subset of a document type declaration. In Example 2.17, all the document type declaration's markup declarations were in an internal subset—that is, they were part of the document file (or rather, part of the document entity) itself.

As the specification tells us, a single document type declaration can both contain an internal subset and point to an external subset. For example, if the `rpt.dtd` file only consisted of the three lines shown in Example 2.24, the document shown in Example 2.25 would still be fine. This is because it both points to the smaller `rpt.dtd` external subset and also has the remaining declarations in its own internal subset.

Example 2.24: Sample three-line `rpt.dtd` file

```
<!ELEMENT rpt (title,par+)>
<!ELEMENT par (#PCDATA)>
<!ENTITY auml "[auml  ]">
```

Example 2.25: Document referencing 2.24 along with its own internal declaration subset

```
<?xml version="1.0"?>
<!DOCTYPE rpt SYSTEM "rpt.dtd" [
<!ELEMENT title (#PCDATA)>
<!ENTITY disclaimer SYSTEM "disclaimer.xml">
<!ENTITY copyright SYSTEM "copyright.xml">
]>
<rpt><title>Snee: A White Paper</title>
&copyright;
<par>Here is the first paragraph. The German word
for "brew" is "br&auml;u."</par>
<par>Here is the second paragraph.</par>
&disclaimer;
</rpt>
```

In a case like this, the last sentence of the specification paragraph above tells us that the "DTD for a document consists of both subsets taken together". More precisely, the DTD is declared by the markup declarations in both subsets taken together.

A *markup declaration* is an element type declaration, an attribute-list declaration, an entity declaration, or a notation declaration. These declarations may be contained in whole or in part within parameter entities, as
described in the well-formedness and validity constraints below. For fuller
information, see **Section 4: Physical Structures**.

The document in Example 2.26 demonstrates all the categories of
markup declaration. Line 10's element type declaration shows that a
`tale` element (the root element, as shown by the DOCTYPE declaration on line 2) is made of a `title` element followed by one or more
`par` and `illus` elements.

The `par` element's declaration is actually a string stored in the `par-
decl` entity by the declaration at line 8; the `%pardecl;` entity refer-
ence at line 12 has the effect of putting that `par` element type
declaration right there between the `title` element type declaration
on line 11 and the `illus` element type declaration on line 13. This
`pardecl` declaration is an example of a parameter entity, because
unlike a general entity that stores a piece of a document instance, a
parameter entity stores a piece of a document type declaration—in
this case, the `par` element type declaration.

**Example 2.26: Sample document with all categories of markup
declaration**

```
1. <?xml version="1.0"?>
2. <!DOCTYPE tale [
3.
4. <!NOTATION EPS PUBLIC "+//ISBN 0-201-18127-4::Adobe//
5. NOTATION PostScript Language Ref. Manual//EN">
6.
7. <!ENTITY glow SYSTEM "img/glow.eps" NDATA EPS>
8. <!ENTITY % pardecl "<!ELEMENT par    (#PCDATA)>">
9.
10. <!ELEMENT tale (title,(par|illus)+)>
11. <!ELEMENT title (#PCDATA)>
12. %pardecl;
13. <!ELEMENT illus EMPTY>
14. <!ATTLIST illus picfile ENTITY #REQUIRED>
15. <!-- End of document type declaration -->
```

```
16. ]>
17.
18. <tale><title>What the Thunder Said</title>
19. <par>After the torchlight red on sweaty faces</par>
20. <illus picfile="glow"/>
21. </tale>
```

The other entity declaration, on line 7, declares the file `glow.eps` in the `img` subdirectory as an entity to be used as needed in the document. The `illus` element type's attribute-list (ATTLIST) declaration on line 14 declares one attribute for the `illus` elements: `picfile`, an attribute whose attribute type of ENTITY shows that each `illus` element must have a declared entity name as its value.

The document's one `illus` element, on line 20, has a `picfile` value of `glow`, which was the first entity to be declared in this document's document type declaration at line 7. This `glow` entity declaration shows that it's an EPS file, but what's an EPS file? This brings us to another category of markup declarations: notation declarations, which identify the format of "unparsed" data (that is, data that the processor shouldn't parse as part of the XML text of this document). Example 2.26's notation declaration on lines 4 and 5 tells us where to find the details on the PostScript format.

Chapter 4, "Physical Structures" and 4.1, "Character and Entity References" describe the use of parameter entities; for more background on the other kinds of declarations, see 3.2, "Element Type Declarations"; 3.3, "Attribute-List Declarations"; 4.2, "Entity Declarations"; and 4.7, "Notation Declarations".

Document Type Definition

[28]`doctypedecl`	::=	`'<!DOCTYPE' S Name (S ExternalID)? S?`
		`('[' (markupdecl | PEReference | S)*`
		`']' S?)? '>'`
			[VC: Root Element Type]

[29]`markupdecl`	::=	`elementdecl	AttlistDecl	EntityDecl` `| NotationDecl	PI	Comment`	[VC: Proper Declaration/PE Nesting] [WFC: PEs in Internal Subset]

We've seen examples of all the **doctypedecl** components:

- **S**, according to production 3, is made up of one or more space characters.

- In Example 2.25 earlier, SYSTEM "rpt.dtd" is an example of an ExternalID.

- Each line between Example 2.25's square brackets ("[]") is a markup declaration, or **markupdecl**.

- A **PEReference** is a parameter-entity reference, like %pardecl; in Example 2.26.

The **markupdecl** production shows that it may be one of six things: one of the four declaration types demonstrated by the tale example, a comment, or a processing instruction (**PI**). Comments (described further in 2.5, "Comments") have no information for the parser, and usually give background to a person reading an XML document. In Example 2.26's tale document, "End of document type declaration" on line 15 is a comment.

Processing instructions contain data that the parser passes on to the system, to the processing application, or to both. The very first line of the tale document, which identifies the release of XML being used, is a processing instruction. See 2.6, "Processing Instructions" for more background.

> The markup declarations may be made up in whole or in part of the replacement text of parameter entities. The productions later in this specification for individual nonterminals (`elementdecl`, `AttlistDecl`, and so on) describe the declarations *after* all the parameter entities have been included.

A parameter entity's replacement text is the resulting text after all applicable replacements have been made (see 4.5, "Construction of Internal Entity Replacement Text", for more on this). In Example 2.26's `tale` example, the `parmodel` parameter entity's replacement text is `<!ELEMENT par (#PCDATA)>`. (See 3.2.2, "Mixed Content", for more on "PCDATA".)

"Nonterminals" are the pieces of a document whose structure is shown by the specification's productions; see "" for more on productions and nonterminals.

The final sentence of the paragraph above tells us that the upcoming productions in the XML specification do not show you where you might put parameter entity references. Instead, they assume that any parameter entity references that may have been in the nonterminal shown have had their replacement text substituted for them.

> **VALIDITY CONSTRAINT: Root Element Type**
>
> The `Name` in the document type declaration must match the element type of the root element.

This is the first of many validity constraints in the XML specification. Productions refer to these constraints (production 28 cites this one) to show further conditions that the defined nonterminal must meet for a parser to consider its document valid. (Well-formedness constraints play a similar role in defining well-formedness.)

This validity constraint tells us that the **Name** in a document type declaration (production 22) can't be just any Name (2.3, "Common Syntactic Constructs", shows exactly what the specification means by

"Name"). It has to be the element type name of the root element of the document: that is, the single main element that encloses all of the document's other elements.

> **VALIDITY CONSTRAINT: Proper Declaration/PE Nesting**
>
> Parameter-entity replacement text must be properly nested with markup declarations. That is to say, if either the first character or the last character of a markup declaration (`markupdecl` above) is contained in the replacement text for a parameter-entity reference, both must be contained in the same replacement text.

If a parameter entity has the beginning or end of a markup declaration, it has to have the other one as well.

We'll see in the next well-formedness constraint that there are certain conditions for storing and using a piece of a markup declaration instead of an entire one. But even when meeting those conditions, the piece being stored can never have the beginning of a markup declaration without also including that declaration's ending, or vice versa. (We'll also see examples after the next well-formedness constraint.)

> **WELL-FORMEDNESS CONSTRAINT: PEs in Internal Subset**
>
> In the internal DTD subset, parameter-entity references can occur only where markup declarations can occur, not within markup declarations. (This does not apply to references that occur in external parameter entities or to the external subset.)

When you use a parameter entity reference in a document type declaration's internal subset, it can't represent merely a portion of a markup declaration. It can when used in an external subset.

This is easier to see with an example. The `ents.xml` file shown in Example 2.27 has an internal subset and refers to the external subset stored in the file `ents-ext.dtd` shown in Example 2.28. (Both files have the interesting parts described in comments and the illegal parts commented out so that the examples will parse properly; more detailed descriptions follow ents-ext.dtd.)

Example 2.27: Parameter entities in internal and external subsets

```
1. <?xml version="1.0"?>
2. <!DOCTYPE a SYSTEM "ents-ext.dtd" [
3. <!ELEMENT a (#PCDATA|b|c|d|e|f|g)*>
4.
5. <!-- The following two lines work fine. -->
6. <!ENTITY % edecl "<!ELEMENT e (#PCDATA)>">
7. %edecl;
8.
9. <!-- The following two declarations are illegal,
10.     so they're commented out and replaced by the
11.     line after them. Note that ents-ext.dtd's
12.     equivalent of this, cdeclpart, works fine.
13. <!ENTITY % fdeclpart "f (#PCDATA)">
14. <!ELEMENT %fdeclpart;>
15. -->
16. <!ELEMENT f (#PCDATA)>
17.
18. <!ELEMENT g (#PCDATA)>
19. ]>
20. <a>
21. <b>How</b> <c>about</c> <d>those</d>
22. <e>parameter</e> <f>entity</f> <g>rules.</g>
23. </a>
```

Example 2.28: The ents-ext.dtd file referenced in Example 2.28

```
1. <!ENTITY % bdecl "<!ELEMENT b (#PCDATA)>">
2. %bdecl;
3.
4. <!-- The following two lines work fine, because
5.     they're in an external declaration subset. -->
6. <!ENTITY % cdeclpart "c (#PCDATA)">
7. <!ELEMENT %cdeclpart;>
8.
9. <!-- The following two lines are illegal, so they're
10.     commented out and replaced by the line after them.
11. <!ENTITY % ddeclpart "<!ELEMENT d ">
```

```
12. %ddeclpart; (#PCDATA)>
13. -->
14. <!ELEMENT d (#PCDATA)>
```

The first entity declaration in Examples 2.27 and 2.28 each store an entire element type declaration in a parameter entity: edecl at line 6 of ents.xml and bdecl at line 1 of ents-ext.dtd. The lines immediately following each of these have references to these entities, in effect declaring the e and b element types whose declarations they store.

Both files then try to declare and use a parameter entity that stores several parameters of an element type declaration. ents-ext.dtd declares cdeclpart as c (#PCDATA) at line 6 and uses it on the following line, and an XML parser has no problem with this. It would have a problem with the ents.xml file's declaration and usage of fdeclpart at lines 13 and 14 because of the last paragraph of the spec shown above: it's referenced within a markup declaration in an internal subset. The cdeclpart parameter entity was not a problem because it was referenced in an external subset.

The final declaration doesn't work in the external subset, so the internal subset doesn't even try it: the ents-ext.dtd file's ddeclpart entity tried to store the beginning and a middle piece of the d element type's declaration at line 11. It didn't work because it was declared illegal by the "Proper Declaration/PE Nesting" validity constraint. (Because it didn't work, I commented it out.)

As the parenthesized final sentence of the specification paragraph above tells us, the "PEs in Internal Subset" well-formedness constraint doesn't apply to parameter-entity references in an external parameter entity or in a DTD external subset, because when an XML processor is checking for well-formedness, it doesn't have to bother with external parameter entities and DTD external subsets.

Like the internal subset, the external subset and any external parameter entities referred to in the DTD must consist of a series of complete markup declarations of the types allowed by the non-terminal symbol `markupdecl`, interspersed with white space or parameter-entity references. However, portions of the contents of the external subset or of external parameter entities may conditionally be ignored by using the conditional section construct; this is not allowed in the internal subset.

The first sentence here sums up what we saw in the Examples 2.27 and 2.28. The second sentence tells us that conditional sections are OK in an external subset but not in an internal subset. Conditional sections (described further in 3.4, "Conditional Sections") let you easily change whether a parser ignores or parses a large block of text. For example, changing the "INCLUDE" to "IGNORE" in Example 2.29 tells the parser not to parse anything between the second `[` and the `]]>` that shows where the conditional section ends.

Example 2.29: An INCLUDE marked section

```
<![INCLUDE[
<!ENTITY sss "Shantih shantih shantih">
<!ENTITY tsepic SYSTEM "img/tse.eps" NDATA EPS>
]]>
```

External Subset

[30] `extSubset`	`::=`	`TextDecl? extSubsetDecl`
[31] `extSubsetDecl`	`::=`	`( markupdecl | conditionalSect | PEReference | S )*`

Production 30 shows that an external subset consists of an optional text declaration followed by an external subset declaration. Production 31 shows that the latter is a combination of zero or more of the markup declarations, conditional sections, and parameter-entity references (with optional white space between them) that we've seen throughout 2.8, "Prolog and Document Type Declaration".

As explained in 4.3.1, "The Text Declaration", a text declaration is a processing instruction telling us the version of XML being used by a particular external parsed entity.

> The external subset and external parameter entities also differ from the internal subset in that in them, parameter-entity references are permitted *within* markup declarations, not only *between* markup declarations.

This restates something that is implied by the "PEs in Internal Subset" well-formedness constraint and demonstrated by the parameter entities in Examples 2.27 and 2.28: references to parameter entities that contain incomplete pieces of markup declarations are only legal in external subsets.

> An example of an XML document with a document type declaration:
>
> ```
> <?xml version="1.0"?>
> <!DOCTYPE greeting SYSTEM "hello.dtd">
> <greeting>Hello, world!</greeting>
> ```
>
> The system identifier "`hello.dtd`" gives the URI of a DTD for the document.

As we saw in the "Status of this Document" section at the beginning of the specification, a "Uniform Resource Identifier" (URI) is a notation for naming resources on the Web. A "Uniform Resource Locator" (URL) such as `http://www.w3.org` is one kind of URI. Even a simple file name can be treated as a Relative URL that points to a file in the same directory as the entity in which the Relative URL is stored. URLs are a good way to identify system identifiers because of the huge HTML world's familiarity with them and because of the ease with which a URL can point to both local and remote addresses.

So, it looks like all those file names we've been seeing in DOC-TYPE declarations to identify the document type declarations' external subsets (like `hello.dtd` in the sample above) were URIs all the time.

Knowing this opens up a lot of possibilities. It means that your document can point to a DTD somewhere else by using a URL, like the one in Example 2.30.

Example 2.30: DOCTYPE declaration using a URL to identify a DTD

```
<!DOCTYPE min
    SYSTEM "http://www.snee.com/dtds/invoice.dtd">
```

This will be common for geographically widespread organizations that want to retain a regular structure for their documents. Different branch offices can point to a centrally maintained collection of DTDs without needing to maintain and update their own copies.

An XML processor treats a relative URI as being relative to the entity where it's stored, not relative to the document entity ultimately containing the reference. For example, say the `catalog.xml` document entity in the `grandfather` directory references the `parts.xml` file in the `father` subdirectory of `grandfather` as `father/parts.xml`, and an entity declaration in `parts.xml` references a file in `son/bolts.xml`. The XML processor will expect `son` to be a child of the `father` directory and not a child of the `catalog.xml` document's `grandfather` directory.

> The declarations can also be given locally, as in this example:
>
> ```
> <?xml version="1.0" encoding="UTF-8" ?>
> <!DOCTYPE greeting [
>   <!ELEMENT greeting (#PCDATA)>
> ]>
> <greeting>Hello, world!</greeting>
> ```
>
> If both the external and internal subsets are used, the internal subset is considered to occur before the external subset. This has the effect that entity and attribute-list declarations in the internal subset take precedence over those in the external subset.

The internal subset pre-empts any attempts to re-declare the same objects. In addition, entities declared in the internal subset can be referenced in the external subset.

Using the `extdecl.dtd` file shown in Example 2.31 as an external subset, this precedence of internal declarations will cause an XML processor to treat the document in Example 2.32 as if the `rutle` entity had the value "Barry" and the single `redecl` element's `flavor` attribute had the default value of "lemon".

Example 2.31: `extdecl.dtd` file with declarations pre-empted by Example 2.32's internal subset declarations

```
<!ATTLIST redecl flavor CDATA "mint">
<!ENTITY  rutle "Stig">
```

Example 2.32: Document with internal subset declarations pre-empting external subset declarations

```
<?xml version="1.0"?>
<!DOCTYPE redecl SYSTEM "extdecl.dtd" [
<!ELEMENT redecl (#PCDATA)>
<!ATTLIST redecl flavor CDATA "lemon">
<!ENTITY rutle "Barry">
]>
<redecl>My favorite Rutle was &rutle;.</redecl>
```

2.9. Standalone Document Declaration

Markup declarations can affect the content of the document, as passed from an XML processor to an application; examples are attribute defaults and entity declarations. The standalone document declaration, which may appear as a component of the XML declaration, signals whether or not there are such declarations which appear external to the document entity.

An XML document can get by with no declarations at all. It can also have declarations as part of an internal subset, and it can have declarations in an external subset such as a separate DTD file. The standalone document declaration, or **SDDecl** (used by production 23, among others) answers the question "can we get by using this document without paying attention to the external declarations?"

> **Tip**   Note that this question may not even be asked—the **SDDecl** provides information in case it's requested; it doesn't mandate behavior.

Standalone Document Declaration

[32] SDDecl	::=	S 'standalone' Eq (("'" ('yes' | 'no') "'") | ('"' ('yes' | 'no') '"'))	[VC: Standalone Document Declaration]

In a standalone document declaration, the value "yes" indicates that there are no markup declarations external to the document entity (either in the DTD external subset, or in an external parameter entity referenced from the internal subset) which affect the information passed from the XML processor to the application. The value "no" indicates that there are or may be such external markup declarations. Note that the standalone document declaration only denotes the presence of external *declarations*; the presence, in a document, of references to external *entities*, when those entities are internally declared, does not change its standalone status.

For example, the document type declaration in Example 2.33 tells us that, although the document may have declarations in an external file, the document can be processed without them. What kind of declarations are optional to document processing? The "Standalone Document Declaration" validity constraint below lists the possible conditions.

Example 2.33: XML declaration with a standalone declaration

```
<?xml version="1.0" standalone="yes"?>
```

If there are no external markup declarations, the standalone document declaration has no meaning. If there are external markup declarations but there is no standalone document declaration, the value "no" is assumed.

An external declaration subset that exists but isn't necessary is really the exceptional case, which is why you can normally omit the standalone document declaration. If there is an external subset and your document needs it, the processor assumes that standalone="no" if you don't specify otherwise; if there is no external subset, the standalone value is moot.

Any XML document for which standalone="no" holds can be converted algorithmically to a standalone document, which may be desirable for some network delivery applications.

By "converted algorithmically", this means that, with no human intervention, a document that depends on external declarations can be mechanically converted to one that doesn't. Basically, such a program would just make a copy of the document with all the external declarations moved to the internal subset (all the external declarations, that is, not pre-empted in the internal subset). Doing so is likely to be common, because storing documents as multiple interrelated pieces often makes sense from a document management viewpoint, while delivering them from one computer to another ("network delivery applications") is easier using documents that are self-contained units. These seemingly contradictory goals can both be achieved on a network by using document servers that can convert non-standalone documents to ones that don't need an external declaration subset.

VALIDITY CONSTRAINT: Standalone Document Declaration

The standalone document declaration must have the value "no" if any external markup declarations contain declarations of:

Now we get specific. Here are the four conditions in which a processor needs access to the markup declarations badly enough that if the declarations are in an external subset, the document being processed can't be considered standalone.

- attributes with default values, if elements to which these attributes apply appear in the document without specifications of values for these attributes, or

---

If the `chapter` element type has the attribute list definition shown in 2.34, then a `chapter` element in a document using this declaration has a `flavor` value of "mint" if its start-tag doesn't list any attribute values (`<chapter>`). A parser knows this from looking at the `chapter` element type's attribute list declaration, which specifies "mint" as the default value. If the parser has to look in an external declaration subset to find this declaration, then it's not a standalone document entity.

Example 2.34: Attribute declaration with default value of "mint"

```
<!ATTLIST chapter flavor CDATA "mint">
```

- entities (other than `amp`, `lt`, `gt`, `apos`, `quot`), if references to those entities appear in the document, or

---

If an XML processor finds the entity reference `&cnote;` in a document, how does it know what it refers to? It does so by looking at the cnote entity's declaration. If the processor has to look outside the document entity in an external declaration subset to find this declaration, then it's not a standalone document. Exceptions are the entity references used to represent the ampersand, less-than, greater-than, apostrophe, and quotation characters, because an XML processor will already know what these refer to. See 4.6, "Predefined Entities", for more on these.

- attributes with values subject to *normalization*, where the attribute appears in the document with a value which will change as a result of normalization, or

Some attribute values can refer to entities, and an important job of attribute value normalization is the resolution of these references. (See 3.3.3, "Attribute-Value Normalization", for more on this.) As with most other entity references, an XML processor needs their declarations to find them in storage. Any need to look at an external declaration subset for these means that the document is not a standalone one.

- element types with element content, if white space occurs directly within any instance of those types.

An element type consisting of element content has only other elements as children, with no character data that is not part of any child element (see 3.2.1, "Element Content", for background on this). Because the processor needs access to the element type declaration to know whether it should treat an element as having only element content, any need to look to an external declaration subset for the declaration means that the document is not a standalone one.

An example XML declaration with a standalone document declaration:

```
<?xml version="1.0" standalone='yes'?>
```

2.10. White Space Handling

In editing XML documents, it is often convenient to use "white space" (spaces, tabs, and blank lines, denoted by the nonterminal s in this specification) to set apart the markup for greater readability. Such white space is typically not intended for inclusion in the delivered version of the document. On the other hand, "significant" white space that should be preserved in the delivered version is common, for example in poetry and source code.

For example, production 28 has many places where **s** indicates required white space. Because **s** means "one or more of the space, tab, and line end characters", the parser doesn't care about the difference between the DOCTYPE declaration shown in Example 2.35 and the one shown in Example 2.36.

Example 2.35: DOCTYPE declaration with minimum required spaces

```
<!DOCTYPE rant SYSTEM "rant.dtd">
```

Example 2.36: DOCTYPE declaration with extra spaces in it

```
<!DOCTYPE     rant
       SYSTEM      "rant.dtd"   >
```

To "set apart the markup for greater readability" refers to the practice of adding disposable spaces to make the marked-up document easier to read. If a discography document type's album element type is declared as shown in Example 2.37 then `album` has element content (see 3.2.1, "Element Content", for more on this). A parser would not care whether an `album` element looks like the one in Example 2.38 or the one in Example 2.39.

Example 2.37: Declaration for `album` element shown in Examples 2.38 and 2.39

```
<!ELEMENT album (song+)>
```

Example 2.38: `album` element conforming to Example 2.37's element type declaration

```
<album><song>Hold My Hand</song><song>Number One</song>
<song>Love Life</song><song>Cheese and Onions</song></album>
```

Example 2.39: Another `album` element conforming to Example 2.37's element type declaration

```
<album>
    <song>Hold My Hand</song>
    <song>Number One</song>
    <song>Love Life</song>
    <song>Cheese and Onions</song>
</album>
```

The carriage returns and indentation in Example 2.39 don't matter to the XML processor.

Sometimes carriage returns and extra spaces are important, and you don't want the processor to throw them out. As examples, the specification mentions poetry (see Example 2.40) and the source code of programming languages. Consider the little Perl program shown in Example 2.41.

Example 2.40: Poem excerpt with meaningful white space

```
<poem>
<verse>'What shall we ever do?'</verse>
<verse>                    The hot water at ten.</verse>
<verse>And if it rains, a closed car at four.</verse>
</poem>
```

Example 2.41: Perl program with meaningful white space

```
#!/usr/local/bin/perl
$i = 0;
while (<>) {
    $i++;
    print "$i:     $_\n";
}
```

White space can be particularly important in program source code. While the difference between one and three spaces after the keyword "DOCTYPE" in a DOCTYPE declaration may not matter, such a cavalier attitude toward the space beginning some program listing lines would make the program difficult to read, and doing it to the space between the quotation marks in the program in Example 2.41's print line would change how the program worked.

The XML Working Group debated long and hard about how XML processors should handle white space characters, especially carriage returns.[†] Issues such as completely blank lines and carriage returns before and after comments make it difficult to lay out simple rules about which white space to preserve and which to throw out. After all

---

† At one point in their e-mail discussion of white space and the Record Start/Record End "characters" that delimit input lines, XML specification co-editor Tim Bray wrote "At this point I'd rather write WordPerfect macros than read another 10 postings about RS/RE".

the debate, the Working Group came up with something simple and straightforward.

> An XML processor must always pass all characters in a document that are not markup through to the application. A validating XML processor must also inform the application which of these characters constitute white space appearing in element content.

Instead of deciding which white space to throw out and which to keep, an XML processor must pass it all to the application.

Earlier drafts of the specification assigned further responsibilities to a validating XML processor: in addition to telling the application which white space characters were in element content, it was supposed to "signal to the application that white space in element content is not significant". The deletion of this line removes the value judgment on element content white space (like the carriage returns after each song element in Example 2.39) while still requiring the processor to identify element content white space for the application to use or ignore as it wishes.

> A special attribute named xml:space may be attached to an element to signal an intention that in that element, white space should be preserved by applications. In valid documents, this attribute, like any other, must be declared if it is used. When declared, it must be given as an enumerated type whose only possible values are "default" and "preserve". For example:
>
> ```
> <!ATTLIST poem    xml:space (default|preserve) 'preserve'>
> ```
>
> The value "default" signals that applications' default white-space processing modes are acceptable for this element; the value "preserve" indicates the intent that applications preserve all the white space. This declared intent is considered to apply to all elements within the content of the element where it is specified, unless overriden with another instance of the xml:space attribute.

This is a nice way to tell the application which elements should have their white space left alone. For most attributes that you define for elements, you'll end up specifying attribute values for each of the elements of that type. By specifying a default value of "preserve" in this attribute list declaration, the processor will treat every <poem> start-tag as if it said <poem xml:space="preserve"> instead. You can override this default by starting a poem with the tag <poem xml:space="default">. (Don't confuse this concept of default attribute values with the permitted value of "default" for the poem element type's xml:space attribute.)

Speaking of overriding, the last sentence of the specification paragraph above tells us that an xml:space value applies to all of an element's child elements and their descendants unless you specify otherwise for a specific element. For example, the xml:space attribute declaration shown for the poem element type in the spec's example above tells an XML processor to keep the extra spaces in its child elements—for example, the verse elements of Example 2.42. That is, unless verse had been declared with an attribute specification overriding this xml:space setting as shown in Example 2.43.

Example 2.42: Poem excerpt whose verse space will be kept because of poem element types xml:space

```
<poem>
<verse>'What is that noise?'</verse>
<verse>               The wind under the door.</verse>
<verse>'What is that noise now? What is the wind doing?'</verse>
<verse>               Nothing again nothing.</verse>
```

Example 2.43: Specifying xml:space value for verse element type

```
<!ATTLIST verse xml:space (default|preserve) 'default'>
```

The root element of any document is considered to have signaled no intentions as regards application space handling, unless it provides a value for this attribute or the attribute is declared with a default value.

If no such xml:space attribute was declared for the root element (the main document element that contains all the other elements in the document), you can't assume anything about what the processor will tell the application regarding the handling of spaces in that document.

Don't worry too much about xml:space, because an XML document that will be formatted for display on a page or screen will probably have a corresponding stylesheet. Part of the point of a stylesheet is to store far more sophisticated instructions about handling of white space than the xml:space attribute ever could. Besides, xml:space does not mandate any particular behavior, anyway; like the standalone document declaration, it merely passes a message along to be used if the application is interested.

2.11. End-of-Line Handling

XML parsed entities are often stored in computer files which, for editing convenience, are organized into lines. These lines are typically separated by some combination of the characters carriage-return (#xD) and linefeed (#xA).

Most text processing programs treat a line of text as the basic unit of a text file. This is part of the legacy of punch cards, which represented each line of a file with a single card. (It's no coincidence that before computers used the windows, icons, and mouse pointers of graphical user interfaces, the old green text-mode computer screens showed up to 80 characters on each line—that's how many characters each punch card stored.)

Different operating systems represent the end of a line in different ways:

- UNIX machines use a line feed (byte 10, or in hexadecimal, "#xA").

- Macintoshes use a carriage return (byte 13, or "#xD" in hex).

- Windows PCs use a carriage return followed by a line feed.

This is why, when a program such as an FTP utility copies files from one computer to another, it often wants to know if they're text or binary—if the latter, they leave every byte alone, but for text files, they need to know about any necessary line end conversions.

In developing the XML specification, some members of the Working Group questioned whether the concept of a "line" was still relevant. After all, an XML document is a collection of elements, entities, and declarations. If a document's DTD has no xml:space attributes declared anywhere, a document without a single carriage return or line feed is functionally the same as a document with a line end character at the last word break before every eightieth character.

The Working Group decided to use the term "for editing convenience", because we still think of a document in terms of lines when we interact with it on the screen, or for that matter, on paper. (Think how often you use word processing commands that deal in terms of lines: jump to the current line's beginning, jump to its end, delete the current line, and so forth.)

> To simplify the tasks of applications, wherever an external parsed entity or the literal entity value of an internal parsed entity contains either the literal two-character sequence "#xD#xA" or a standalone literal #xD, an XML processor must pass to the application the single character #xA. (This behavior can conveniently be produced by normalizing all line breaks to #xA on input, before parsing.)

No matter which representation of a line end is encountered by an XML processor, it passes along a single line feed character (ASCII character 10) to the application. Therefore, the XML application—unlike an FTP program—doesn't have to worry about different possible representations. This simplifying of the application's job is another example of the effort to ease the development of small yet effective applications.

Tip   *The processor still understands all three representations of line ends, but it must always pass a single* #xA *(line feed) character to the application.*

2.12. Language Identification

In document processing, it is often useful to identify the natural or formal language in which the content is written. A special attribute named xml:lang may be inserted in documents to specify the language used in the contents and attribute values of any element in an XML document. In valid documents, this attribute, like any other, must be declared if it is used. The values of the attribute are language identifiers as defined by [IETF RFC 1766], "Tags for the Identification of Languages":

XML's country and language identifiers can give an application important information that it needs for tasks like case conversion, because two countries that speak the same language may have different case conversion rules. (For example, an upper-case "è" is "E" in Montreal but "È" in Paris.)

In eastern alphabets, knowing the specific language and country is particularly important, because certain Unicode characters may be used in Chinese, Japanese, or Korean language documents. Displaying them properly requires a knowledge of which language is in use.

Language Identification

[33] `LanguageID`	`::=`	`Langcode ('-' Subcode)*`
[34] `Langcode`	`::=`	`ISO639Code	IanaCode	UserCode`
[35] `ISO639Code`	`::=`	`([a-z] | [A-Z]) ([a-z] | [A-Z])`
[36] `IanaCode`	`::=`	`('i' | 'I') '-' ([a-z] | [A-Z])+`
[37] `UserCode`	`::=`	`('x' | 'X') '-' ([a-z] | [A-Z])+`
[38] `Subcode`	`::=`	`([a-z] | [A-Z])+`

The `Langcode` may be any of the following:

- a two-letter language code as defined by [ISO 639], "Codes for the representation of names of languages"
- a language identifier registered with the Internet Assigned Numbers Authority [IANA]; these begin with the prefix "`i-`" (or "`I-`")
- a language identifier assigned by the user, or agreed on between parties in private use; these must begin with the prefix "`x-`" or "`X-`" in order to ensure that they do not conflict with names later standardized or registered with IANA

The term "tag" in the title of the Internet Engineering Task Force's (IETF) Request for Comment (RFC) 1766 has nothing to do with the XML sense of the term. This RFC defines a standard for identifying a language using one or more words: the first identifies the language and the optional second one identifies the country in which the language is being spoken and optional additional information. The language "tag" should be the two-letter code specified in ISO 639, "Codes for the representation of names of languages". For example, "fr" is French, "en" is English, and "sa" is Sanskrit.

Tip   The **langcode** uses the two-letter language codes from version 1 of ISO 639, not version 2's three-letter codes.

> There may be any number of `Subcode` segments; if the first subcode segment exists and the Subcode consists of two letters, then it must be a country code from [ISO 3166], "Codes for the representation of names of countries". If the first subcode consists of more than two letters, it must be a subcode for the language in question registered with IANA, unless the `Langcode` begins with the prefix "x-" or "X-".

The optional second "tag" specifies the country using either an abbreviation from ISO 3166, "Codes for the representation of names of countries" (for example, "BE" for Belgium or "US" for the United States) or some other code registered with the Internet Assigned Numbers Authority (the group responsible for first-level domain names like com, edu, and org). According to IETF RFC 1766, subsequent "tags" can be anything you like.

> It is customary to give the language code in lower case, and the country code (if any) in upper case. Note that these values, unlike other names in XML documents, are case insensitive.

For example, if Celine Dion, Jean-Claude Van Damme, and Johnny Halliday were each going to author XML essays on Proust's use of smell imagery, the French-Canadian ballad belter would use a language code of fr-CA to indicate "Canadian French", the muscles from Brussels would use fr-BE to show that his essay was in Belgian French, and aging rock star Johnny Halliday, being the most French of the three, would use fr-FR. On the other hand, an XML document about the "Code Talkers" (the Navajo U.S. Marines who transmitted coded radio messages in the Pacific during World War II) could use the language code i-navajo because the Navajo language has an entry registered with the IANA. Or, if you and a client had agreed to transmit documents in pig latin, and found no existing ISO or IANA code for pig latin, you could make up and use your own, as long as you preceded it with x- or X- (for example, x-pgl).

For example:

```
<p xml:lang="en">The quick brown fox jumps over the lazy dog.</p>
<p xml:lang="en-GB">What colour is it?</p>
<p xml:lang="en-US">What color is it?</p>
<sp who="Faust" desc='leise' xml:lang="de">
   <l>Habe nun, ach! Philosophie,</l>
   <l>Juristerei, und Medizin</l>
   <l>und leider auch Theologie</l>
   <l>durchaus studiert mit heißem Bemüh'n.</l>
</sp>
```

The intent declared with xml:lang is considered to apply to all attributes and content of the element where it is specified, unless overridden with an instance of xml:lang on another element within that content.

In the specification's example above, the four l elements written in German are children of the sp element. Because they have no xml:lang attribute of their own to specify their language, an application must treat them as if they had the xml:lang value of de, as their parent does.

A simple declaration for xml:lang might take the form

```
xml:lang   NMTOKEN   #IMPLIED
```

but specific default values may also be given, if appropriate. In a collection of French poems for English students, with glosses and notes in English, the xml:lang attribute might be declared this way:

```
<!ATTLIST poem   xml:lang NMTOKEN 'fr'>
<!ATTLIST gloss  xml:lang NMTOKEN 'en'>
<!ATTLIST note   xml:lang NMTOKEN 'en'>
```

Note that the attribute declared default of #IMPLIED in that first example makes that xml:lang attribute optional. For the poem, gloss, and note examples, including this attribute in element start-tags is also optional, but for a different reason: because defaults are supplied. If no xml:lang value is specified for any poem, gloss, or note elements in the document, they'll each have the default value shown in their declarations.

Logical Structures

- Start-Tags, End-Tags, and Empty-Element Tags
- Element Type Declarations
- Attribute-List Declarations
- Conditional Sections

his chapter covers the markup used to indicate the kinds of information stored in a document and their relationship. For example, to describe a book as being composed of a title followed by chapters, with each chapter being a title followed by paragraphs with optional illustrations, is to describe the "book" document type's logical structure.

Each XML document contains one or more *elements*, the boundaries of which are either delimited by start-tags and end-tags, or, for empty elements, by an empty-element tag. Each element has a type, identified by name, sometimes called its "generic identifier" (GI), and may have a set of attribute specifications. Each attribute specification has a name and a value.

For example, the document in Example 3.1 is one big `addrbook` element. It has three `entry` elements as children, and each `entry` element has a `name` element followed by a `phone` element.

Example 3.1: `addrbook` element containing three `entry` child elements, each with its own child elements

```
<addrbook>

<entry><name>Dirk</name>
<phone number="423-0532"/></entry>

<entry><name instrument="drums">Barry</name>
<phone number="423-4634"/></entry>

<entry><name instrument="guitar">Stig</name>
<phone number="423-9915"></phone></entry>

</addrbook>
```

The `addrbook` element and all the `entry` and `name` elements each have start-tags (for example, `<addrbook>`, `<entry>`, and `<name instrument="drums">`) and end-tags (for example, `</addrbook>` and `</name>`).

Tip   *The empty phone element can either be represented by a start- and end-tag pair, as in Stig's case in Example 3.1, or by an empty-element tag, as in Dirk and Barry's case. (Note that the empty-element tag has a slash before its closing ">" and that an empty element represented by a start- and end-tag pair has nothing between those two tags.)*

The first (or only) name in the tag tells us the type of element the tag starts, ends, or, in the case of an empty-element tag, both starts and ends. This name is the element type name, or "generic identifier". It's "generic" because it identifies the element as a member of a particular element type, unlike a "unique identifier" that identifies one specific element. You can create unique identifiers using an attribute of type `ID`; see 3.3.1, "Attribute Types", for more on this.

An element *may* have one or more attributes. For example, Barry and Stig's `name` elements in Example 3.1 each exhibit values for the attribute `instrument`, while Dirk's doesn't. All the `phone` elements exhibit values for the `number` attribute. These attributes are always specified in the start-tag, or in the case of empty elements, in the empty-element tag.

Element

[39]`element`	`::=`	`EmptyElemTag`	
		`| STag content ETag`	[WFC: Element Type Match] [VC: Element Valid]

This specification does not constrain the semantics, use, or (beyond syntax) names of the element types and attributes, except that names beginning with a match to `(('X'\|'x')('M'\|'m')('L'\|'l'))` are reserved for standardization in this or future versions of this specification.

Element type and attribute names can mean anything you want them to, and you can make up any names you like, as long as these names conform to the syntax laid out in the specification. In Example 3.1 I could have called the `name` element type "thnad" and the `instrument` attribute "snee" and then had elements like the one shown in Example 3.2.

Example 3.2: Using alternative names for Example 3.1's `name` element and its `instrument` attribute

---

```
<thnad snee="drums">Barry</thnad>
```

I could not, however, call an element type or attribute `96Tears`. The next section shows that an attribute or element type name must be a **Name**, which according to 2.3, "Common Syntactic Constructs", must start with a letter, underscore, or colon.

Certain element types and attributes (such as the `xml:lang` attribute described in 2.12, "Language Identification") start with the letters "xml", and the future may bring more special element type or attribute names that begin this way. To avoid running into problems with this practice, you must avoid starting your own element type or attribute names with the letters "xml" in any combination of upper- or lower-case.[†]

> **WELL-FORMEDNESS CONSTRAINT: Element Type Match**
>
> The Name in an element's end-tag must match the element type in the start-tag.

Elements must nest properly—in other words, if one element starts inside of another element, it must finish before its containing element finishes. An XML processor will choke on the entry end-tag in Example 3.3 because it hasn't found the </name> end-tag yet.

Example 3.3: entry element ending before its child name element does

```
<entry><name>Stig</entry>
```

If the processor finds an end-tag for an element that never even got started, like the </snee> end-tag in Example 3.4, that's even worse.

Example 3.4: End-tag with no corresponding start-tag

```
<entry><name>Stig</snee>
```

(Well, it's not really worse—they're both illegal, period; XML has no degrees of illegality.) Why will the processor reject them? Because the well-formedness constraint above tells it to.

---

† See Chapter 6, "Notation", for an explanation of how (('X'|'x')('M'|'m')('L'|'l')) means "the letters 'xml' in any combination of upper- or lower-case".

This explains the key difference between merely well-formed documents and valid documents: a valid document's elements must also follow one of the rules listed later in this Validity Constraint. These rules all describe an element's relationship to its element type declaration.

Production 45 in 3.2, "Element Type Declarations", shows that one part of an element type declaration is its **contentspec**. Production 46 shows that a **contentspec** may have a value of "EMPTY" or "ANY" or match the productions for **Mixed** (production 51) or **children** (production 47). See 3.2, "Element Type Declarations", for these productions and more on how element type declarations should look.

The descriptions below of these four **contentspec** types include commentary that refers to Example 3.5.

Example 3.5: Document demonstrating all four contentspec categories

```
1.  <?xml version="1.0"?>
2.  <!DOCTYPE note [
3.  <!ELEMENT note (img?, para, desc)>
4.  <!ELEMENT img EMPTY>
5.  <!ATTLIST img src CDATA #REQUI RED>
6.  <!ELEMENT para (#PCDATA|img)*>
7.  <!ELEMENT desc ANY>
8.  ]>
9.  <note><img src="a.jpg"/>
10.    <para>A para can mix up PCDATA text with imgs.
11.     <img src="b.jpg"></img>
12.     That was an img, and here's another: <img src="c.jpg"/>
13.    </para>
14.    <desc>A desc can have anything,<img src="d.jpg"/> as long as
15.     its children are declared and <desc></desc> valid.
```

```
16.     <note>
17.     <para>Even a note!</para>
18.     <desc>So versatile--maybe too versatile!</desc>
19.     </note>
20.   </desc>
21. </note>
```

> 1.   The declaration matches EMPTY and the element has no content.

The img elements in Example 3.5's note document meets these conditions: their name matches the name in the document's second element type declaration at line 4 ("img"), the img declaration "matches EMPTY", and the elements have no content.

Note that the second img element (line 11) is shown as a pair of start- and end-tags with nothing between them, while the others (lines 9, 12, and 14) are represented by empty-element tags.

> 2.   The declaration matches children and the sequence of child elements belongs to the language generated by the regular expression in the content model, with optional white space (characters matching the nonterminal S) between each pair of child elements.

For an element's child elements to belong "to the language generated by the regular expression in the content model", they would fit the pattern expressed by the syntax of the content model in that element type's declaration. In Example 3.5, the note element type's content model on line 3 shows that it consists of an optional img followed by a para and a desc, in that order. The main note element that contains the rest of the document (lines 9 - 21) is an img (line 9) followed by a para (lines 10 - 13) and a desc (lines 14 - 20); the note element inside that desc (lines 16 - 19) is just a para followed by a desc. Since the img is optional, both of these note elements belong "to the language generated by the regular expression" (img?, para, desc) in the note element type's declaration.

> 3. The declaration matches `Mixed` and the content consists of character data and child elements whose types match names in the content model.

The corresponding element type declaration for Example 3.5's para elements (line 6) matches the **Mixed** nonterminal (production 51). It allows each para element to mix character data, or PCDATA, with zero or more occurrences of a child element declared elsewhere in the DTD: img.

> 4. The declaration matches `ANY`, and the types of any child elements have been declared.

An element with a content specification of ANY can have any mix of character data and child elements, as long as those children are properly declared elsewhere in the DTD. This is generally only used for development or temporary emergency purposes; a DTD for serious production work rarely has element types with a content specification of ANY, because they almost contradict the point of having a DTD: to constrain the elements' structures so that automated systems can more easily manipulate documents. Example 3.5's desc element type has a content specification of ANY, and the three desc elements in the document (two at lines 15 and 18 inside of another one at lines 14 to 20) show how much leeway it gives you.

3.1. Start-Tags, End-Tags, and Empty-Element Tags

The beginning of every non-empty XML element is marked by a *start-tag*.

Tip *Empty elements can have start-tags too, because the empty element* <img src="a.jpg"/> *could also be written as* <img src="a.jpg"></img>.

Start-tag

[40]STag	::= '<' Name (S Attribute)* S? '>'	[WFC: Unique Att Spec]
[41]Attribute	::= Name Eq AttValue	[VC: Attribute Value Type] [WFC: No External Entity References] [WFC: No < in Attribute Values]

The Name in the start- and end-tags gives the element's *type*. The Name-AttValue pairs are referred to as the *attribute specifications* of the element, with the Name in each pair referred to as the *attribute name* and the content of the AttValue (the text between the ' or " delimiters) as the *attribute value*.

For example, in the start-tag <chapter author="BD">, the first name (or "generic identifier") chapter tells us the element's type. In the **Name-AttValue** attribute specification pair author="BD" the attribute name is author and the attribute value is BD.

The * in production 40 shows that a start-tag can have zero or more **Attribute** specifications with some space before each one.

> **WELL-FORMEDNESS CONSTRAINT: Unique Att Spec**
>
> No attribute name may appear more than once in the same start-tag or empty-element tag.

A start-tag with more than one attribute specification for the same attribute, such as `<chapter author="BD" author="DB">` is not permitted.

> **VALIDITY CONSTRAINT: Attribute Value Type**
>
> The attribute must have been declared; the value must be of the type declared for it. (For attribute types, see **Section 3.3: Attribute-List Declarations**.)

In a merely well-formed document, elements can have any attributes you want, as long as their names conform to the syntax of an attribute name. However, in a valid XML document, the processor has to know about an element's possible attribute names in advance from its attribute list declaration. See 3.3, "Attribute-List Declarations" for more on these.

> **WELL-FORMEDNESS CONSTRAINT: No External Entity References**
>
> Attribute values cannot contain direct or indirect entity references to external entities.

Because an external general entity may not be text, or may be encoded differently from the document entity, it's inappropriate for an attribute value. (See 4.3.3, "Character Encoding in Entities", for more on entity encoding.)

While it's OK for an attribute value to have a reference to an internal entity, that internal entity better not have a reference to an external entity, because that would be make an indirect reference to an external entity.

For example, the item element on line 12 of the document in Example 3.6 has a reference to the internal entity intent1 in its topic attribute, and that's fine. The remaining item elements are commented out because they're illegal: the one on line 17 has a topic attribute whose value has a direct reference to the extent1 external entity, and the one on line 19's topic attribute has a reference to the intent2 entity—an internal entity, sure, but one whose value has a reference to the external entity extent1, making that intent2 entity reference an indirect reference to an external entity and therefore illegal.

Example 3.6: Various successful and unsuccessful entity references

```
 1. <?xml version="1.0"?>
 2. <!DOCTYPE list [
 3. <!ELEMENT list    (item+)>
 4. <!ELEMENT item (#PCDATA)>
 5. <!ATTLIST item topic CDATA #IMPLIED>
 6. <!ENTITY  extent1 SYSTEM "extfile.ent">
 7. <!ENTITY  intent1 "the intent1 text">
 8. <!ENTITY  intent2 "a reference to &extent1;">
 9. ]>
10.
11. <list>
12. <item topic="reference to &intent1;">
13. Sample item 1. &extent1;</item>
14.
15. <!-- illegal, and commented out:
16.
17. <item topic="reference to &extent1;">
18. Sample item 2.</item>
19. <item topic="reference to &intent2;">
20. Sample item 3.</item>
21.
```

22. `-->`
23.
24. `</list>`

> **WELL-FORMEDNESS CONSTRAINT: No < in Attribute Values**
>
> The replacement text of any entity referred to directly or indirectly in an attribute value (other than "`&lt;`") must not contain a <.

In the entity declaration in Example 3.7 "the intent1 text" is the replacement text. If any entity in a document has replacement text with a "<" in it, the document isn't well-formed. The exception, of course, is the `lt` entity, whose only replacement text is "<", so use that when you need this character in an attribute value.

Example 3.7: Entity declaration with "the intent1 text" as its replacement text

```
<!ENTITY    intent1 "the intent1 text">
```

> An example of a start-tag:
>
> ```
> <termdef id="dt-dog" term="dog">
> ```
>
> The end of every element that begins with a start-tag must be marked by an *end-tag* containing a name that echoes the element's type as given in the start-tag:

Start- and end-tags always come in pairs.

End-tag

[42]ETag   `::=  '</' Name S? '>'`

> An example of an end-tag:
>
> ```
>   </termdef>
> ```
>
> The text between the start-tag and end-tag is called the element's *content*:

An end-tag looks just like the corresponding start-tag except that it has a slash (/) after its opening "<" and will never have attribute specifications.

Content of Elements

```
[43] content        ::=   (element | CharData | Reference | CDSect | PI |
                           Comment)*
```

An element's content can consist of the following:

- Other elements.
- Character data. (See 2.4, "Character Data and Markup", for more. The presence of character data is what prevents an element's content from being considered "element content". I told you it could be confusing.)
- Entity or character references (see 4.1, "Character and Entity References").
- Processing instructions (see 2.6, "Processing Instructions") and comments (see 2.5, "Comments").

■ CDATA sections (see 2.7, "CDATA Sections").

> ***Tip*** *Don't confuse the phrase "element's content" here with "element content", which is described on page 142.*

Surrounding production 43's list in parentheses and putting an asterisk after the right parenthesis means "zero or more of any combination of these".

> If an element is *empty*, it must be represented either by a start-tag immediately followed by an end-tag or by an empty-element tag. An *empty-element tag* takes a special form:

This means that a document could use both `<img></img>` and `<img/>` to represent an empty `img` element. (Note that, when using a start- and end-tag together to represent an empty element, there must be *nothing* between them—not even a space.)

Tags for Empty Elements

```
[44]EmptyElemTag   ::=  '<' Name (S Attribute)* S? '/>'    [WFC: Unique Att Spec]
```

An empty-element tag looks pretty much like a start-tag with a slash before the closing >. After the opening < it has the generic identifier that shows the element type, then zero or more attribute specifications.

> Empty-element tags may be used for any element which has no content, whether or not it is declared using the keyword EMPTY. For interoperability, the empty-element tag must be used, and can only be used, for elements which are declared EMPTY.

You can use an empty-element tag for any empty element, even if it's not declared as empty. For example, the third item element in Example 3.8 is perfectly valid XML.

Example 3.8: Using an empty element for an element not declared as always empty

```
<!DOCTYPE list [
<!ELEMENT list (item+)>
<!ELEMENT item (#PCDATA)>
]>
<list>
<item>Here is item 1.</item>
<item>Here is item 2.</item>
<item/>
<item>Here is item 4. The third one was empty.</item>
</list>
```

This is a big jump from original SGML practice, which is why "for interoperability" (that is, if you're going to use SGML software that hasn't been upgraded to WebSGML) you should only use the empty-element tag to represent elements that were declared to always be empty.

> Examples of empty elements:
>
> ```
> <IMG align="left"
>  src="http://www.w3.org/Icons/WWW/w3c_home" />
> <br></br>
> <br/>
> ```

Note the extra space before the `/>` that closes the `IMG` empty-element tag. This is optional, as shown by the `?` in production 44.

3.2. Element Type Declarations

The element structure of an XML document may, for validation purposes, be constrained using element type and attribute-list declarations. An element type declaration constrains the element's content.

An element type declaration specifies constraints, or rules, for the elements of a particular type—for example, all the `par` elements or all the `chapter` elements. Attribute-list declarations tell us about each of an element type's attributes. This is the crux of XML's power, because a program that can read these rules knows what to expect when it reads the documents that conform to a particular set of rules. The tools that build on this knowledge let us create systems that can use XML documents in any medium that exists or may exist in the future.

Element type declarations often constrain which element types can appear as children of the element. At user option, an XML processor may issue a warning when a declaration mentions an element type for which no declaration is provided, but this is not an error.

One of the most important jobs of an element type declaration is specifying the content of the elements of a given type, or the element type's content model. The content model might specify which elements can go inside of elements of a certain type and their possible ordering, but it doesn't have to do this—the keyword `ANY` tells the processor that anything can go inside of a particular element type. (See the spec's `container` example on page 142.) The element type declaration in Example 3.9 tells us that a `chapter` element is composed of a `title` element followed by one or more `para` elements.

Example 3.9: Three element type declarations

```
<!ELEMENT chapter (title,para+)>
<!ELEMENT title   (#PCDATA)>
<!ELEMENT para    (#PCDATA)>
```

The `chapter` element in Example 3.10 conforms to the declarations in Example 3.9 and is therefore valid.

Example 3.10: `chapter` element conforming to Example 3.9's declarations

```
<chapter><title>The Fire Sermon</title>
<para>The river's tent is broken: the last fingers of leaf
clutch and sink into the wet bank. The wind crosses the
brown land, unheard. The nymphs have departed.</para>
</chapter>
```

The `chapter` element in Example 3.11, while well-formed, doesn't conform to the element type declaration, and is therefore not valid.

Example 3.11: Well-formed `chapter` element that doesn't conform to Example 3.9's element type declaration

```
<chapter><title flavor="mint">The Fire Sermon</title>
The river's tent is broken: the last fingers of leaf
clutch and sink into the wet bank. The wind crosses the
brown land, unheard. The <emph>nymphs</emph> have departed.
</chapter>
```

 *Tip*   An XML document that isn't valid isn't worthless, the way an invalid C++ program or RTF document is. It might still be well-formed and perfectly useful to many applications. A well-formed XML document is a legal, useful one; being valid is a more demanding condition that offers greater possibilities to software manipulating the documents.

According to the last specification sentence above, if a content model mentions element types that don't have their own declarations it's not an error, but the processor may issue a warning, and the user should be able to turn off this warning. However, if any elements of those types occur in the document instance, the document would not be valid.

An *element type declaration* takes the form:

An element type declaration is a way of saying "here's an element type that can be used in this document, and here's the form it can take".

Element Type Declaration

[45] elementdecl	::=	'<!ELEMENT' S Name S contentspec S? '>'	[VC: Unique Element Type Declaration]
[46] contentspec	::=	'EMPTY' | 'ANY' | Mixed | children	

where the Name gives the element type being declared.

The **contentspec** specifies the possible children of an element of the type being declared. Of the four categories of **contentspec**,

- EMPTY is described further near the end of 3.1, "Start-Tags, End-Tags, and Empty-Element Tags".
- ANY (the most permissive of the four) is described on page 131.
- **Mixed** is described in 3.2.2, "Mixed Content".

- **children** is described in 3.2.1, "Element Content".

> **VALIDITY CONSTRAINT: Unique Element Type Declaration**
>
> No element type may be declared more than once.
>
> Examples of element type declarations:
>
> ```
> <!ELEMENT br EMPTY>
> <!ELEMENT p (#PCDATA|emph)* >
> <!ELEMENT %name.para; %content.para; >
> <!ELEMENT container ANY>
> ```

Note the third of those four sample element type declarations, which has parameter-entity references. The processor will replace these reference with whatever text was used to declare them. For example, if they had been defined with the declarations shown in Example 3.12, the processor would treat that third element type declaration in the spec's example above as being equivalent to the second one.

Example 3.12: Sample declarations for the name.para and content.para parameter entities

```
<!ENTITY % name.para "p">
<!ENTITY % content.para "(#PCDATA|emph)*">
```

3.2.1. Element Content

An element type consisting of element content is declared to have only other elements as children, with no character data that is not part of a child element. In other words, its content model only shows child elements and not #PCDATA. Any carriage returns, tabs, and other white space between its child elements are only there to make it easier for people to read the marked-up data. For example, the para element in Example 3.13 does not have element content because it has character data in addition to the emph child element.

Example 3.13: `para` element whose content is not element content

```
<para>This element does <emph>not</emph> have
element content.</para>
```

Knowing this, would you consider Example 3.14's `list` element to have element content?

Example 3.14: `list` element: element content?

```
<list>
<item>garlic</item>
<item>sapphires</item>
<item>item</item>
</list>
```

It's a trick question: you can't tell whether it has element content without looking at its declaration. If it was declared with the declaration shown in Example 3.15, it's obviously element content, and the carriage returns between the child elements should be ignored. If it was declared with the declaration shown in Example 3.16, however, that same `list` element is still perfectly valid, although it no longer has element content.

Example 3.15: Declaration for Example 3.14's `list` element that gives it element content

```
<!ELEMENT list (item)+>
```

Example 3.16: Declaration for Example 3.14's `list` element that gives it mixed, not element content

```
<!ELEMENT list (#PCDATA|item)*>
```

Does the `list` element have any PCDATA in it? Yes, if a document type declaration used that second declaration to define it—the carriage returns between the child elements qualify as PCDATA.

> An element type has *element content* when elements of that type must contain only child elements (no character data), optionally separated by white space (characters matching the nonterminal S). In this case, the constraint includes a content model, a simple grammar governing the allowed types of the child elements and the order in which they are allowed to appear. The grammar is built on content particles (cps), which consist of names, choice lists of content particles, or sequence lists of content particles:

In computer science and linguistics, a "grammar" is a set of rules defining a vocabulary of symbols or words and their possible orderings. An element type declaration's content model tells us two things:

- The "allowed types of the child elements", or the element types of the children that may appear within a particular element. In Example 3.9, `title` and `para` are the "vocabulary" of element types allowed in a `chapter` element.

- The "order in which [these children] are allowed to appear". If your `chapter` element type consists of a `title` followed by one or more `para` elements, the syntax of a content model lets you specify that the `title` must come first.

Content model syntax gives you a way to say "a `ingredients` element consists of any number of `fruit`, `vegetable`, and `grain` elements in any order". Or, you could say "a `titlepage` element has to have exactly one `title` element followed by exactly one `author` element followed by exactly one `publisher` element". It also offers various degrees of freedom between these two extremes, so that you could specify that a `notice` element starts with either a `warning` or a `cau-`

tion element, then has zero or more para elements, then a severity element, then … you get the idea. The concept of "content particles" is the specification's way of spelling out where and how you can take advantage of this flexibility.

The following productions are easier to understand if you first look at Examples 3.17 through 3.22.

Element-content Models

[47]`children`	`::=`	`(choice | seq) ('?' | '*' | '+')?`
[48]`cp`	`::=`	`(Name | choice | seq) ('?' | '*' ` `| '+')?`
[49]`choice`	`::=`	`'(' S? cp ( S? '|' S? cp )* S?` `')'` [VC: Proper Group/PE Nesting]
[50]`seq`	`::=`	`'(' S? cp ( S? ',' S? cp )* S?` `')'` [VC: Proper Group/PE Nesting]

where each `Name` is the type of an element which may appear as a child. Any content particle in a choice list may appear in the element content at the location where the choice list appears in the grammar; content particles occurring in a sequence list must each appear in the element content in the order given in the list. The optional character following a name or list governs whether the element or the content particles in the list may occur one or more (+), zero or more (*), or zero or one times (?). The absence of such an operator means that the element or content particle must appear exactly once. This syntax and meaning are identical to those used in the productions in this specification.

Production 47 shows that the content model for an element type that consists of element content (see productions 45 and 46) consists of either a choice of content particles or a sequence of content particles. (The specification paragraph above refers to the latter as a "sequence list".) The ?, *, and + punctuation marks on the right of production 47 let you specify how many times this particular choice or sequence can occur (see Chapter 6, "Notation" for more on this syntax, with examples):

- A question mark (?) shows that the choice or sequence is optional—in other words, that it should show up either zero times or once.

- An asterisk (*) shows that the choice or sequence can appear zero or more times.

- A plus sign (+) shows that the choice or sequence must show up one or more times.

Note the two question marks in production 47. The second one is part of the syntax of the production to show you that everything in the parenthesized expression preceding it is optional. The first question mark, being inside of quotation marks, is part of the text that you may put in your element type declaration's content model to show that the content particle preceding it represents an optional part of the element being declared.

The last sentence of the specification paragraph above tries to make these two different uses of the question mark seem helpful to you: "See! This syntax for showing how an element type's children may repeat is the same as the syntax that we're using to show you what syntax you can use!"

To understand these productions, let's first look at some simple examples. Example 3.17's declaration shows that a `section` element has a single child, which can be either a `chapter` or an `appendix` element.

Example 3.17: Demonstrating productions 47 through 49

```
<!ELEMENT section (chapter|appendix)>
```

The | character shows that you can choose between the `chapter` and `appendix` elements. Production 48 shows that a **Name** can serve as a **cp**, so both `chapter` and `appendix` can be **cp** expressions. Production 49 shows that a **choice** expression is made of one content particle (**cp**) followed by zero or more content particles separated by the |

character. Therefore, (chapter|appendix) is a legal **choice** expression.

Finally, production 47 shows that a **children** expression can be made of a single **choice** expression. That means (chapter|appendix) is also a legal **children** expression for a **contentspec** as defined in production 46.

Let's look at some variations on this. The asterisk in production 49 shows that the chapter element in the section element type's content model could be followed by zero or more other element type names separated by the | character. Both the section element type declarations shown in Example 3.18 would therefore be legal (but not in the same DTD!).

Example 3.18: Two possible section declarations, the second one demonstrating production 49

```
<!ELEMENT section (chapter)>

<!ELEMENT section (chapter|appendix|glossary)>
```

Production 47 shows that the **choice** or **seq** expression can have a question mark after it to show that the whole thing is optional, so Example 3.19 would also be legal.

Example 3.19: section declaration demonstrating production 47

```
<!ELEMENT section (chapter|appendix)?>
```

Unlike a **choice** expression, a **seq** expression lists child content particle expressions (which may themselves be **choice** or **seq** expressions) in the order that they must appear. As production 50 shows, commas separate the listed children. For example, Example 3.20 shows a section that consists of a single chapter followed by a single appendix.

Example 3.20: `section` declaration demonstrating production 50

```
<!ELEMENT section (chapter,appendix)>
```

In Example 3.21's `section` element type declaration, the plus sign tells us that the `chapter`, `appendix`, and `glossary` sequence must appear at least once in that order, and this sequence of three elements can be repeated additional times.

Example 3.21: Using the plus sign in a content model

```
<!ELEMENT section (chapter,appendix,glossary)+>
```

These examples only scratch the surface of what's possible. Production 48 shows that a content particle can be another **choice** or **seq** instead of always being a **Name**, as it is in all the examples above. This allows more complex content models. In Example 3.22, a `section` element is a single `chapter` followed by zero or more `appendix` and `index` elements, with a single `glossary` required at the `section` element's end.

Example 3.22: A more complex content model

```
<!ELEMENT section (chapter,(appendix|index)*,glossary)>
```

The parentheses, which productions 49 and 50 tell us to put around these groups, make the more complicated productions a little easier to read.

The content of an element matches a content model if and only if it is possible to trace out a path through the content model, obeying the sequence, choice, and repetition operators and matching each element in the content against an element type in the content model. For compatibility, it is an error if an element in the document can match more than one occurrence of an element type in the content model. For more information, see **Appendix E: Deterministic Content Models (Non-Normative)**.

A parser's first task is breaking down its input into pieces and making sure that each pattern of those pieces fits a variation allowed by the rules of the language's syntax. The variations on a pattern are often represented by a graph known as a "transition graph" to computer scientists. For example, we can represent the content model of the element type declaration shown in Example 3.23 with the graph shown in Figure 3–1.

Example 3.23: Element type declaration whose content model is diagrammed in Figure 3–1

```
<!ELEMENT chapter (intro,map,(poem|para+),endnotes)>
```

The numbers in each circle identify the various states of the parser as it figures out whether the chapter being parsed is a valid one. In each state, the parser has a new set of valid choices. The double circle represents the final state of one of these graphs.

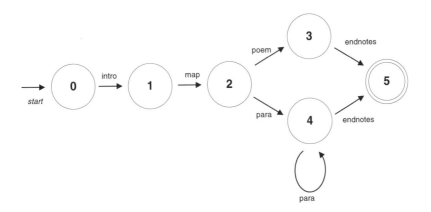

Figure 3–1 Sample content model transition graph

For the chapter element shown in Example 3.24, we can trace a path on the diagram from the starting position to the final state reached by finding an endnotes element, so it's a valid chapter element.

Example 3.24: Sample chapter conforming to Example 3.23's element type declaration

```
<chapter>
  <intro/>
  <map/>
  <para/>
  <para/>
  <endnotes/>
</chapter>
```

For the chapter shown in Example 3.25, however, we would get stuck at state 2. After the map, the parser expects to find either a poem or a para, so it will output an error message about the unexpected endnotes. The first sentence of the above specification paragraph now makes more sense: because it's not "possible to trace out a path through the content model" for this last chapter element, it doesn't match its content model.

Example 3.25: Sample chapter that doesn't conform to Example 3.23's element type declaration

```
<chapter>
  <intro/>
  <map/>
  <endnotes/>
</chapter>
```

The second sentence of that specification paragraph requires the content model to be "deterministic". In other words, there should never be any question about which path to take from one state to another. As an example of a nondeterministic content model, Appendix E, "Deterministic Content Models (Non-Normative)" provides the one in Example 3.26. It has the transition graph shown in Figure 3–2.

Example 3.26: A nondeterministic content model

```
((b, c) | (b, d))
```

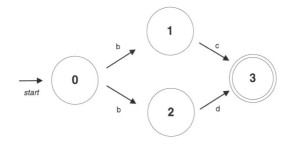

Figure 3–2 Nondeterministic transition graph

It's nondeterministic because after that first b element comes along, the parser won't know whether it's in state 1 and looking for a c to come along or in state 2 and waiting for a d element.

Nondeterminism is not an insoluble problem for parser writers, but forbidding nondeterministic content models makes XML parsers much easier to write. It also makes the models easier for humans to understand.

> **VALIDITY CONSTRAINT: Proper Group/PE Nesting**
>
> Parameter-entity replacement text must be properly nested with parenthetized groups. That is to say, if either of the opening or closing parentheses in a choice, seq, or Mixed construct is contained in the replacement text for a parameter entity, both must be contained in the same replacement text.

In Example 3.27, the chapter element type declaration references the chapbody parameter entity, which references the body parameter entity.

Example 3.27: Nested parameter entities

```
<!ENTITY % body "(poem | para+)">
<!ENTITY % chapbody "(intro, map, %body;, endnotes)">
<!ELEMENT chapter %chapbody;>
```

"Proper nesting" means that a parenthesized expression that begins in a particular parameter entity's replacement text must end in the same replacement text.

> For interoperability, if a parameter-entity reference appears in a `choice`, `seq`, or `Mixed` construct, its replacement text should not be empty, and neither the first nor last non-blank character of the replacement text should be a connector (| or ,).

While Example 3.28's type of declarations are legal in XML, you should avoid them "for interoperability" (that is, if you want the document to work with SGML software that lacks support for Web-SGML). An older SGML parser won't like the end parameter entity, which has an empty string for replacement text, and it won't like the start parameter entity, which has replacement text that ends with a comma.

Example 3.28: A parameter entity with replacement text ending in a comma connector, and another with no replacement text

```
<!ENTITY % start "intro,">
<!ENTITY % end "">
<!ELEMENT chapter  (%start; map,(poem|para+),endnotes %end;)>
```

> Examples of element-content models:
>
> ```
> <!ELEMENT spec (front, body, back?)>
> <!ELEMENT div1 (head, (p | list | note)*, div2*)>
> <!ELEMENT dictionary-body (%div.mix; | %dict.mix;)*>
> ```

Actually, the `dictionary-body` element type above may not be element content, depending on the replacement text of the two entities referenced in its content model.

3.2.2. Mixed Content

An element type has *mixed content* when elements of that type may contain character data, optionally interspersed with child elements. In this case, the types of the child elements may be constrained, but not their order or their number of occurrences:

The spec's sample declarations for element types p and b on page 155 at the end of this section show the two basic forms of mixed-content element types: either just PCDATA (character data) or a list of elements that can show up and repeat in any order with any amount of PCDATA mixed in between them.

Note that for PCDATA mixed with other components, PCDATA is always listed first. If there are no components besides PCDATA, there is nothing particularly "mixed" about purely PCDATA content, but it is still considered mixed content.

Mixed-content Declaration

```
[51]Mixed   ::=  '(' S? '#PCDATA' (S? '|' S? Name)* S?
                 ')*'
             | '(' S? '#PCDATA' S? ')'        [VC: Proper Group/PE Nesting]
                                              [VC: No Duplicate Types]
```

where the Names give the types of elements that may appear as children.

The five p elements in Example 3.29 all conform to the first sample element type declaration in the specification on page 155.

Example 3.29: Different p elements

```
<p>This one only has character data.</p>

<p>Character data <b>a b element in the middle</b>
and some more character data.</p>

<p><b>A b element</b>, <i>an i element</i>,
<b>another b element</b>.</p>
```

```
<p></p>
```

```
<p/>
```

The declaration's * shows that you can have zero or more of these components, which is why the last two p elements shown in Example 3.29 are OK. The components can also be repeated, which is why two (or more) b elements in a row are fine. So are two b elements with an i element between them, as in the third p element shown above.

The "P" in "PCDATA" shows that it's *parsed* character data: the result of fully parsing the original XML text to look for tags, processing instructions, other markup, and—of course—character data. (In contrast, no real parsing occurs in XML's CDATA sections, just a scan for]]>. See 2.7, "CDATA Sections", for more on this.)

Note that a parser treats extra white space and carriage returns between child elements in mixed content as data, just like it treats any letters and numbers between them. This is one of the most important distinctions between mixed-content and element content. See 3.2.1, "Element Content" for more explanation, with examples.

VALIDITY CONSTRAINT: No Duplicate Types

The same name must not appear more than once in a single mixed-content declaration.

For example, the declaration in Example 3.30 is invalid because the emph element type name appears more than once.

Example 3.30: Element type declaration violating "No Duplicate Types" validity constraint

```
<!ELEMENT para (#PCDATA | emph | keyword | emph | ref)*>
```

Examples of mixed content declarations:

```
<!ELEMENT p (#PCDATA|a|ul|b|i|em)*>
<!ELEMENT p (#PCDATA | %font; | %phrase; | %special; | %form;)* >
<!ELEMENT b (#PCDATA)>
```

3.3. Attribute-List Declarations

Attributes are used to associate name-value pairs with elements. Attribute specifications may appear only within start-tags and empty-element tags; thus, the productions used to recognize them appear in **Section 3.1: Start-Tags, End-Tags, and Empty-Element Tags**. Attribute-list declarations may be used:

- To define the set of attributes pertaining to a given element type.
- To establish type constraints for these attributes.
- To provide default values for attributes.

Attributes are properties of elements. They are specified as named pieces of information in an element's start-tag, or in the case of empty elements, in the empty-element tag. The empty phone element in Example 3.31 has three attribute specifications: who, number, and where.

Example 3.31: Empty element with three attribute specifications

```
<phone who="Dirk" number="970-LOVE" where="home"/>
```

The pairing of an attribute's name and the quoted value that goes with it is called an attribute specification.

Why store information in an attribute instead of in an element's content? After all, you could also store the information from Example 3.31 in child elements as shown in Example 3.32.

Example 3.32: Storing a phone element's information in child elements instead of in attributes

```
<phone>
  <who>Dirk</who>
  <number>970-LOVE</number>
  <where>home</where>
</phone>
```

The question has no simple answer, and is a popular debate topic for XML and SGML people.[†] Paragraphs of text should obviously be stored in an element's content, and information about the element that can be limited to short strings of characters—for example, element IDs, revision dates, and approval status—are typically stored in attributes. Ideally, data is represented as content if you consider it to be part of the element. It would be represented as attributes if it is information *about* the element.

But there are implementation considerations as well.

One great reason to store information in an attribute instead of in an element's content is listed in the spec's second bulleted item above: you can use built-in XML facilities to constrain the allowable values so that validating software can identify inappropriate values for you. In 3.3.1, "Attribute Types", we'll see how you can specify a certain type for an attribute so that a phone element's number attribute is not allowed to have spaces in it and the where attribute is limited to the values home, work, fax, and car.

> *Attribute-list declarations* specify the name, data type, and default value (if any) of each attribute associated with a given element type:

As with element type names, you can make up attribute names as you go along when creating a merely well-formed document instance.

---

† Books have been written on the topic. See Megginson, *Structuring XML Documents*, and Jelliffe, *The XML and SGML Cookbook*, both in this series.

Declaring each element type's attributes in the document type declaration, however, gives you the advantages listed in the bulleted list on page 155:

- You're enumerating specific possibilities so that processing software knows what it has to work with.

- You can define limitations on the values that can be entered.

- You can define default values that will be used when no value is specified in the markup of an element of that type.

Attribute-list Declaration

[52]AttlistDecl	::=	'<!ATTLIST' S Name AttDef* S? '>'
[53]AttDef	::=	S Name S AttType S DefaultDecl

The Name in the AttlistDecl rule is the type of an element. At user option, an XML processor may issue a warning if attributes are declared for an element type not itself declared, but this is not an error. The Name in the AttDef rule is the name of the attribute.

The sample document shown in Example 3.33 and the DTD file in Example 3.34 that it uses should make productions 52 and 53 easier to understand.

Example 3.33: Sample poem.xml file

```
1. <?xml version="1.0"?>
2. <!DOCTYPE poem SYSTEM "poem.dtd" [
3. <!ENTITY % titleatts 'note CDATA "not checked"'>
4. ]>
5. <poem author="GZ"><title>What the Thunder Said</title>
6. <verse flavor="chocolate" hatsize="7.75">
7. If there were rock</verse>
8. <verse>And also water</verse>
9. </poem>
```

poem.xml has one entity declaration on line 3. We can assume that the other element type and attribute list declarations are in the poem.dtd file declared on its second line.

Example 3.34: poem.dtd file referenced by Example 3.33

```
1. <!ELEMENT poem   (title,verse+)>
2. <!ELEMENT verse (#PCDATA)>
3. <!ATTLIST poem   author NMTOKEN  #REQUIRED>
4. <!ATTLIST verse flavor (chocolate | vanilla | mint) "mint"
5.                 hatsize CDATA #IMPLIED>
6. <!ELEMENT title (#PCDATA)>
7. <!ENTITY % titleatts "">
8. <!ATTLIST title %titleatts;>
```

According to the first line of poem.dtd in Example 3.34, a poem element consists of a single title followed by one or more verse elements. The poem element type's attribute list declaration (line 3 of Example 3.34) has one attribute definition in its "list": author, which has an attribute type of NMTOKEN and is a required attribute for all poem elements. See 3.3.1, "Attribute Types" for more on these.

The verse element type's attribute list declaration (lines 4 and 5) has two attribute definitions in its list:

- flavor, an enumerated attribute type with three possible values and a default value of "mint".

- hatsize, which has an attribute type of CDATA and is optional ("IMPLIED").

The poem element that starts at line 5 of poem.xml in Example 3.33 has the required author attribute. Its first verse element start-tag (line 6) has attribute specifications for both flavor and hatsize, while the second verse (line 8) has neither. Note that while this second verse element has no hatsize specified, it does exhibit a flavor value of "mint", because this was specified as a default in the attribute list declaration (line 4 of poem.dtd in Example 3.34).

The `title` element's attribute list declaration at line 8 of `poem.dtd` demonstrates that these declarations don't require any attribute definitions. (Note that, in production 52, **AttDef** has a "*" after it meaning "*zero* or more **AttDef** expressions".) After defining the `titleatts` parameter entity as an empty string at line 7, `titleatts` is used in place of the attribute definition for the `title` element's attribute list declaration at line 8.

The `poem` document in `poem.xml` takes advantage of this flexibility by redeclaring `titleatts` at line 3 of Example 3.33 so that the `title` attribute list declaration does contain an attribute definition. (Note that 2.8, "Prolog and Document Type Declaration", tells us that an entity declaration in the internal subset takes precedence over one in the external subset.) With this new attribute declaration at line 3, the document's `title` element on line 5 has a `note` attribute with a value of `not checked`, the default, because its start-tag specifies no other value for `note`.

What if you add an attribute list declaration for an element type that hasn't been declared? As the specification paragraph above tells us, this isn't an error. However, a document is invalid if it contains an element of that type.

Examples 3.33 and 3.34 merely demonstrate the declaration and use of attribute lists. See 3.3.1, "Attribute Types" for details on the broad range of control that you can exercise over attribute use in your documents.

When more than one `AttlistDecl` is provided for a given element type, the contents of all those provided are merged. When more than one definition is provided for the same attribute of a given element type, the first declaration is binding and later declarations are ignored. For interoperability, writers of DTDs may choose to provide at most one attribute-list declaration for a given element type, at most one attribute definition for a given attribute name, and at least one attribute definition in each attribute-list declaration. For interoperability, an XML processor may at user option issue a warning when more than one attribute-list declaration is provided for a given element type, or more than one attribute definition is provided for a given attribute, but this is not an error.

Why would you have more than one attribute list declaration for a single element type? Let's say you're writing a chapter for a book in collaboration with several other authors. The publisher sends you a `chapter.dtd` DTD file that includes the element type and attribute list declarations shown in Example 3.35.

Example 3.35: Element type declaration with an attribute list declaration that you want to extend

```
<!ELEMENT section (title,par+)>
<!ATTLIST section ID ID #IMPLIED>
```

You might want to customize it by adding your own attribute, such as a `draft` number to help you remember which draft stage each section has reached. A good place for this would be the internal declaration subset preceding your chapter, as shown in Example 3.36.

Example 3.36: Adding a new attribute specification to Example 3.35's attribute list specification

```
<!DOCTYPE chapter SYSTEM "chapter.dtd" [
<!ATTLIST section draft NMTOKEN "1">
]>
<chapter><title>What the Thunder Said</title>
<section ID="s2.1" draft="2"><title>Death by Water</title>
<par><!-- section continues here... -->
```

As the beginning of the specification paragraph above tells us, an XML processor will treat the two attribute list declarations for `section` as one list of two attribute definitions. If the second one, in the external subset, also redefined the ID attribute declared in the `chapter.dtd` file, the processor would ignore the attempted redefinition.

A DTD designer who needs interoperability with pre-WebSGML software should avoid:

- Multiple attribute list declarations for the same element type (as with `section` in the above example).

- Multiple definitions for the same attribute.

- Attribute list declarations with no attribute definitions (as with `title` in Example 3.34).

An XML processor can warn about the first two conditions if its designer wishes, but this is optional.

3.3.1. Attribute Types

XML attribute types are of three kinds: a string type, a set of tokenized types, and enumerated types. The string type may take any literal string as a value; the tokenized types have varying lexical and semantic constraints, as noted:

Assigning a type to each attribute definition gives you the same benefit that it does when defining the fields of a traditional database: it's a way to say "make sure that any values stored here meet these conditions". The software that manipulates those values can make certain assumptions and be more efficient than it would if it had to do lots of error checking.

A "string" is a sequence of characters—any characters, including white space characters. The CDATA attribute type, the only string attribute type, is the most forgiving, allowing virtually any characters.

A tokenized type is a more restricted form of string. An attribute value of this type must match the **Name** production (production 5) or the **Nmtoken** production (production 7). Generally, this means that no spaces and only a limited number of punctuation characters (the period, hyphen, underscore, and colon) are allowed. A **Name** has the additional requirement that it begin with a letter, underscore, or colon. These restrictions are what the spec means by "lexical constraints".

NMTOKEN and NMTOKENS aren't the only tokenized types; the validity constraints for all the other types besides CDATA show that they must match the **Name** or **Nmtoken** productions. Some must also meet certain semantic constraints—in other words, they have to mean something to the parser. (For example, an ENTITY attribute value's name must be the name of a declared unparsed entity.)

Enumerated types, the most restrictive of all, are those for which the attribute definition lists the possible values. For example, you could declare an approved attribute that required either the value "yes" or the value "no" and processing software would flag any other values as an error.

Attribute Types

[54]AttType	::=	StringType | TokenizedType | EnumeratedType	
[55]StringType	::=	'CDATA'	
[56]TokenizedType	::=	'ID'	[VC: ID] [VC: One ID per Element Type] [VC: ID Attribute Default]
		| 'IDREF'	[VC: IDREF]
		| 'IDREFS'	[VC: IDREF]
		| 'ENTITY'	[VC: Entity Name]
		| 'ENTITIES'	[VC: Entity Name]
		| 'NMTOKEN'	[VC: Name Token]
		| 'NMTOKENS'	[VC: Name Token]

NMTOKENS and two other attribute types are plural forms, which means that their values can contain more than one token. For example, the memo element type's authors attribute in Example 3.37 is declared as having an NMTOKENS type. The sample memo element's authors attribute in Example 3.37 has four tokens specified in the value.

Example 3.37: Declaring and using an NMTOKENS attribute

```
<?xml version="1.0"?>
<!DOCTYPE memo [
<!ELEMENT memo (#PCDATA)>
<!ATTLIST memo authors NMTOKENS #IMPLIED>
```

```
]>
<memo authors="RN DM SO BW">The awful daring of a
moment's surrender</memo>
```

Because authors was declared as a plural NMTOKENS type, an XML parser will know that "RN DM SO BW" is four tokens and not one eleven-character string.

Besides CDATA (described above) the other attribute types are described further after their corresponding validity constraints in the next few pages.

> **VALIDITY CONSTRAINT: ID**
>
> Values of type ID must match the Name production. A name must not appear more than once in an XML document as a value of this type; i.e., ID values must uniquely identify the elements which bear them.

If an element has an empnum attribute with a value of "X" and empnum is an ID attribute type, then no other elements in the same document can have "X" as the value of an ID attribute type.

This is the whole point of an ID attribute: to uniquely identify the element. Linking to an element is unambiguous when that element has its own unique identifier, just as mailing a letter is reliable because no other house in the same town can have the same address.

Unique identifiers can have other advantages. For example, this annotation that I'm typing now is an element whose start-tag is shown in Example 3.38.

Example 3.38: Start-tag for this annotation in this book

```
<annot id="a3.3.1-2">
```

A program combines these annotations with the specification in order to create this book. It knows that the annot element with an id value of a3.3.1-2 goes after the first validity constraint in 3.3.1, "Attribute

Types". In other words, it uses these id attributes to know which elements are which, much like an employee database uses employee ID numbers to keep track of employee records. In fact, the value of an ID attribute is commonly referred to as the ID of the element.

Tip   Note that the annot element type's attribute has the same name ("id") as the attribute type itself—"id" is a common name for unique identifier attributes. Some members of the XML Working Group wanted to hardcode this into XML so that even with documents that have no DTD, an XML processor would treat any attribute named id as being of the ID attribute type.

The last sentence in the specification paragraph above tells us that every value of an ID attribute type must be completely unique. Even if two attribute values are for two different attributes for two different elements of two different element types, they still can't be the same.

In other words, the value of an ID attribute functions as the name of the element—it distinguishes that element from all others. (This is very different from the generic identifier, which is the name of the element *type*.) For example, in Example 3.39's joke document, the "a1" value for the punchline element's pid attribute on line 12 is illegal, because "a1" was already used as the value for another ID attribute: the setup element's sid attribute on line 10.

Example 3.39: Illegal assignment of the same value ("a1") to two different ID attributes

```
1. <?xml version="1.0"?>
2. <!DOCTYPE joke [
3. <!ELEMENT joke (setup,punchline)>
4. <!ELEMENT setup (#PCDATA)>
5. <!ATTLIST setup sid ID #REQUIRED>
6. <!ELEMENT punchline (#PCDATA)>
7. <!ATTLIST punchline pid ID #REQUIRED>
8. ]>
9. <joke>
10.   <setup sid="a1">My apartment is so small</setup>
```

```
11.    <!-- !!! Following pid value illegal !!! -->
12.    <punchline pid="a1">The mice are
13. round-shouldered</punchline>
14. </joke>
```

> **VALIDITY CONSTRAINT: One ID per Element Type**
>
> No element type may have more than one ID attribute specified.

Once you declare an attribute of type ID for an element type, you can't declare any more for that element type. For example, the picture element type in 3.40 has two ID attributes declared, which is illegal.

Example 3.40: Illegally declaring two ID attributes for the same element type

```
<!ATTLIST picture uid     ID #IMPLIED
                  picnum  ID #IMPLIED> <!-- illegal -->
```

It's also unnecessary—once an element is uniquely identified, another unique identifier won't add any capabilities that were not possible with the first one.

> **VALIDITY CONSTRAINT: ID Attribute Default**
>
> An ID attribute must have a declared default of #IMPLIED or #REQUIRED.

As you'll see in 3.3.2, "Attribute Defaults", #IMPLIED means that specifying the attribute is optional, and the meaning of #REQUIRED is obvious. The other choices—#FIXED or a default value to use when no explicit value is included with an element—allow the possibility of two different elements having the same value for that attribute, which contradicts the purpose of a unique ID attribute.

> **VALIDITY CONSTRAINT: IDREF**
>
> Values of type `IDREF` must match the `Name` production, and values of type `IDREFS` must match `Names`; each `Name` must match the value of an ID attribute on some element in the XML document; i.e. `IDREF` values must match the value of some ID attribute.

Use an `IDREF` attribute to refer to another element with a unique ID. For example, the XML version of the XML spec itself has a `specref` element for "specification reference". The line shown in Example 3.41, from 1.2, "Terminology", refers to a constraint element by using its `id` attribute: elementvalid.

Example 3.41: Using an element with an IDREF attribute

```
An element matches its declaration when it
conforms in the fashion described in the
constraint <specref ref='elementvalid'/>.
```

The ID doesn't appear in the PostScript, Acrobat, or HTML versions of the spec. The programs that create those versions use the `id` value to look up the constraint's actual title and put it where that `specref` element is. If the title of that constraint ever changes, the author won't have to update those references by hand. (The ease or difficulty of these automated lookups is an important consideration when evaluating XML tools.)

If an `IDREF` value is not some element's `ID` attribute value, it's part of a validating XML processor's job to flag this mistake as an error. That's because the document doesn't satisfy the conditions of this validity constraint and is therefore not a valid document.

Although no two `ID` values in a document's elements can be the same, there's nothing wrong with more than one element having the same IDREF attribute value. For example, two sections of your book may want to refer to the same third section.

The plural form version of the IDREF attribute type, IDREFS, lets you include references to multiple elements at once. In Example 3.42, the portfolio document's title element has a pics attribute that references the uid attribute (another popular name for unique ID attributes) of the document's three picture elements.

Example 3.42: Declaring and using an IDREFS attribute

```
<?xml version="1.0"?>
<!DOCTYPE portfolio  [
<!ELEMENT portfolio  (title,picture+)>
<!ELEMENT title    (#PCDATA)>
<!ATTLIST title   pics IDREFS #REQUIRED>
<!ELEMENT picture (#PCDATA)>
<!ATTLIST picture uid ID #REQUIRED>
]>
<portfolio>
<title pics="y1 y2 y3">My Vacation</title>
<picture uid="y1">La Brea Tar Pits</picture>
<picture uid="y2">Land of Little Horses</picture>
<picture uid="y3">South of the Border</picture>
</portfolio>
```

VALIDITY CONSTRAINT: Entity Name

Values of type ENTITY must match the Name production, values of type ENTITIES must match Names; each Name must match the name of an unparsed entity declared in the DTD.

The value used for an ENTITY attribute type must be the name of a properly declared unparsed entity. In line 9 of Example 3.43, the "clownpic" attribute value is valid because:

- It's declared on line 5 so that the parser recognizes clownpic as an entity name.

- It's the name of an unparsed entity—in other words, it's an entity that the parser doesn't parse as XML text for this document. That status is indicated by the presence of the NDATA keyword in the entity declaration on line 5. After this keyword, the declaration names the notation used for this entity: JPEG. The entity's notation must also be declared so that the parser knows what "JPEG" is; this declaration is on lines 3 and 4.

Example 3.43: Declaring and using an unparsed entity

```
1. <?xml version="1.0"?>
2. <!DOCTYPE illustration [
3. <!NOTATION JPEG SYSTEM
4.           "Joint Photographic Experts Group">
5. <!ENTITY clownpic SYSTEM "clown.jpg" NDATA JPEG>
6. <!ELEMENT illustration EMPTY>
7. <!ATTLIST illustration picfile ENTITY #REQUIRED>
8. ]>
9. <illustration picfile="clownpic"/>
```

As with IDREF and IDREFS, the ENTITY attribute type has a plural form: ENTITIES. With Example 3.44's declaration, Example 3.45's precedents element would be valid, assuming that the c3874, c2217, and c9311 entities had been properly declared the way clownpic was in Example 3.43.

Example 3.44: Declaring an ENTITIES attribute

```
<!ELEMENT precedents EMPTY>
<!ATTLIST precedents cases ENTITIES #REQUIRED>
```

Example 3.45: Using the ENTITIES attribute declared in Example 3.44

```
<precedents cases="c3874 c2217 c9311"/>
```

See 4.2.2, "External Entities", for more on declaring these types of entities. See also 4.7, "Notation Declarations".

> **VALIDITY CONSTRAINT: Name Token**
>
> Values of type NMTOKEN must match the *Nmtoken* production; values of type NMTOKENS must match Nmtokens.

A **Nmtoken** is one or more **NameChar** characters. According to 2.3, "Common Syntactic Constructs", **NameChar** characters consist of letters, numbers, the period, hyphen, underscore, and colon, plus other miscellaneous characters listed in Appendix B, "Character Classes". When you declare an attribute of type NMTOKEN or NMTOKENS, document authors can make up any attribute values they want, as long as they fit production 7, the **Nmtoken** production. Unlike most other attribute types, they don't have to follow any other special rules—for example, the value doesn't have to match something declared somewhere else.

Example 3.37, which shows a memo element with an authors attribute, demonstrates a NMTOKENS attribute type.

> *Enumerated attributes* can take one of a list of values provided in the declaration. There are two kinds of enumerated types:

In Webster's New World College Dictionary, definition 2 of "enumerate" is "to name one by one". The declaration of an enumerated attribute type names all the possible values that may be assigned to that attribute. As production 57 shows, the two types are **NotationType** and **Enumeration**.

Enumerated Attribute Types

[57] EnumeratedType	::=	NotationType | Enumeration	
[58] NotationType	::=	'NOTATION' S '(' S? Name (S? '|'	[VC: Notation Attributes]
		S? Name)* S? ')'	
[59] Enumeration	::=	'(' S? Nmtoken (S? '|' S?	[VC: Enumeration]
		Nmtoken)* S? ')'	

Production 59 shows the kind of enumeration where you can specify any **Nmtoken** values you like in the list. Example 3.46's maincourse attribute list declaration has three enumerated attribute types:

- The kosher attribute offers a choice of the **Nmtoken** values yes and no and has a default value of no.

- The flavor attribute, which offers a choice of mint, chocolate, and cherry, doesn't assume or require any value to be specified.

- For the cooked attribute, all maincourse elements must have a value of rare, medium, or well-done specified.

Example 3.46: Declaring enumerated attribute types

```
<!ATTLIST maincourse
            kosher (yes|no) "no"
            flavor (mint|chocolate|cherry) #IMPLIED
            cooked (rare|medium|well-done) #REQUIRED>
```

A NOTATION attribute identifies a notation, declared in the DTD with associated system and/or public identifiers, to be used in interpreting the element to which the attribute is attached.

Production 58 shows a special case of enumerated types in which the choices must be declared notation names. In Example 3.47, the quote element has a NOTATION attribute called format.

Example 3.47: Declaring and using a NOTATION attribute type

```
<?xml version="1.0"?>
<!DOCTYPE message [
<!NOTATION TEX   PUBLIC
    "+//ISBN 0-201-13448-9::Knuth//NOTATION The TeXbook//EN">
<!NOTATION RTF   PUBLIC "Rich Text Format v1.4">
<!ELEMENT message (#PCDATA|quote)*>
<!ELEMENT quote    (#PCDATA)>
<!ATTLIST quote    format NOTATION (TEX|RTF) "TEX">
]>
<message>Here is some sample text.
<quote format="RTF">{\rtf1 That's really rich.}</quote>
This concludes our test.</message>
```

VALIDITY CONSTRAINT: Notation Attributes

Values of this type must match one of the *notation* names included in the declaration; all notation names in the declaration must be declared.

Note that both the TEX and RTF notations that are listed as possibilities for the quote element type's format attribute in Example 3.47 are declared as notations in the DTD. (See 4.7, "Notation Declarations", for more on this.)

VALIDITY CONSTRAINT: Enumeration

Values of this type must match one of the *Nmtoken* tokens in the declaration.

For interoperability, the same *Nmtoken* should not occur more than once in the enumerated attribute types of a single element type.

In SGML before the WebSGML adaptations, two enumerated attribute types for the same element type couldn't use the same **Nmtoken** as one of their choices. For example, the attribute list specification shown in Example 3.48 was illegal because once the chapter element's `reviewed` attribute listed `yes` and `no` as its possible values, no other enumerated attribute for the `chapter` element could use either of those tokens in its choices.

Example 3.48: Re-using name tokens in the same attribute list declaration

```
<!ATTLIST chapter reviewed (yes|no) "no"
                  printed  (yes|no) "no">
```

Luckily, this is not a problem in XML, but the spec warns you to avoid the practice if you're interested in interoperability with pre-WebSGML SGML systems.

3.3.2. Attribute Defaults

An attribute declaration provides information on whether the attribute's presence is required, and if not, how an XML processor should react if a declared attribute is absent in a document.

As production 53 showed, the information about an attribute's default value comes right after the name of the attribute's type. Production 60 shows the possible attribute default value prescriptions:

Attribute Defaults

```
[60] DefaultDecl  ::=  '#REQUIRED'  |  '#IMPLIED'
                     |  (('#FIXED' S)? AttValue)   [VC: Required Attribute]
                                                    [VC: Attribute Default Legal]
                                                    [WFC: No < in Attribute Values]
                                                    [VC: Fixed Attribute Default]
```

In an attribute declaration, #REQUIRED means that the attribute must
always be provided, #IMPLIED that no default value is provided. If the
declaration is neither #REQUIRED nor #IMPLIED, then the AttValue
value contains the declared *default* value; the #FIXED keyword states
that the attribute must always have the default value. If a default value is
declared, when an XML processor encounters an omitted attribute, it is to
behave as though the attribute were present with the declared default
value.

There are three ways to describe default values, with one variation
on the third way available:

- #REQUIRED means that for every element of this type, a
  value must be specified for that attribute. In the spec's
  example after the "Fixed Attribute Default" Validity
  Constraint below, the termdef element type's id attribute
  definition requires every single termdef element to have
  an id value specified in its start-tag (or, if the element is
  empty, in its empty-element tag).

- #IMPLIED means the attribute need not be specified
  because if it isn't, the application will imply a value. In
  other words, as far as the markup goes, the attribute
  specification is optional. In the spec's example below, the
  termdef element type's name attribute is #IMPLIED.

- If you name a specific, valid **AttValue** (attribute value) as
  the default, the processor will use this value when no
  other is specified. In the spec's example below, the list
  element type's type attribute has a default value of
  ordered. For any list element with no type attribute

specified, the processor must treat it as if it had
type="ordered" in its start- or empty-element tag.

VALIDITY CONSTRAINT: Required Attribute

If the default declaration is the keyword #REQUIRED, then the
attribute must be specified for all elements of the type in the attribute-
list declaration.

VALIDITY CONSTRAINT: Attribute Default Legal

The declared default value must meet the lexical constraints of the
declared attribute type.

VALIDITY CONSTRAINT: Fixed Attribute Default

If an attribute has a default value declared with the #FIXED keyword,
instances of that attribute must match the default value.

Examples of attribute-list declarations:

```
<!ATTLIST termdef
          id       ID        #REQUIRED
          name     CDATA     #IMPLIED>
<!ATTLIST list
          type     (bullets|ordered|glossary)   "ordered">
<!ATTLIST form
          method   CDATA     #FIXED "POST">
```

Inserting the keyword #FIXED in front of the default value means
that the value is more than the default: it's the only value allowed for
that attribute. In the spec's example above, the form element type's
method attribute will always have a value of POST. Therefore, there's
no need to specify method="POST" for each form element.

Why define an attribute that has the same value for all of its element instances? A common use is a predefined attribute that tells a
processor to take advantage of certain software features associated
with that attribute.

For example, if you want an XLink-compliant browser to know that your `fnote` elements are always simple links, you could include the attribute specification `xml:link="simple"` in all your `fnote` start-tags. Alternatively, you could just include the line shown in Example 3.49 in the `fnote` element type's attribute list declaration.

Example 3.49: Specifying a fixed value for the `xml:link` attribute

```
xml:link CDATA #FIXED "simple"
```

3.3.3. Attribute-Value Normalization

Normalizing is the process of converting something to a standard form. If two things are essentially the same but expressed differently, normalizing puts them in a form in which they look the same and can be more easily compared.

Before the value of an attribute is passed to the application or checked for validity, the XML processor must normalize it as follows:

- a character reference is processed by appending the referenced character to the attribute value

For example, when encountering a character reference such as `&#xE4;` in an attribute specification, the processor appends the referenced character ä onto the attribute value. The XML processor doesn't pass the character reference text to the application, which only sees ä. See 4.1, "Character and Entity References" for more information on these.

- an entity reference is processed by recursively processing the replacement text of the entity

Recursive processing means that if the cnotice entity was declared as shown in Example 3.50, a processor that found a reference to cnotice in an attribute value would replace it with the declared entity value. It would then replace the &cdate; entity reference in the cnotice entity value, and continue replacing entity references it found within entity values as long as it found them.

Example 3.50: Using a reference to one entity in another entity's replacement text

```
<!ENTITY cnotice "Copyright &cdate; all rights reserved">
```

- a whitespace character (#x20, #xD, #xA, #x9) is processed by appending #x20 to the normalized value, except that only a single #x20 is appended for a "#xD#xA" sequence that is part of an external parsed entity or the literal entity value of an internal parsed entity

A spacebar space (#x20), carriage return (#xD), line feed (#xA), or tab character (#x09) will be replaced by a single spacebar space.

When there's a carriage return and a line feed together (as you'll find at the end of lines in text files created using DOS or Windows) in an entity that is meant to be parsed as XML, they're not both replaced by space characters. Instead, the processor replaces the pair of characters with a single spacebar space. See 2.11, "End-of-Line Handling", for more on how an XML processor handles line endings.

- other characters are processed by appending them to the normalized value

Characters that don't fall into one of these categories are added to the accumulating normalized value as the processor comes across them.

> If the declared value is not CDATA, then the XML processor must further process the normalized attribute value by discarding any leading and trailing space (#x20) characters, and by replacing sequences of space (#x20) characters by a single space (#x20) character.

If the attribute is not of the CDATA type, it's either of type ID, IDREF, IDREFS, ENTITY, ENTITIES, NMTOKEN, or NMTOKENS. Any attribute value used for one of these types is ultimately either a **Name** (production 5), a **Nmtoken** (production 7), or a list of one of them. Spaces can play no part in such attribute values other than delimiting tokens.

This paragraph of the spec describes how to deal with extraneous spaces in these cases. It tells us that, in Example 3.51, an XML processor must remove the leading and trailing spaces around the poem element's date value specification of " 1922 " to effectively treat the date attribute as having "1922" for its value.

The processor will also remove all but one space from between the three **Name** values in the verse element's reviewers attribute value specification, treating the total reviewers list as "BW DM RN".

Example 3.51: Name token attribute values with extraneous spaces

```
<?xml version="1.0"?>
<!DOCTYPE poem [
<!ELEMENT poem (verse+)>
<!ATTLIST poem date   NMTOKEN #IMPLIED>
<!ELEMENT verse (#PCDATA)>
<!ATTLIST verse reviewers NMTOKENS #IMPLIED>
]>
<poem date="   1922     ">
<verse reviewers="BW        DM        RN">
unshaven, with a pocket full of currants</verse>
</poem>
```

See 3.3.1, "Attribute Types" for more on these various types.

> All attributes for which no declaration has been read should be treated by a non-validating parser as if declared CDATA.

A non-validating parser won't necessarily read any attribute declarations, so it cannot know which attribute values are CDATA and which are supposed to have more constraints enforced on them. So, it treats all attributes as CDATA.

3.4. Conditional Sections

Conditional sections are portions of the document type declaration external subset which are included in, or excluded from, the logical structure of the DTD based on the keyword which governs them.

Conditional sections provide you with an easy way to tell a parser to use or to ignore part of a DTD stored in an external entity. For example, with Example 3.52's lines in an external file, an XML processor would declare the entity author with the value "Dirk" and the entity status with "final" as its value.

Example 3.52: Using conditional sections

```
<![IGNORE[
<!ENTITY author "Barry">
<!ENTITY status "first draft">
]]>

<![INCLUDE[
<!ENTITY author "Dirk">
<!ENTITY status "final">
]]>
```

If you reversed the keywords IGNORE and INCLUDE in that example, the entities would be declared with the values "Barry" and "first draft".

Conditional Section

[61] conditionalSect	::=	includeSect | ignoreSect
[62] includeSect	::=	'<![' S? 'INCLUDE' S? '[' extSubsetDecl ']]>'
[63] ignoreSect	::=	'<![' S? 'IGNORE' S? '[' ignoreSectContents* ']]>'
[64] ignoreSectContents	::=	Ignore ('<![' ignoreSectContents ']]>' Ignore)*
[65] Ignore	::=	Char* - (Char* ('<![' | ']]>') Char*)

Like the internal and external DTD subsets, a conditional section may contain one or more complete declarations, comments, processing instructions, or nested conditional sections, intermingled with white space.

Tip   Note that the specification says "complete" declarations, comments, processing instructions, or nested conditional sections. A conditional section cannot begin or end in the middle of one of these DTD components.

If the keyword of the conditional section is INCLUDE, then the contents of the conditional section are part of the DTD. If the keyword of the conditional section is IGNORE, then the contents of the conditional section are not logically part of the DTD. Note that for reliable parsing, the contents of even ignored conditional sections must be read in order to detect nested conditional sections and ensure that the end of the outermost (ignored) conditional section is properly detected. If a conditional section with a keyword of INCLUDE occurs within a larger conditional section with a keyword of IGNORE, both the outer and the inner conditional sections are ignored.

By "not *logically* part of the DTD", the spec means that the conditional section is still physically part of the set of DTD declarations. However, the declarations in an ignored conditional section do not affect the DTD properties used by the processor when parsing the document.

Conditional sections may be nested in XML documents. Everything inside of an IGNORE section is ignored, which includes any INCLUDE sections. For example, the "Stig" and "second draft" declarations in Example 3.53 will be ignored, because although they're inside of an INCLUDE conditional section, that entire INCLUDE section is inside of an IGNORE section.

Example 3.53: An INCLUDE section inside of an IGNORE section

```
<![IGNORE[

<!ENTITY author "Barry">
<!ENTITY status "first draft">

<![INCLUDE[
<!ENTITY author "Stig">
<!ENTITY status "second draft">
]]>


]]>
```

Actually, the processor doesn't completely ignore the contents of an IGNORE section, because, "for reliable parsing", it has to look for the]]> that ends it. This has one important implication that explains the role of the <![and]]> in productions 64 and 65: the contents of an ignored section can have a <![followed eventually by a matching]]> (production 64), but either one without the other is not allowed (hence the minus sign in 65).

If the processor sees a <![inside of an ignored section (like the one before the word "INCLUDE" in Example 3.53) it will expect to find a matching]]> before the end of the ignored section enclosing it. If it finds a]]> in an XML DTD, it's an error if there isn't a currently open marked section that needs closing.

> If the keyword of the conditional section is a parameter-entity reference, the parameter entity must be replaced by its content before the processor decides whether to include or ignore the conditional section.
>
> An example:
>
> ```
> <!ENTITY % draft 'INCLUDE' >
> <!ENTITY % final 'IGNORE' >
> <![%draft;[
> <!ELEMENT book (comments*, title, body, supplements?)>
> ]]>
> <![%final;[
> <!ELEMENT book (title, body, supplements?)>
> ]]>
> ```

Or, in terms of the example shown, %draft; and %final; have to refer to declared entities that the processor knows about.

Instead of the literal keywords INCLUDE and IGNORE at the beginning of a conditional section, you can use a parameter entity with one of these terms as its replacement text. Imagine a dozen marked sections sprinkled throughout a long, complex DTD that are all used in the annotated version of your book but not the basic version. When switching back and forth, a global replace of "[IGNORE[" for "[INCLUDE[" might affect marked sections that are unrelated to whether you are processing the basic or annotated versions.

Instead, you should declare the parameter entity shown in Example 3.54 in your DTD and then begin those twelve marked sections with [%annotver;[. You can then safely ignore or include those twelve marked section by simple switching the value in the annotver declaration between IGNORE and INCLUDE.

Example 3.54: Declaring an entity for use in controlling conditional sections

```
<!ENTITY % annotver 'INCLUDE'>
```

Physical Structures

T his chapter covers issues related to a document's relationship to the system where it resides. If the host operating system stores information in files, the markup for a document's physical structure will identify the files and their location. If certain files are encoded for non-Western alphabets, markup must be included to identify the encoding. Markup for defining a document's physical structure also lets you identify pieces of documents for re-use.

An XML document may consist of one or many storage units. These are called *entities*; they all have *content* and are all (except for the document entity, see below, and the external DTD subset) identified by *name*. Each XML document has one entity called the document entity, which serves as the starting point for the XML processor and may contain the whole document.

Most operating systems these days use the term "files" for their "storage units", but not all of them. For example, MVS mainframes refer to them as "data sets", and the AS/400's OS/400 operating system calls them "members".

XML uses the term "entity" more broadly: it refers to a named collection of information stored somewhere in a computer. The named collection might not even be stored as a unit; it may be generated upon a request to a particular program such as a database front end or an unarchiving program. To take this wide range of information storage possibilities into account, XML interposes its own virtual storage model and naming system for collections of information. XML uses each entity declaration to assign its own name to a particular collection of stored XML text or non-XML data.

Two entities don't need entity names: the document entity and its external DTD subset, if it has one. For example, assuming the existence of a valid memos.dtd external subset, Example 4.1 is a valid document entity. Neither it nor memos.dtd need to have entity names assigned to them by entity declarations.

Example 4.1: Document entity with no entity name assigned to it

```
<?xml version="1.0"?>
<!DOCTYPE msg SYSTEM "memos.dtd">
<msg>There is not even silence in the mountains
But dry sterile thunder without rain</msg>
```

You could assign a name such as msgdtd to the memos.dtd file and declare and reference it as an external parameter entity easily enough, as shown in 4.2, but you don't have to.

Example 4.2: Assigning an entity name to an external declaration subset

```
<?xml version="1.0"?>
<!DOCTYPE msg [
<!ENTITY % msgdtd SYSTEM "memos.dtd">
%msgdtd;
]>
<msg>There is not even silence in the mountains
But dry sterile thunder without rain</msg>
```

How does an XML processor know which entity is the document entity? Perhaps users enter a file name as a parameter to a command-line program. Maybe they enter a file name in some field on a dialog box, or they drag one icon on top of another. Maybe the document is in a stream of data piped to the processor from another process or read in from a communications port. Essentially, the method of identifying the document entity is left up to the choices offered by the host operating system.

The processor can find out about an external DTD subset from the document type declaration, just as Example 4.1 has its `memos.dtd` external DTD subset. Any other entities that contain part of the document must have entity declarations, which assign entity names to the stored information so that the document has some way to refer to it.

An external subset can declare and refer to other external parameter entities. For example, the `memos.dtd` file in Examples 4.1 and 4.2 could declare and reference other files full of declarations. These other files could in turn refer to others, with no specified limit to how many entity references the processor can follow. This makes the document entity's role as a "starting point" clearer, because once the processor starts there it can find the declarations that directly or indirectly lead to other entities.

Entities may be either parsed or unparsed. A *parsed entity's* contents are referred to as its replacement text; this text is considered an integral part of the document.

In earlier, draft versions of the specification, this paragraph said that "entities may be either binary or text". This was changed to "parsed or unparsed" (note that the order was reversed; "binary" was changed to "unparsed" and "text" was changed to "parsed"). The key distinction is not whether the entity notation is binary or character-based, but whether or not the XML processor is supposed to parse it—that is, to treat it as XML text, looking for markup and data and processing them according to the spec.

As we'll see in the spec's next paragraph, "an unparsed entity is a resource whose contents may or may not be text". It may be binary, but it may be character-based (for example, RTF, LaTeX, HTML, or even XML)—the important thing is, the processor isn't supposed to parse it as part of the current document. It is declared to be data.

An entity reference is essentially an instruction for the parser saying "this is the name of an entity whose contents should replace this reference". This is why the parsed entity's contents are known as its replacement text. The text might be included right in the entity declaration, which makes it an internal entity; or, it might be stored in an a separate, external storage object such as a file. In Example 4.3, `cpinfo` is declared as an internal entity with the contents "1999" and `pubyear` is declared as an external entity, with its contents stored in the file `copyright.txt`.

Example 4.3: Declaring an internal and an external general entity

```
<!ENTITY pubyear "1999">
<!ENTITY cpinfo  SYSTEM "copyright.txt">
```

See 4.2.1, "Internal Entities", and 4.2.2, "External Entities", for more on these.

> An *unparsed entity* is a resource whose contents may or may not be text, and if text, may not be XML. Each unparsed entity has an associated notation, identified by name. Beyond a requirement that an XML processor make the identifiers for the entity and notation available to the application, XML places no constraints on the contents of unparsed entities.

The last sentence of the specification paragraph above tells us that the data in the unparsed entity can be absolutely anything. Since it isn't parsed as XML, what does the parser do with it?

Example 4.4 demonstrates what the parser does. The clownpic entity has a declared notation of JPEG which has its own NOTATION declaration on the previous line.

Example 4.4: Declaring and using an unparsed entity

```
<?xml version="1.0"?>
<!DOCTYPE illus [
<!NOTATION JPEG SYSTEM "viewjpg.exe">
<!ENTITY clownpic SYSTEM "clown.jpg" NDATA JPEG>
<!ELEMENT illus EMPTY>
<!ATTLIST illus picfile ENTITY #REQUIRED>
]>
<illus picfile="clownpic"/>
```

The processor's only obligation is to make sure that the application can find out the entity's identifiers (clownpic and the system identifier clown.jpg in the above example) and those of its notation (JPEG and viewjpg.exe). The application might have a reaction along the lines of "JPEG file? Then I'll start up the viewjpg program and pass it clown.jpg as a parameter!"

> Parsed entities are invoked by name using entity references; unparsed entities by name, given in the value of ENTITY or ENTITIES attributes.

You can't just stick a reference to an unparsed entity in the middle of element content, because an XML processor wouldn't know what to do with it. As with the clownpic example above, it has to be named in the value of an attribute declared as being of the ENTITY or ENTITIES type.

General entities are entities for use within the document content. In this specification, general entities are sometimes referred to with the unqualified term *entity* when this leads to no ambiguity. Parameter entities are parsed entities for use within the DTD. These two types of entities use different forms of reference and are recognized in different contexts. Furthermore, they occupy different namespaces; a parameter entity and a general entity with the same name are two distinct entities.

Tip   *Because general entities are used more commonly than parameter entities, the specification tells us that the term "entity" without the words "general" or "parameter" usually refers to a general entity.*

"Different namespaces" refers to a processor's obligation to keep track of general and parameter entities separately, so that you could actually have a general entity and a parameter entity with the same name in the same DTD. For example, see the two `sampleEnt` entities in Example 4.5.

Example 4.5: Declaring and using general and parameter entities with the same name: `sampleEnt`

```
1. <?xml version="1.0"?>
2. <!DOCTYPE item [
3. <!ENTITY % sampleEnt "<!ELEMENT item (para+)>">
4. <!ENTITY sampleEnt "the hyacinth girl">
5. %sampleEnt;
6. <!ELEMENT para (#PCDATA)>
7. ]>
8. <item><para>'They called me &sampleEnt;.'</para></item>
9.
```

> **Tip**   A general entity and a parameter entity with the same name in the same DTD are not a problem for the parser, but may confuse someone reading the DTD.

An XML processor knows that the `sampleEnt` entity reference at line 5 is a parameter-entity reference because of its %, and that it's declared at line 3. The second `sampleEnt` entity declaration at line 4 declares a general entity. Its replacement text will replace any `&sampleEnt;` entity reference that properly occurs in the document—for example, at line 8.

4.1. Character and Entity References

A *character reference* refers to a specific character in the ISO/IEC 10646 character set, for example one not directly accessible from available input devices.

"Not directly accessible from available input devices", for most people, means "not on your keyboard".

Character Reference

```
[66] CharRef   ::=   '&#' [0-9]+ ';'
                 |   '&#x' [0-9a-fA-F]+ ';'          [WFC: Legal Character]
```

The ISO/IEC 10646 character set standard assigns a character number, or "code point", to each character in its repertoire. Humans can identify a character unambiguously, when speaking or writing about it, by using its character number.

How do you enter a character not on your keyboard? Your editor may have some sort of menu offering characters to pick from, but what if it does not? You can enter a string called a *character reference* consisting of the character's number preceded by an ampersand and pound sign and followed by a semicolon. For example, you could represent an "a" with an umlaut ("ä") as `&#228;`. (For more on this topic, see 2.2, "Characters".)

> **WELL-FORMEDNESS CONSTRAINT: Legal Character**
>
> Characters referred to using character references must match the production for Char.
>
> If the character reference begins with "`&#x`", the digits and letters up to the terminating `;` provide a hexadecimal representation of the character's code point in ISO/IEC 10646. If it begins just with "`&#`", the digits up to the terminating `;` provide a decimal representation of the character's code point.

Character set tables often show the hexadecimal (base 16) version of the number. When using the hex version of the number in a character reference, add an "x" after the pound sign. For example, "ä" would be `&#xE4;` because `xE4` is the hexadecimal representation of the decimal value 228.

In hexadecimal notation, the first two digits of a four-digit number (for example, the `00` in `&#x00e4;`) tell which grouping of ISO 10646 the character belongs to. "00" is used for the "Basic Latin" and "Latin 1 Supplement" groups; others include "05" for the Armenian and Hebrew characters and "0e" for the Thai and Lao characters.

The well-formedness constraint above shows that the numbers must fall in one of the ranges defined by production 2.

> An *entity reference* refers to the content of a named entity. References to parsed general entities use ampersand (`&`) and semicolon (`;`) as delimiters. *Parameter-entity references* use percent-sign (`%`) and semicolon (`;`) as delimiters.

For example, in Example 4.5 earlier, the `&sampleEnt;` entity reference in the document instance was a reference to the `sampleEnt` general entity that had "the hyacinth girl" as its replacement text. Also, `%sampleEnt;` in the DTD was a reference to the `sampleEnt` parameter entity that had "`<!ELEMENT item (para+)>`" as its replacement text.

Entity Reference

[67]`Reference`	`::=`	`EntityRef | CharRef`	
[68]`EntityRef`	`::=`	`'&' Name ';'`	[WFC: Entity Declared] [VC: Entity Declared] [WFC: Parsed Entity] [WFC: No Recursion]
[69]`PEReference`	`::=`	`'%' Name ';'`	[VC: Entity Declared] [WFC: No Recursion] [WFC: In DTD]

WELL-FORMEDNESS CONSTRAINT: Entity Declared

In a document without any DTD, a document with only an internal DTD subset which contains no parameter entity references, or a document with "`standalone='yes'`", the `Name` given in the entity reference must match that in an *entity declaration*, except that well-formed documents need not declare any of the following entities: `amp`, `lt`, `gt`, `apos`, `quot`. The declaration of a parameter entity must precede any reference to it. Similarly, the declaration of a general entity must precede any reference to it which appears in a default value in an attribute-list declaration.

Note that if entities are declared in the external subset or in external parameter entities, a non-validating processor is *not obligated to* read and process their declarations; for such documents, the rule that an entity must be declared is a well-formedness constraint only if *standalone='yes'*.

To sum up, an entity reference in a document that only has an internal DOCTYPE declaration subset must refer to an entity that's been previously declared.

The exceptions are references to the five entities described in 4.6, "Predefined Entities", which don't need to be declared:

- amp for &, the ampersand

- lt for <, the less-than symbol

- gt for >, the greater-than character

- apos for ', the apostrophe

- quot for ", the quotation mark

The final sentence of the well-formedness constraint above reminds us of the possibility that an entity may be declared where a non-validating processor is not required to read it. Even if an entity is declared before any reference to it, as the constraint requires, an XML processor that's only checking for well-formedness need not process that declaration if it's in an external declaration subset or an external parameter entity. It also ignores any references to such an entity, and to any undeclared entities.

In other words, when there is an external declaration subset or an external parameter entity, this well-formedness constraint only applies if the document has a **standalone** declaration specifying that it can get by without them. See 2.9, "Standalone Document Declaration", for more information.

VALIDITY CONSTRAINT: Entity Declared

In a document with an external subset or external parameter entities with "standalone='no'", the Name given in the entity reference must match that in an *entity declaration*. For interoperability, valid documents should declare the entities amp, lt, gt, apos, quot, in the form specified in **Section 4.6: Predefined Entities**. The declaration of a parameter entity must precede any reference to it. Similarly, the declaration of a general entity must precede any reference to it which appears in a default value in an attribute-list declaration.

In a valid document whose **standalone** declaration indicates a dependence on an external subset or external parameter entities, all entities must be declared before they are referenced. If an XML document references the entities amp, lt, gt, apos, or quot and you want to use that document with SGML software from before the Web-SGML Adaptations were approved, the document's DTD needs declarations for those entities.

The last two sentences in the specification paragraph above tell us that you can't reference entities until after they're declared. In the case of general entities, this seems obvious. After all, a document instance comes after a DTD, and general entities are declared in a DTD and usually referenced in a document instance. But they're not always referenced in a document instance; an attribute default value specification may reference a general entity, and these are specified in the DTD.

In Example 4.6, the faveColor entity is declared before the &faveColor; entity reference on line 4. Otherwise, it would have caused an error, because the processor wouldn't know what to do with the entity reference in the color attribute declaration's default value specification.

Example 4.6: Declaring a general entity before its use in an attribute default

```
<?xml version="1.0"?>
1.<!DOCTYPE para [
2.<!ELEMENT para (#PCDATA)>
3.<!ENTITY faveColor "burgundy">
4.<!ATTLIST para color CDATA "&faveColor;">
5.]>
6.<para>Shall I at least set my lands in order?</para>
```

Tip   *Note that this is a validity constraint, and not a well-formedness constraint as it was in earlier drafts of the XML spec. As a well-formedness constraint, it forced XML processors to reject documents with any inaccessible external entities. As a validity constraint, it allows such documents to be considered well-formed, so that XML software can (for example) represent inaccessible entities with a special icon and still let you work with the document.*

> **WELL-FORMEDNESS CONSTRAINT: Parsed Entity**
>
> An entity reference must not contain the name of an unparsed entity. Unparsed entities may be referred to only in attribute values declared to be of type ENTITY or ENTITIES.

An entity reference (for example, &faveColor;) cannot refer to an unparsed entity, because the processor will parse the text that replaces the reference as part of the XML document. If non-XML data is part of the document, it must be named (as opposed to referenced) in an attribute value of type ENTITY or ENTITIES. See 3.3.1, "Attribute Types", for more on unparsed entities and naming them in ENTITY or ENTITIES attributes.

> **WELL-FORMEDNESS CONSTRAINT: No Recursion**
>
> A parsed entity must not contain a recursive reference to itself, either directly or indirectly.

In Example 4.7, the outer entity refers to itself indirectly, because it has a reference to the inner entity, which references the outer entity.

Example 4.7: An entity (outer) with an indirect reference to itself

```
<!ENTITY outer "This is bad, &inner;">
<!ENTITY inner  "So &outer; bad that it's ill-formed">
```

According to 3.3.3, "Attribute-Value Normalization", "an entity reference is processed by recursively processing the replacement text of the entity". If it weren't for this constraint, a processor that found `&inner;` in a document using these two declarations would replace it with `"So &outer; bad that it's ill-formed"`. It would then replace the `&outer;` reference in that replacement text with `"This is bad, &inner;"`, and then replace the `&inner;` in that replacement text and continue these steps in an unending cycle.

That's an indirect reference. A direct reference would mean referring to an entity in it's own replacement text, as shown in Example 4.8.

Example 4.8: An entity with a direct reference to itself

```
<!ENTITY dirref "This is bad, &dirref;">
```

WELL-FORMEDNESS CONSTRAINT: In DTD

Parameter-entity references may only appear in the DTD.

This is what parameter entities are for: storing strings of text to be reused within a DTD. If you want to declare a string of text to use within the document instance, declare it as a general entity.

Examples of character and entity references:

```
Type <key>less-than</key> (&#x3C;) to save options.
This document was prepared on &docdate; and
is classified &security-level;.
```

`&#x3C;` is the character reference, and will be replaced by the `<` character. `&security-level;` is a general entity reference; its replacement text depends on how it was declared.

Example of a parameter-entity reference:

```
<!-- declare the parameter entity "ISOLat2"... -->
<!ENTITY % ISOLat2
        SYSTEM "http:&sol;/www.xml.com&sol;iso&sol;isolat2-
xml.entities" >
<!-- ... now reference it. -->
%ISOLat2;
```

`ISOLat2` is the parameter-entity; the example shows both its entity declaration declaration and a reference to it (`%ISOLat2;`).

4.2. Entity Declarations

Entities are declared thus:

Except for the five predeclared entities described in 4.6, "Predefined Entities", all entities must be declared so that when the processor finds a reference to a given entity it knows what to replace the reference with.

Entity Declaration

[70]**EntityDecl**	::=	GEDecl | PEDecl	
[71]**GEDecl**	::=	'<!ENTITY' S Name S EntityDef S? '>'	
[72]**PEDecl**	::=	'<!ENTITY' S '%' S Name S PEDef S? '>'	
[73]**EntityDef**	::=	EntityValue | (ExternalID NDataDecl?)	
[74]**PEDef**	::=	EntityValue | ExternalID	

Production 70 shows that an entity declaration is either a general entity declaration (**GEDecl**) or a parameter entity declaration (**PEDecl**).

Productions 71 and 72 show that the way to tell a general entity declaration from a parameter entity declaration is the percent sign (%) just before the entity name (with some space on either side of it). For example, in Example 4.9, the first line declares jogg as a general entity, and the second declares it as a parameter entity.

Example 4.9: Declaring general and a parameter internal entities

```
<!ENTITY jogg "All rights reserved.">
<!ENTITY % jogg "(#PCDATA)">
```

The syntax for defining general and parameter entity values differs a little, too: production 71 shows an **EntityDef** there, while 72 shows a **PEDef**. Productions 73 and 74 show that an **EntityDef** and a **PEDef** are similar, although an **EntityDef** offers you the option of identifying the notation (**NDataDecl**) of an external entity (**ExternalID**). (For unparsed entities, the notation isn't optional, because if the entity isn't XML, the document must tell the processor what format it is. 4.2.2, "External Entities", tells us that the presence of a declared notation name is what makes it an unparsed entity. See that section and 4.4.6, "Notify" for more on this.)

 *Tip*   Despite the similarity in the syntax for declaring general and parameter entities, their purposes are very different. A parameter entity stores text for use within a DTD, so an external parameter entity would refer to a file (or some other external storage unit) that stores one or more declarations to plug into a DTD.

An external file for reference within a DTD is declared in Example 4.10.

Example 4.10: Declaring a parameter entity for a DTD

```
<!ENTITY % tableDecls "calsdefs.dtd">
```

A general entity stores text for use with a document instance. The entity name could be the value of an attribute declared to be of type ENTITY or ENTITIES (in which case the declaration needs that **NData-**

Decl shown in production 73 and defined in production 76 to identify the format). A general entity can also be referenced from the content of the document, in which case the entity must have well-formed XML text.

> The Name identifies the entity in an entity reference or, in the case of an unparsed entity, in the value of an ENTITY or ENTITIES attribute. If the same entity is declared more than once, the first declaration encountered is binding; at user option, an XML processor may issue a warning if entities are declared multiple times.

To paraphrase the first sentence here, the entity name in an entity declaration is the one that an entity reference or the value of an ENTITY or ENTITIES attribute will use to refer to that entity. If there is more than one declaration for the same parameter entity or general entity, the processor will ignore any after the first one and may output a warning message. It must give the user a way to suppress these error messages.

> ### 4.2.1. Internal Entities
>
> If the entity definition is an EntityValue, the defined entity is called an *internal entity*. There is no separate physical storage object, and the content of the entity is given in the declaration. Note that some processing of entity and character references in the literal entity value may be required to produce the correct replacement text: see **Section 4.5: Construction of Internal Entity Replacement Text**.

There's nothing special about the way **EntityValue** (production 9) is defined that makes it an internal entity; it's an internal entity because, as productions 73 and 74 show, if it's an **EntityValue** it's not an **ExternalID**. It's not stored externally in its own entity; an internal entity declaration, instead of saying "this entity's value is stored in the following location" tells us "this entity's value is the following string of characters right here in this declaration". In the spec's

Pub-Status example below, the entity value is the string
"This is a pre-release of the specification."

> An internal entity is a parsed entity.

A "parsed entity" is text for the XML processor to parse as part of
the document. The only kinds of entities that the processor doesn't
parse are the entities that are named (as opposed to referenced) as values of attributes declared with an attribute type of ENTITY or ENTI-
TIES. General entity references—for example, &entname;—always
refer to parsed entities.

> Example of an internal entity declaration:
>
> ```
> <!ENTITY Pub-Status "This is a pre-release of the
>    specification.">
> ```

Example 4.11 shows how the spec's Pub-Status example might be
used.

Example 4.11: Using the spec's Pub-Status example

```
<p>Status of this document: &Pub-Status;</p>
```

4.2.2. External Entities

If the entity is not internal, it is an *external entity*, declared as follows:

An external entity is stored outside the entity where its declaration
is stored.

External Entity Declaration

[75]ExternalID	::=	'SYSTEM' S SystemLiteral | 'PUBLIC' S PubidLiteral S SystemLiteral	
[76]NDataDecl	::=	S 'NDATA' S Name	[VC: Notation Declared]

A **SystemLiteral** and a **PubidLiteral**, both described further below, are the two approaches to telling the parser where to look for the entity.

> If the NDataDecl is present, this is a general unparsed entity; otherwise it is a parsed entity.

Production 73 shows that an **EntityDef** can have an **NDataDecl** after its **ExternalID**. This shows that the entity being defined is not text for the XML processor to parse in the context of the current document. It could be a separate XML document, but usually it's not even XML. It could be a bitmapped picture file, a sound or movie file, or any type of data that you want your applications to incorporate into your document.

The term NDATA means "Non-XML Data", or more precisely, "Not XML text to be parsed as part of this document". The replacement text for all entities declared without an **NDataDecl** (which includes all internal entities) is treated as part of the document where it is inserted to replace the entity references.

> ### VALIDITY CONSTRAINT: Notation Declared
>
> The Name must match the declared name of a notation.

Just as an entity reference must refer to an existing (that is, declared) entity, the **Name** of a notation specified in an **NDataDecl** must refer to a properly declared notation. See 4.7, "Notation Declarations", for more on this.

> The `SystemLiteral` is called the entity's *system identifier*. It is a URI, which may be used to retrieve the entity. Note that the hash mark (#) and fragment identifier frequently used with URIs are not, formally, part of the URI itself; an XML processor may signal an error if a fragment identifier is given as part of a system identifier. Unless otherwise provided by information outside the scope of this specification (e.g. a special XML element type defined by a particular DTD, or a processing instruction defined by a particular application specification), relative URIs are relative to the location of the resource within which the entity declaration occurs. A URI might thus be relative to the document entity, to the entity containing the external DTD subset, or to some other external parameter entity.

"URI" stands for "Uniform Resource Identifier", the system for naming resources on the Web. A resource is usually a file, but its full meaning is broader to allow for greater flexibility in the future. One form of URI is the URL, or "Uniform Resource Locator", more popularly known as a "Web address" (such as `http://www.w3.org/XML`).

If a URL locates a particular HTML document, you can make it locate a specific element in that document (an `a` anchor element with a `name` attribute value specified). This is done by adding a pound sign (#) and the target point's `name` attribute value to the URL that locates the document.

For example, `http://www.snee.com/catalog/products.html#cable` locates the `<a name="cable">` element in the `http://www.snee.com/catalog/products.html` document. This `#cable` is one of the "fragment identifiers" described above, and therefore not considered part of the URI; an XML processor may even (note the use of "may") treat it as an error.

The spec tells us that a URI is "relative to the location of the source within which the entity declaration occurs". This means that an XML processor fills out a partial URI by looking at the corresponding pieces of the URI for the entity holding the declaration.

For example, if a file at `http://www.snee.com/dtds/pr.dtd` holds the declaration shown in Example 4.12, an XML processor treats the `cals.dtd` system identifier as though it were actually `http://www.snee.com/dtds/cals.dtd`.

Example 4.12: Using a system identifier

```
<!ENTITY % tabledecls SYSTEM "cals.dtd">
```

This is similar to HTML's practice; if a Web document at `http://www.snee.com/catalog/products.html` contains the link anchor element `<A HREF="cable.html">` then a Web server assumes that this Web page has the full URL `http://www.snee.com/catalog/cable.html`.

Because an entity declaration can be in an XML document's internal declaration subset, that same `tabledecls` declaration in Example 4.12 might be in a document with the URI `http://www.snee.com/catalog/products.xml`. In that case, the XML processor treats the `cals.dtd` system identifier as though it were actually `http://www.snee.com/products/cals.dtd`. This is worth noting because the last sentence of the specification paragraph above points out that a "URI might be thus relative to the document entity" (as with the `products.xml` case), "the entity containing the external DTD subset, or to some other external parameter entity".

Tip   Keep in mind that this whole system for interpreting relative URIs can be overridden ("Unless otherwise provided..."). The tremendous promise of hypertext and multimedia systems in the future means that a lot of work will be done on ways to address units of information. This part of the XML spec is very careful about not locking systems down to an overly rigid way of resolving incomplete URIs.

An XML processor should handle a non-ASCII character in a URI by representing the character in UTF-8 as one or more bytes, and then escaping these bytes with the URI escaping mechanism (i.e., by converting each byte to %HH, where HH is the hexadecimal notation of the byte value).

The ISO ASCII standard assigns specific octets to represent specific characters. For example, the octet `01100001`, which has the decimal value 97, represents the letter "a", and octet `01100010` (98) represents a "b". Only 127 characters were assigned, which just about covers the characters that you can enter with an English-language computer keyboard. Various companies and organizations have developed their own encodings for using octets above 127 to represent other characters. (For example, an "ä" is represented by byte 138 on a Macintosh, 228 on a Windows system, and 132 in DOS.)

To allow the use of characters with numbers higher than 127 in URLs, while avoiding the confusion of these different encodings, the IETF RFC 1738 URL standard tells us that we can represent URL characters as a percent sign (`%`) followed by a hexadecimal representation of the character's number. For example, because the hexadecimal version of 97 is 61, the URL `http://www.%61cm.org` sends a browser to the Association for Computing Machinery's home page just as `http://www.acm.org` does.

The above specification paragraph stipulates that for a system identifier character whose number is greater than 127, an XML processor should use this IETF technique to represent each octet of the UTF-8 encoding of the character.

In addition to a system identifier, an external identifier may include a *public identifier*. An XML processor attempting to retrieve the entity's content may use the public identifier to try to generate an alternative URI. If the processor is unable to do so, it must use the URI specified in the system literal. Before a match is attempted, all strings of white space in the public identifier must be normalized to single space characters (#x20), and leading and trailing white space must be removed.

One disadvantage of using system identifiers is apparent if someone renames a directory. All the XML documents that contain system identifiers that point to files in that directory (or any of its subdirectories) must be edited and fixed, because they're no longer pointing at the right place.

Using a public identifier allows you to assign a separate name to a resource (in the specification's example below, `-//Textuality//TEXT Standard open-hatch boilerplate//EN`); the processor or application then looks this name up somewhere to see which system identifier it refers to. This way, when you rename a directory, you only have to edit the lookup table file to ensure that all the XML documents pointing to system entities within that directory still point to the right place.

Public identifiers sound more sensible than system identifiers, but I've glossed over a few points: what are the parts of a public identifier name, and what do they mean? How does the processor know where to find the lookup table? What is the syntax of the lookup table?

Although the SGML world has used public identifiers for a decade (many HTML people wonder about the public identifier `-//W3C//DTD HTML 3.2//EN` that begins so many HTML files), the few conventions in place for each of these questions were only that: conventions. That's because no industry-wide standards have ever been established.

The XML Working Group debated the point, but decided that nailing down definite, usable rules in the timeframe that they had was not realistic. Instead, they decided to require a system identifier after any public identifier to ensure that an XML processor wouldn't be too dependent on the currently vague practices for implementing public identifiers.

Before looking up the system resource represented by a particular public identifier, an XML processor must first delete any white space characters (carriage returns, tabs, or the spacebar space) at the very beginning or end of the public identifier. It also must convert any combination of white space characters within the identifier into a single spacebar space.

Examples of external entity declarations:

```
<!ENTITY open-hatch SYSTEM
    "http://www.textuality.com/boilerplate/OpenHatch.xml">
<!ENTITY open-hatch PUBLIC
    "-//Textuality//TEXT Standard open-hatch boilerplate//EN"
        "http://www.textuality.com/boilerplate/OpenHatch.xml">
<!ENTITY hatch-pic SYSTEM "../grafix/OpenHatch.gif"
        NDATA gif >
```

The spec's first example above shows an ENTITY declaration with a system identifier that has a complete URI. The second shows a public identifier followed by a system identifier.

The third example, hatch-pic, shows a system identifier with a relative URI that must be interpreted in the context of the URI of the entity where the hatch-pic declaration is stored. For example, if this third entity declaration is in a file located at http://www.textuality.com/boilerplate/index.xml, then the OpenHatch.gif file's full URI would be http://www.textuality.com/grafix/OpenHatch.gif. (The ../grafix part shows that Openhatch.gif is in a sibling of the boilerplate directory.)

4.3. Parsed Entities

4.3.1. The Text Declaration

External parsed entities may each begin with a *text declaration*.

Example 4.13 shows a text declaration.

Example 4.13: A text declaration

```
<?xml version="1.0" encoding="ISO-8859-1"?>
```

Text Declaration

| [77] `TextDecl` | ::= | `'<?xml' VersionInfo? EncodingDecl S? '?>'` |

This looks a lot like the XML declaration that should begin all XML documents (see production 23), and many text declarations could serve as valid XML declarations. There are three possible differences in the information they provide:

- The version information parameter (for example, `version="1.0"`) is required in a document's XML declaration but optional in an external parsed entity's text declaration. If an external text entity doesn't have this, the XML parser assumes that it conforms to the same specification release as the document referencing it.

- The encoding declaration, which is optional in a document's XML declaration, is required in a parsed entity's text declaration. The text declaration itself is optional; its reason for being is to declare an alternative encoding. Therefore, it would be pointless to allow a text declaration without an encoding declaration.

- An XML declaration may include a standalone document declaration, which is irrelevant in an external parsed entity's text declaration.

> The text declaration must be provided literally, not by reference to a parsed entity. No text declaration may appear at any position other than the beginning of an external parsed entity.

You can't store your text declaration in a parameter entity and then plug it into a file with an entity reference. Also, the only legal place for a text declaration is the very beginning of an external parsed entity. That's because the processor may use the literal declaration to determine the encoding automatically. (See Appendix F, "Autodetection of Character Encodings (Non-Normative)", for more information.)

4.3.2. Well-Formed Parsed Entities

The document entity is well-formed if it matches the production labeled document. An external general parsed entity is well-formed if it matches the production labeled extParsedEnt. An external parameter entity is well-formed if it matches the production labeled extPE.

The first sentence here amplifies item 3 of 2.1, "Well-Formed XML Documents", by stating the well-formedness requirements for referenced parsed entities.

Well-Formed External Parsed Entity

```
[78] extParsedEnt  ::=  TextDecl? content
[79] extPE         ::=  TextDecl? extSubsetDecl
```

The content of an external parsed entity may be one big element, as with a document entity or with Example 4.14, or it may be multiple elements, or it may be character data with no markup at all.

Example 4.14: A small, simple, well-formed external parsed entity

```
<msg>The barges drift</msg>
```

In fact, because the text declaration is optional, you could store the word "hello" in a file all by itself and it would be a well-formed external parsed entity.

An external parameter entity must match production 79, which shows that it consists of an optional text declaration followed by an external subset declaration. Production 31 shows that an external subset declaration consists of zero or more markup declarations (and possibly parameter entities and conditional sections, which help control the use of the markup declarations). Because a parameter entity reference is used to plug something into a DTD, an external parameter entity is something that you treat as a piece of a DTD.

Why are these useful? Many DTD authors group their declarations into different, re-usable entities according to their purpose so that they can create more complex yet compatible DTDs by combining these building blocks. For example, let's say you have the following four files of declarations:

- Declarations for paragraphs of text, bulleted and numbered lists, and hierarchical headings in a file called `textdecl.dtd`.

- Declarations for tables with their rows, entries, and column specifications in `cals.dtd`.

- Declarations for pictures and different kinds of captions in `illus.dtd`.

- Declarations for storing information about graphs in `graphs.dtd`.

When it's time to design a document type for financial reports, you know it will need hierarchical text, tables, and graphs, but not illustrations, so you create the document type declaration shown in Example 4.15. It defines an element type for the `finrpt` document type and indicates which building blocks to incorporate into this document type.

Example 4.15: Combining several "building block" DTD files into a new one

```
<?xml version="1.0"?>
<!DOCTYPE finrpt [

<!ELEMENT finrpt (chapter+)>
<!-- chapter declared in textdecl.dtd -->

<!ENTITY % TextDeclarations SYSTEM "textdecl.dtd">
<!ENTITY % GraphDecls       SYSTEM "graphs.dtd">
```

```
<!ENTITY % TableDecls        SYSTEM "cals.dtd">

<!-- References to external parameter entities. -->
%TextDeclarations;
%GraphDecls;
%TableDecls;
]>
```

With very little work, you've declared a large, powerful document type definition by using external parameter entities.

> An internal general parsed entity is well-formed if its replacement text matches the production labeled `content`. All internal parameter entities are well-formed by definition.

An internal general parsed entity is just like an external one, except that it never has a text declaration. (It doesn't need its own production because production 43 for **content** defines it.) An internal entity doesn't need a text declaration because it will have the same encoding as the document entity or external entity that contains its declaration.

> A consequence of well-formedness in entities is that the logical and physical structures in an XML document are properly nested; no start-tag, end-tag, empty-element tag, element, comment, processing instruction, character reference, or entity reference can begin in one entity and end in another.

This makes the parser's job easier, because when it finishes reading one entity, it doesn't have to keep track of incomplete structures that must be finished up in another entity. More importantly, it means that the well-formedness of an entity is not affected by any failure to resolve external references made within it.

4.3.3. Character Encoding in Entities

Each external parsed entity in an XML document may use a different encoding for its characters. All XML processors must be able to read entities in either UTF-8 or UTF-16.

UTF-8 and UTF-16 are two sets of character encodings (defined as part of the ISO/IEC 10646 standard) that assign characters to specific octets and octet sequences. See 2.2, "Characters", for more on this standard's role in determining character encodings.

The long fight to keep XML usable for people all over the world, regardless of their language and way of representing it, has resulted in some of the spec's more complex aspects. But don't panic: if you don't fool around with any of these settings and leave them at their defaults, using plain old ASCII text won't break any rules. When you're ready to use non-Western content in your documents, XML will be ready for you.

Entities encoded in UTF-16 must begin with the Byte Order Mark described by ISO/IEC 10646 Annex E and Unicode Appendix B (the ZERO WIDTH NO-BREAK SPACE character, #xFEFF). This is an encoding signature, not part of either the markup or the character data of the XML document. XML processors must be able to use this character to differentiate between UTF-8 and UTF-16 encoded documents.

In general, characters stored using UTF-16 take up twice as much room as characters using UTF-8. The good news is that UTF-16 can represent a much wider repertoire of characters than UTF-8. When creating documents using Western, Latin-style alphabets, you will almost always use UTF-8, whether you know it or not.

"Whether you know it or not" is important: you shouldn't have to worry about it. When you save a document written using the Japanese Kanji alphabet, your XML software may store it in UTF-16, in which case it will begin the document entity with the special Byte

Order Mark described above. When XML software reads a document, it will check for the Byte Order Mark to find out whether the document is stored in UTF-16 or the default UTF-8. This means a little more work for the people designing this software, and this part of the spec spells out their responsibilities.

Although an XML processor is required to read only entities in the UTF-8 and UTF-16 encodings, it is recognized that other encodings are used around the world, and it may be desired for XML processors to read entities that use them. Parsed entities which are stored in an encoding other than UTF-8 or UTF-16 must begin with a *text declaration* containing an encoding declaration:

Encoding Declaration

```
[80] EncodingDecl  ::=  S 'encoding' Eq ('"' EncName '"'
                        | "'" EncName "'" )
[81] EncName       ::=  [A-Za-z] ([A-Za-z0-9._] | '-')*   /* Encoding name con-
                                                             tains only Latin
                                                             characters */
```

An encoding declaration within an XML declaration or a text declaration lets an external entity specify other possible encodings. Encodings like the Japanese EUC-JP existed before UTF-8 and UTF-16, and there's a lot of existing data that we don't want to prohibit from use in XML documents.

Tip   An XML processor is not required to handle all of these other encodings ("an XML processor is required to read only entities in the UTF-8 and UTF-16 encodings"), but the XML Working Group did make provisions so that applications could be built around them.

In the document entity, the encoding declaration is part of the XML declaration. The EncName is the name of the encoding used.

In an encoding declaration, the values "UTF-8", "UTF-16", "ISO-10646-UCS-2", and "ISO-10646-UCS-4" should be used for the various encodings and transformations of Unicode / ISO/IEC 10646, the values "ISO-8859-1", "ISO-8859-2", … "ISO-8859-9" should be used for the parts of ISO 8859, and the values "ISO-2022-JP", "Shift_JIS", and "EUC-JP" should be used for the various encoded forms of JIS X-0208-1997. XML processors may recognize other encodings; it is recommended that character encodings registered (as *charsets*) with the Internet Assigned Numbers Authority [IANA], other than those just listed, should be referred to using their registered names. Note that these registered names are defined to be case-insensitive, so processors wishing to match against them should do so in a case-insensitive way.

In the absence of information provided by an external transport protocol (e.g. HTTP or MIME), it is an error for an entity including an encoding declaration to be presented to the XML processor in an encoding other than that named in the declaration, for an encoding declaration to occur other than at the beginning of an external entity, or for an entity which begins with neither a Byte Order Mark nor an encoding declaration to use an encoding other than UTF-8. Note that since ASCII is a subset of UTF-8, ordinary ASCII entities do not strictly need an encoding declaration.

There are three things that can go wrong with an encoding declaration. An XML processor must treat each as an error:

- If the encoding declaration is wrong—that is, if the entity uses one encoding and the encoding declaration names another.

- If the encoding declaration isn't the first thing in the entity.

- If the entity isn't in UTF-8 and doesn't have either a Byte Order Mark or an encoding declaration to specify which encoding it uses. This is why you can ignore these encoding details for simple ASCII documents: with no Byte Order Mark or encoding declaration, an XML

processor assumes a UTF-8 encoding, and ASCII is a
subset of UTF-8.

This is all subject to a big qualifier: it doesn't apply if a transport
protocol supplies information that overrides the encoding declara-
tion. Transport protocols such as the HyperText Transport Protocol
(HTTP) and Multipurpose Internet Mail Extensions (MIME) are sets
of rules that enable computers to have conversations like this:
"Can I send you a file now?"
"Yes, you can send a file".
"Here comes the first 512 bytes".
"OK, I got the first 512 bytes, I'm ready for more if you have it".
The conversations may include the equivalent of "Can you handle
this particular type of file?" If a transmitting program converts a
UTF-8 file to a UTF-16 file as it sends it, the XML processor at the
other end has no control over this, and will hopefully be told some-
how that the entity it is reading does not conform to the
`<?xml encoding='UTF-8'?>` declaration that begins it.

> It is a fatal error when an XML processor encounters an entity with an
> encoding that it is unable to process.

If an XML processor sees an encoding declaration that names an
encoding it doesn't recognize, it can't continue processing the document as if nothing's wrong. This should be obvious, but a standard
needs to specify everything.

> Examples of encoding declarations:
>
> ```
> <?xml encoding='UTF-8'?>
> <?xml encoding='EUC-JP'?>
> ```

EUC-JP is the Japanese version of the "Extended UNIX Code"
developed by several UNIX organizations to enable the use of Japa-

nese on UNIX workstations. It complies with ISO standard 2022, "Character code structure and extension techniques".

4.4. XML Processor Treatment of Entities and References

The table below summarizes the contexts in which character references, entity references, and invocations of unparsed entities might appear and the required behavior of an XML processor in each case. The labels in the leftmost column describe the recognition context:

The `entdemo` document in Example 4.16 on page 217 demonstrates the use (or misuse—illegally used references are commented out) of all the entities and references in the table immediately preceding the document. The annotations to the spec's descriptions of "recognition contexts" in the table's first column ("Reference in Content", "Reference in Attribute Value", etc.) refer often to this sample document.

Reference in Content

as a reference anywhere after the start-tag and before the end-tag of an element; corresponds to the nonterminal `content`.

In the `entdemo` document, see the parameter-entity reference `%parameterEnt;` on line 27, the internal general-entity reference `&intGenEnt;` on line 25, the external parsed general reference `&extParsedGE;` on line 24, the attempted unparsed entity reference

`&unparsedEnt;` on line 31, and the character reference `&#241;` on line 25.

> **Reference in Attribute Value**
>
> as a reference within either the value of an attribute in a start-tag, or a default value in an attribute declaration; corresponds to the nonterminal `AttValue`.

In Example 4.16's `entdemo` document, the examples are all used within the attribute value for the `style` attribute, which is declared on line 6 to have a CDATA attribute value. See the attempted parameter-entity reference `%parameterEnt;` on line 28, the internal general-entity reference `&intGenEnt;` on line 26, the attempted external parsed general entity reference `&extParsedGE;` near the beginning of line 34, the attempted unparsed entity reference `&unparsedEnt;` on line 33, and the character reference `&#241;` on line 26.

> **Occurs as Attribute Value**
>
> as a `Name`, not a reference, appearing either as the value of an attribute which has been declared as type `ENTITY`, or as one of the space-separated tokens in the value of an attribute which has been declared as type `ENTITIES`.

In the `entdemo` document, the examples are all used as values for the attribute `picfile`, which is declared on line 7 to have an attribute type of `ENTITY`. See the attempted parameter-entity usage `parameterEnt` on line 32, the attempted internal general-entity usage `intGenEnt` on line 31, the attempted external parsed general entity usage `extParsedGE` near the end of line 34, the unparsed entity usage `unparsedEnt` on line 26, and the attempt to use character number 241 on line 33.

Reference in Entity Value

as a reference within a parameter or internal entity's literal entity value in the entity's declaration; corresponds to the nonterminal `Entity-Value`.

In Example 4.16's `entdemo` document, see the parameter-entity reference `%parameterEnt;` on line 12 as part of the `intGenEnt4` entity's value (which is then referenced on line 28), the internal general-entity reference `&intGenEnt;` on line 10, the external parsed general entity reference `&extParsedGE;` on line 10, the attempted unparsed entity reference `&unparsedEnt;` on line 20, and the two `&#97;` character references on line 11.

Reference in DTD

as a reference within either the internal or external subsets of the DTD, but outside of an `EntityValue` or `AttValue`.

In the `entdemo` document, see the parameter-entity reference `%parameterEnt` on line 5, the attempted internal general-entity reference `&intGenEnt;` on line 17, the attempted external parsed general reference `&extParsedGE;` on line 18 (even if its `newdata.xml` file had valid DTD declarations, the parser would still choke on the `&` that starts the `&extParsedGE;` entity reference), the attempted unparsed entity reference `&unparsedEnt;` on line 21, and the attempted character reference `&#97;` on line 19. Note that, unlike most other entity references within the DTD, none of these occur within an entity value or attribute value.

	Entity Type				Character
	Parameter	Internal General	External Parsed General	Unparsed	
Reference in Content	*Not recognized*	*Included*	*Included if validating*	*Forbidden*	*Included*
Reference in Attribute Value	*Not recognized*	*Included in literal*	*Forbidden*	*Forbidden*	*Included*
Occurs as Attribute Value	*Not recognized*	*Forbidden*	*Forbidden*	*Notify*	*Not recognized*
Reference in Entity Value	*Included in literal*	*Bypassed*	*Bypassed*	*Forbidden*	*Included*
Reference in DTD	*Included as PE*	*Forbidden*	*Forbidden*	*Forbidden*	*Forbidden*

Example 4.16's `entdemo` document demonstrates all the entity and character references described in the table above. After the sample document, the specification (and annotations) give further details on the meaning of the table's entries: "Not recognized", "Included", "Included if validating", etc.

Example 4.16: Demonstrating all the successful and unsuccessful entity and character references

```
1. <?xml version="1.0"?>
2. <!DOCTYPE entdemo [
3. <!ELEMENT entdemo (para+)>
4. <!ENTITY % parameterEnt "#PCDATA">
5. <!ELEMENT para (%parameterEnt;)>
6. <!ATTLIST para style   CDATA #IMPLIED
7.                picfile ENTITY #IMPLIED>
```

```
 8. <!ENTITY extParsedGE SYSTEM "newdata.xml">
 9. <!ENTITY intGenEnt   "Spanish">
10. <!ENTITY intGenEnt2 "&intGenEnt; and &extParsedGE;">
11. <!ENTITY intGenEnt3 "C&#97;t in the H&#97;t">
12. <!ENTITY intGenEnt4 "text: %parameterEnt;">
13. <!NOTATION JPEG SYSTEM "JPGView">
14. <!ENTITY unparsedEnt SYSTEM "clown.jpg" NDATA JPEG>
15.
16. <!--    ===== commented out, forbidden in a DTD: =====
17. <!ELEMENT &intGenEnt; (#PCDATA)>
18. &extParsedGE;
19. <!ELEMENT &#97;bcdef (#PCDATA)>
20. <!ENTITY intGenEnt5 "forbidden:  &unparsedEnt;">
21. &unparsedEnt;                                      -->
22. ]>      <!-- ===== end of DTD ===== -->
23.
24. <entdemo><para>&extParsedGE;
25. "Spain" in &intGenEnt; is "Espa&#241;a."</para>
26. <para style="&#241;  &intGenEnt;" picfile="unparsedEnt">
27. Not recognized: %parameterEnt;</para>
28. <para style="That's %parameterEnt;">&intGenEnt4;</para>
29.
30. <!-- ===== commented out, forbidden in a document: ====
31. <para picfile="intGenEnt">&unparsedEnt;</para>
32. <para picfile="parameterEnt"></para>
33. <para style="Look: &unparsedEnt;" picfile="#241"></para>
34. <para style="My &extParsedGE;" picfile="extParsedGE">
35. </para> --> </entdemo>
```

4.4.1. Not Recognized

Outside the DTD, the % character has no special significance; thus, what would be parameter entity references in the DTD are not recognized as markup in content. Similarly, the names of unparsed entities are not recognized except when they appear in the value of an appropriately declared attribute.

When it's not processing a DTD, an XML processor isn't looking for parameter entities, so a percent sign is just a percent sign. In line

27 of Example 4.16, the attempted parameter entity reference `%parameterEnt;` will not be treated as an entity reference.

4.4.2. Included

An entity is *included* when its replacement text is retrieved and processed, in place of the reference itself, as though it were part of the document at the location the reference was recognized. The replacement text may contain both character data and (except for parameter entities) markup, which must be recognized in the usual way, except that the replacement text of entities used to escape markup delimiters (the entities `amp`, `lt`, `gt`, `apos`, `quot`) is always treated as data. (The string "AT&T;" expands to "AT&T;" and the remaining ampersand is not recognized as an entity-reference delimiter.) A character reference is *included* when the indicated character is processed in place of the reference itself.

To summarize, an included entity is one that replaces a reference to it.

If the replacement text contains markup, that markup will be interpreted as part of the document's markup after the entity replaces the entity reference. For example, after a `listitem` general entity is declared as shown in Example 4.17, an `item` element had better be legal wherever the document has a `&listitem;` entity reference.

This doesn't apply to the predefined entities. If the `listitem` entity value had included the string `&lt;item&gt;` the processor would not have treated it as an `item` start-tag. (If it did, your document could never have a less-than symbol as data—an XML processor would always treat it as the beginning of a tag.) See 4.6, "Predefined Entities", for more on these.

Example 4.17: An entity replacement value that incorporates markup

```
<!ENTITY listitem "<item>Here is an item</item>">
```

4.4.3. Included If Validating

When an XML processor recognizes a reference to a parsed entity, in order to validate the document, the processor must include its replacement text. If the entity is external, and the processor is not attempting to validate the XML document, the processor may, but need not, include the entity's replacement text. If a non-validating parser does not include the replacement text, it must inform the application that it recognized, but did not read, the entity.

If an application only requires that a document is well-formed, it doesn't have to read in external entities. If it finds a reference to an external entity and chooses not to read it in, it has to tell the application "Hey! There's an external entity reference to listitem here, but I'm not going to read it!" (Or something along those lines.)

This rule is based on the recognition that the automatic inclusion provided by the SGML and XML entity mechanism, primarily designed to support modularity in authoring, is not necessarily appropriate for other applications, in particular document browsing. Browsers, for example, when encountering an external parsed entity reference, might choose to provide a visual indication of the entity's presence and retrieve it for display only on demand.

The XML Working Group made this allowance because a browser or editor might not want to read in all the entities of a large document before it shows the viewer anything. It might be more efficient to display the document entity and an icon or hypertext link for any external entity references (both examples of a "visual indication of the entity's presence") for users to click when and if they're ready to see that particular entity.

4.4.4. Forbidden

The following are forbidden, and constitute fatal errors:

- the appearance of a reference to an unparsed entity.

An XML document can only point to an unparsed entity from an attribute declared as an ENTITY or ENTITIES attribute, because then the XML processor knows that it's supposed to check the entity's declaration for a NOTATION value. It can then cross-reference this value with a NOTATION declaration to see how to handle the entity.

If the processor sees an entity reference in the middle of a document, it assumes that it's a reference to a block of parseable XML. If it's not (as on line 21 of the `entdemo` document in Example 4.16) it won't know what to do with the entity. See below in 4.4.6, "Notify", for more.

- the appearance of any character or general-entity reference in the DTD except within an `EntityValue` or `AttValue`.

Character references and general entity references are for plugging text into document instances, not DTDs. You can reference them from within an **EntityValue** or **AttValue** in a DTD because these are mechanisms for specifying text to plug into the document instance later. In Example 4.16's `entdemo` document, the `&intGenEnt;` entity reference on line 10 and the two character references on line 11 are OK because they're in entity values, but in lines 17 and 19 they're illegal.

- a reference to an external entity in an attribute value.

Note the distinction, in the chart on page 217, between an entity that is referenced from within an attribute value and an entity whose name occurs as an attribute value. In Example 4.16's `entdemo` document, there is an entity *name* as the value of a `picfile` attribute `unparsedEnt` on line 26 and an entity *reference* within the `style` attribute value (the `&intGenEnt;` on the same line).

4.4.5. Included in Literal

When an entity reference appears in an attribute value, or a parameter entity reference appears in a literal entity value, its replacement text is processed in place of the reference itself as though it were part of the document at the location the reference was recognized, except that a single or double quote character in the replacement text is always treated as a normal data character and will not terminate the literal. For example, this is well-formed:

```
<!ENTITY % YN '"Yes"' >
<!ENTITY WhatHeSaid "He said &YN;" >
```

while this is not:

```
<!ENTITY EndAttr "27'" >
<element attribute='a-&EndAttr;'>
```

Lines 5 and 26 of the `entdemo` document in Example 4.16 (reproduced in Example 4.18) are processed as though `%parameterEnt;` is replaced with the `#PCDATA` text declared for it on line 4, `&#241;` is replaced with the ñ character that it represents, and `&intGenEnt;` is replaced with the text string "`Spanish`" declared as its replacement on line 9. The result looks like the `para` element shown in Example 4.19.

Example 4.18: Excerpts from Example 4.16

```
 4. <!ENTITY  % parameterEnt "#PCDATA">
 5. <!ELEMENT para (%parameterEnt;)>

 9. <!ENTITY intGenEnt  "Spanish">

26. <para style="&#241;  &intGenEnt;" picfile="unparsedEnt">
```

Example 4.19: para element from Example 4.18 after entity replacements are made

```
<!ELEMENT para (#PCDATA)>

<para style="ñ  Spanish" picfile="unparsedEnt">
```

4.4.6. Notify

When the name of an unparsed entity appears as a token in the value of an attribute of declared type ENTITY or ENTITIES, a validating processor must inform the application of the system and public (if any) identifiers for both the entity and its associated notation.

The whole point of unparsed entities is to provide XML documents with a method for incorporating non-XML data, whether it's sound, movies, or plain text files. If it's not XML, the XML processor won't know what to do with it, and must pass information on to the application about what to do with it.

For example, when an XML parser sees unparsedEnt as a value for the picfile attribute on line 26 of Example 4.16 (shown again in Example 4.20), it knows that picfile was declared as an ENTITY attribute. It therefore checks the picfile declaration for a NOTATION value, and finds it on line 14 (shown again in Example 4.21).

Example 4.20: Line 26 of Example 4.16

```
<para style="&#241;  &intGenEnt;" picfile="unparsedEnt">
```

Example 4.21: Line 14 of Example 4.16: declaring the unparsedEnt entity

```
<!ENTITY unparsedEnt SYSTEM "clown.jpg" NDATA JPEG>
```

So it uses the "JPEG" notation. What's that? It looks for a declaration for this notation, and finds it on line 13 (shown again in Example 4.22).

Example 4.22: Line 13 of Example 4.16: declaring the JPEG notation

```
<!NOTATION JPEG SYSTEM "JPGView">
```

The notation declaration tells us to use something called "JPG-View" to deal with entities of the JPEG notation type. The XML processor passes the following information along to the application software:

- The system identifier of the unparsed entity `unparsedEnt: clown.jpg`.

- The system identifier of the notation: "JPGView". The application should know what to do with `clown.jpg` based on this information.

4.4.7. Bypassed

When a general entity reference appears in the `EntityValue` in an entity declaration, it is bypassed and left as is.

Entity declarations go in DTDs, and an XML processor doesn't even look for general-entity references until it gets to the actual document element. When an XML processor sees a general-entity reference in an entity declaration, like the two on line 10 of the `entdemo` document (reproduced in Example 4.23), it leaves them alone.

Example 4.23: Line 10 of Example 4.16: using general-entity references

```
<!ENTITY intGenEnt2 "&intGenEnt; and &extParsedGE;">
```

In this case, when and if the XML processor comes across an `&intGenEnt2;` entity reference (in the `entdemo` document, it never actually does) it replaces the reference with the "`&intGenEnt; and &extParsedGE;`" entity value. Then, it looks for XML markup within that replacement value to parse, and only then finds the `&intGenEnt;` and `&extParsedGE;` general-entity references. It replaces these references with the appropriate text.

4.4.8. Included as PE

Just as with external parsed entities, parameter entities need only be *included if validating*. When a parameter-entity reference is recognized in the DTD and included, its replacement text is enlarged by the attachment of one leading and one following space (#x20) character; the intent is to constrain the replacement text of parameter entities to contain an integral number of grammatical tokens in the DTD.

By "integral number", it means "a number that's an integer and not a fraction". In Example 4.24, the `ent1` parameter entity's replacement text contains a single token: the name `para`.

Example 4.24: Parameter entity replacement text with exactly one token in it: "para"

```
<!ENTITY % ent1 "para">
<!ELEMENT notice (title,%ent1;) >
```

An XML parser would have no problem with these two lines as long as they're in an external declaration subset. As the spec describes in 2.8, "Prolog and Document Type Declaration", a well-formed document's internal declaration subset can only have parameter-entity references in places where it can have an entire declaration. In other words, the internal subset doesn't permit parameter-entity references that only represent a piece of a declaration, like the example above.

If the `ent1` parameter entity only stored part of the name `para`, as shown in Example 4.25, it would not work. That's because half of a grammatical token (in this case, half of an element type name) is not an integral number of tokens.

Example 4.25: Attempting to reference a parameter entity with a partial token

```
<!ENTITY % ent1 "ra">
<!ELEMENT notice (title,pa%ent1;) > <!-- Won't work. -->
```

To make this situation easier for parsers to detect, the parser adds a space (#x20) before and after the replacement text. Replacing %ent1; with " para " (note the leading and trailing spaces) in the second line of Example 4.24 would be fine, but plugging " ra " into Example 4.25's notice element type declaration would result in the invalid declaration shown in Example 4.26.[†]

Example 4.26: Example 4.25 after plugging in the partial token stored by the parameter entity

```
<!ELEMENT notice (title,pa ra ) > <!-- Won't work. -->
```

4.5. Construction of Internal Entity Replacement Text

In discussing the treatment of internal entities, it is useful to distinguish two forms of the entity's value. The *literal entity value* is the quoted string actually present in the entity declaration, corresponding to the non-terminal EntityValue. The *replacement text* is the content of the entity, after replacement of character references and parameter-entity references.

The literal entity value and the replacement text may be the same thing, as with the rights general entity defined in the spec's example below. The pub parameter entity preceding it, however, has a character reference in its entity value, which makes its replacement text different from the literal entity value. After replacing the É in the

---

† Note that spaces are not added when a parameter entity reference occurs in an entity value.

entity's literal value "Éditions Gallimard", the entity has "Éditions Gallimard" as its replacement text.

> The literal entity value as given in an internal entity declaration (Entity-Value) may contain character, parameter-entity, and general-entity references. Such references must be contained entirely within the literal entity value. The actual replacement text that is included as described above must contain the *replacement text* of any parameter entities referred to, and must contain the character referred to, in place of any character references in the literal entity value; however, general-entity references must be left as-is, unexpanded. For example, given the following declarations:
>
> ```
> <!ENTITY % pub     "&#xc9;ditions Gallimard" >
> <!ENTITY   rights "All rights reserved" >
> <!ENTITY   book   "La Peste: Albert Camus,
> &#xA9; 1947 %pub;. &rights;" >
> ```
>
> then the replacement text for the entity "book" is:
>
> ```
> La Peste: Albert Camus,
> © 1947 Éditions Gallimard. &rights;
> ```
>
> The general-entity reference "&rights;" would be expanded should the reference "&book;" appear in the document's content or an attribute value.

When the XML processor replaces a parameter entity reference, it plugs in the replacement text. In the example above, the processor won't replace %pub; with the pub parameter entity's literal value of "Éditions Gallimard", but with its replacement text of "Éditions Gallimard" instead.

The exception is general-entity references, which are only replaced when the finds processor references to them in the document instance content or in an attribute value. This is why, in the spec's examples above, the book general entity's replacement text has &rights; in it and not the rights entity's replacement text of "All rights reserved". The XML processor will deal with the &rights; reference only after it replaces the &book; entity reference.

These simple rules may have complex interactions; for a detailed discussion of a difficult example, see **Appendix D: Expansion of Entity and Character References (Non-Normative)**.

Appendix D, "Expansion of Entity and Character References (Non-Normative)", shows two examples that combine character, general-entity, and parameter-entity references, and describes the substitutions made by the XML processor and the order in which it performs them.

4.6. Predefined Entities

Entity and character references can both be used to *escape* the left angle bracket, ampersand, and other delimiters. A set of general entities (amp, lt, gt, apos, quot) is specified for this purpose. Numeric character references may also be used; they are expanded immediately when recognized and must be treated as character data, so the numeric character references "<" and "&" may be used to escape < and & when they occur in character data.

Because XML markup uses the ampersand (&), less-than symbol (<), greater-than symbol (>), apostrophe ('), and quotation mark (") so often, the entity references predefined for those characters should—and sometimes must—be used in locations in which the characters are to occur as actual data. Otherwise, the XML processor might think that they are markup. (See page 81 for a list of situations where you may safely use them in their literal form.)

For a real-life example, I used predefined references five times in the previous paragraph: I didn't want the processor to treat the ampersand between that first pair of parentheses as the beginning of an entity reference, I didn't want it to treat the less-than sign between that second pair of parentheses as the beginning of a start- or end-tag, and so forth.

As explained further in 2.4, "Character Data and Markup", to "escape" text is to identify it as something that should escape parsing. In other words, if there's anything in text that would normally be considered XML markup, escaping it causes it to be treated as character data.

Doing this with numbers instead of entity references is another option. 60 is the Unicode value for the less-than character and 38 is the value for the ampersand, which is why the spec uses those examples. (These are decimal values—if they were hexadecimal, they'd have an "x" prefix.) Entity references are easier to read and remember than numeric character entity references. For example, it's much easier to remember what < represents than <.

> All XML processors must recognize these entities whether they are declared or not. For interoperability, valid XML documents should declare these entities, like any others, before using them. If the entities in question are declared, they must be declared as internal entities whose replacement text is the single character being escaped or a character reference to that character, as shown below.

SGML originally required all entities to be explicitly declared, so for interoperability with older SGML systems, include the entity declarations for the five characters as shown here.

```
<!ENTITY lt    "&#38;#60;">
<!ENTITY gt    "&#62;">
<!ENTITY amp   "&#38;#38;">
<!ENTITY apos  "&#39;">
<!ENTITY quot  "&#34;">
```

> Note that the < and & characters in the declarations of "lt" and "amp" are doubly escaped to meet the requirement that entity replacement be well-formed.

Note that the declarations for the amp and lt entities include an "extra" #38; in their entity values. When an entity declaration is parsed, character references in its entity value are replaced. Because of the extra character reference, the declaration's replacement text for amp is &#38 rather than &, and the replacement text for lt is &#60 rather than <.

The reason for this is that replacement text of a general entity must be well-formed. As the well-formedness rules prohibit & and < as data characters, they can only appear as markup. This rule even applies to the replacement text of entities, since that text must be parsed as though it had appeared in the document element.

Because the replacement text strings of these entities are character references, rather than actual characters, they satisfy the well-formedness constraints.

4.7. Notation Declarations

Notations identify by name the format of unparsed entities, the format of elements which bear a notation attribute, or the application to which a processing instruction is addressed.

A notation, sometimes called a "data format", is a set of rules governing the representation of data. Documents use them in several ways:

- Unparsed entities are external entities such as image or sound files that typically store binary data. An XML document can only refer to one by having that entity's name as the value of an attribute that was declared to be of type ENTITY or ENTITIES. The entity's declaration must name the notation that governs the unparsed entity's data.

- Elements may have an attribute of the enumerated type NOTATION, which identifies the element type's data notation. See 3.3.1, "Attribute Types", for more on this.

- In both situations named above, a notation name tells the XML processor (and hence the application it passes the data to) about a data notation so that the application knows what program to invoke when dealing with that data. Processing instructions also identify information for the XML parser to pass along to an application. Each instruction may have an associated notation, identifying its format. Because (as we'll see below) a notation declaration often identifies a particular external program that will help the application process the non-XML data, it can be valuable information for a processing instruction. 2.6, "Processing Instructions", tells you more, although it has nothing about the role of notations in processing instructions.

> *Notation declarations* provide a name for the notation, for use in entity and attribute-list declarations and in attribute specifications, and an external identifier for the notation which may allow an XML processor or its client application to locate a helper application capable of processing data in the given notation.

An external identifier "*may* allow an XML processor or its client application to locate a helper application". Or it may not. There are no definite rules about the responsibilities of a notation declaration's external identifier. There are two common practices:

- It could point to information about the notation, such as a specification version number or information about the book with the specification. A popular public identifier for the PostScript notation is "`+//ISBN 0-201-18127-4::Adobe//NOTATION PostScript Language Ref. Manual//EN`". This makes it clear where the notation came from and how humans can find out more about it;

unfortunately, it doesn't help a processing program to tell it the name of a book where it can look up a specification.

- It could name a program on the system that can process data in the specified notation. This makes it possible to build a more automated system to handle multimedia documents—if the document's creator knows what kind of operating system will be used to read the document and the programs available on it. That's a lot to assume. However, as with entity declarations, public identifiers can be used in the declarations and the system identifiers can be looked up in a local table.

Notation Declarations

```
[82] NotationDecl   ::=   '<!NOTATION' S Name S (ExternalID | PublicID) S? '>'
[83] PublicID       ::=   'PUBLIC' S PubidLiteral
```

XML processors must provide applications with the name and external identifier(s) of any notation declared and referred to in an attribute value, attribute definition, or entity declaration. They may additionally resolve the external identifier into the system identifier, file name, or other information needed to allow the application to call a processor for data in the notation described. (It is not an error, however, for XML documents to declare and refer to notations for which notation-specific applications are not available on the system where the XML processor or application is running.)

In fact, unlike external entities and document type declarations (see 4.2.2, "External Entities", and 2.8, "Prolog and Document Type Declaration"), notation declarations can include a public identifier with no system identifier.

While a system identifier can help an XML processor that doesn't know what to do with the public identifier, there are no hard and fast rules for their use. Nevertheless, notations have been used successfully in SGML systems since the 1980's, and the Internet has used a similar system for MIME-types for many years.

Note that it's not an error for a document to use a notation that is unknown to the processor.

4.8. Document Entity

The *document entity* serves as the root of the entity tree and a starting-point for an XML processor. This specification does not specify how the document entity is to be located by an XML processor; unlike other entities, the document entity has no name and might well appear on a processor input stream without any identification at all.

Once an XML processor is parsing a document entity, it follows the rules laid out in the spec for finding any other entities used by that document. Because most operating systems offer multiple ways to tell a program "here's a stream of data to process", the XML spec doesn't dictate how the XML processor is supposed to find the document entity. Perhaps a name gets entered in a dialog box, or a user drags a file's icon on top of a program's icon, or output from one command line program is piped to be the input of another, or a program capable of communicating over a network reads the data from a port.

Conformance

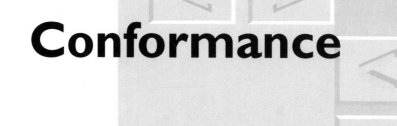

■ Validating and Non-Validating Processors
■ Using XML Processors

his chapter lays down the law about what constitutes a legal, working XML processor. In particular, it spells out the different requirements for validating and non-validating processors. Because the specification's distinction between well-formed and valid documents may cause confusion, this section spells out their relationship.

5.1. Validating and Non-Validating Processors

Conforming XML processors fall into two classes: validating and non-validating.

Validating and non-validating processors alike must report violations of this specification's well-formedness constraints in the content of the document entity and any other parsed entities that they read.

Writing a "well-formedness checker", or a non-validating parser that merely checks for well-formedness, is a fairly simple exercise. This is the whole point of the two-tiered (valid documents and well-formed documents) system of conformance: so that certain classes of XML application are very little trouble to develop.

Of course, finding a free well-formedness checker is even simpler than writing one. The source code to one of these programs, which is often freely available, gives a developer a big head start in creating a customized XML application.

> *Validating processors* must report violations of the constraints expressed by the declarations in the DTD, and failures to fulfill the validity constraints given in this specification. To accomplish this, validating XML processors must read and process the entire DTD and all external parsed entities referenced in the document.

The first part of that first sentence summarizes a validating parser's principal job: to make sure that a document's elements conform to the DTD's element type declarations. A validating parser must read and process each external parsed entity referenced from within the document directly or indirectly. (An indirect reference would be a reference within a referenced entity.) The details of a validating parser's responsibilities are spelled out by the spec's 21 validity constraints.

> Non-validating processors are required to check only the document entity, including the entire internal DTD subset, for well-formedness. While they are not required to check the document for validity, they are required to *process* all the declarations they read in the internal DTD subset and in any parameter entity that they read, up to the first reference to a parameter entity that they do *not* read; that is to say, they must use the information in those declarations to *normalize* attribute values, *include* the replacement text of internal entities, and supply *default attribute values*. They must not process entity declarations or attribute-list declarations encountered after a reference to a parameter entity that is not read, since the entity may have contained overriding declarations.

Tip *It's a common mistake to think that a non-validating parser doesn't need to bother at all with a document's DTD.*

Even a non-validating parser has responsibilities with respect to the DTD declarations that occur in the internal subset (that is, within the square brackets) of the DOCTYPE declaration. It also has responsibilities for any external parameter entities that it chooses to read (up until the first reference to a parameter entity that it does *not* read). These responsibilities are:

- Check the declarations for well-formedness.
- Normalize attribute values—that is, perform any entity replacement and deal with potentially extraneous spaces. See 3.3.3, "Attribute-Value Normalization", for more on this.
- Remember the replacement text of any internal entities so that it can replace references to those entities.
- Remember any default attribute values for use when an element's start-tag or empty-element tag does not include some attribute specification.

In the `list` document shown in Example 5.1, a non-validating parser will know about the first `item` element's `flavor` attribute value of "mint" at line 9 because it was declared as the default value in the internal subset at line 5. It will also know to place the text "cherry" into the content of the second `item` element at line 10, as well as into the `flavor` attribute value, in order to replace the two occurrences of `&xflav;`. It will also get rid of that attribute value's leading spaces as part of the attribute value normalization.

Example 5.1: A document whose DTD has plenty for a non-validating parser to do

```
 1. <?xml version="1.0"?>
 2. <!DOCTYPE list [
 3. <!ELEMENT list (item+)>
 4. <!ELEMENT item (#PCDATA)>
 5. <!ATTLIST item flavor (mint|cherry|lemon) "mint">
 6. <!ENTITY  xflav "cherry">
 7. ]>
 8. <list>
 9. <item>This list item has a mint flavor.</item>
10. <item flavor="  &xflav;">This one is &xflav;.</item>
11. </list>
```

As soon as a non-validating parser finds a reference to an external parameter entity that it chooses not to read, it cannot process any remaining declarations, except to check the remainder of the internal subset for well-formedness.

These remaining declarations may attempt to redeclare objects that were declared in the earlier unread declarations. When a declaration is repeated the first one takes precedence, but if you can't read the first one and do read the second one…well, as you can see, it gets complicated, so the non-validating parser is absolved of responsibility for declarations after a parameter entity reference that it chooses not to resolve.

5.2. Using XML Processors

The behavior of a validating XML processor is highly predictable; it must read every piece of a document and report all well-formedness and validity violations. Less is required of a non-validating processor; it need not read any part of the document other than the document entity. This has two effects that may be important to users of XML processors:

Because non-validating parsers don't have to read external entities, they can miss certain errors and useful information.

> ● Certain well-formedness errors, specifically those that require reading external entities, may not be detected by a non-validating processor. Examples include the constraints entitled *Entity Declared*, *Parsed Entity*, and *No Recursion*, as well as some of the cases described as *forbidden* in **Section 4.4: XML Processor Treatment of Entities and References**.

A non-validating processor must check for well-formedness errors in a document, but a validating processor may find well-formedness errors that a non-validating processor won't find. Why? Because a non-validating processor doesn't have to read external entities, and an external entity may not be well-formed.

> ● The information passed from the processor to the application may vary, depending on whether the processor reads parameter and external entities. For example, a non-validating processor may not *normalize* attribute values, *include* the replacement text of internal entities, or supply *default attribute values*, where doing so depends on having read declarations in external or parameter entities.

For example, in Example 5.2's `zlist` document, a well-formedness checker doesn't have to read the declarations in the `extPE.dtd` file.

Example 5.2: A document with some declarations in an external subset, which a non-validating parser doesn't have to read

```
<?xml version="1.0"?>
<!DOCTYPE zlist [
<!ELEMENT zlist (item+)>
<!ELEMENT item (#PCDATA)>
<!ENTITY % extPE SYSTEM "extPE.dtd">
%extPE;
]>
<zlist>
<item color="        blue">item 1</item>
```

```
<item>item 2</item>
<item>item 3</item>
</zlist>
```

What if this `extPE.dtd` has the attribute declaration list for the `item` element shown in Example 5.3?

Example 5.3: Potential declaration from the `extPE.dtd` referenced in Example 5.2

```
<!ATTLIST item color (red|blue|green) "red">
```

A non-validating parser that fails to read `extPE.dtd` won't know that the second and third `item` elements have a `color` attribute of "red". It also won't know that because this attribute is enumerated and not a CDATA attribute, it's supposed to delete the leading spaces from the value of "   blue" for the first `item` element.

> For maximum reliability in interoperating between different XML processors, applications which use non-validating processors should not rely on any behaviors not required of such processors. Applications which require facilities such as the use of default attributes or internal entities which are declared in external entities should use validating XML processors.

It may seem like an advantage if a non-validating processor does perform some of these jobs even though the specification doesn't list them among its responsibilities. (Many vendors will undoubtedly try to brag about this being an asset of their products—"Well-formedness checking, plus these fabulous extra features!"). But doing so can lead to problems.

For all XML software to work together well without any surprises ("for maximum reliability in interoperating between different XML processors") an application shouldn't be built around a non-validating processor that has two or three features of validating processors necessary for that application. There shouldn't be any gray area; an application should either be built around a non-validating processor that does not read external entities or do anything else optional, or around a validating processor.

Notation

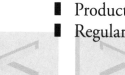
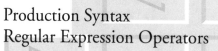

■ Production Syntax
■ Regular Expression Operators

T his chapter explains the rules of the formal grammar used in the specification's productions.

The formal grammar of XML is given in this specification using a simple Extended Backus-Naur Form (EBNF) notation. Each rule in the grammar defines one symbol, in the form

```
symbol ::= expression
```

This section of the spec describes the syntax used by the productions to show the possible makeup of each component of an XML document. "" in the "Supplementary Annotations" appendix of this book describes the role of productions, the history of EBNF, and who these "Backus" and "Naur" guys were.

Symbols are written with an initial capital letter if they are defined by a regular expression, or with an initial lower case letter otherwise. Literal strings are quoted.

This uses the term "regular expression" in a fairly technical sense. When you compare productions 27 and 29 (both shown in Example 6.1), it's not immediately obvious why the first is defined using a regular expression and the second isn't.

Example 6.1: Production defining a regular expression nonterminal and one defining a non-regular expression nonterminal

```
[27] Misc ::= Comment | PI | S

[29] markupdecl ::= elementdecl | AttlistDecl | EntityDecl |
                    NotationDecl | PI | Comment
```

Misc is defined completely in terms of other regular expressions (note that all of its components begin with capital letters). However, **markupdecl** has the non-regular expression **elementdecl** as a component, which means that **markupdecl** isn't one either.

But this just begs the question. Why isn't **elementdecl** a regular expression? Because it has **contentspec** in its production, which has **children** in its production, which has **choice** and **seq** in its production, which both have **cp** in their productions, which has **choice** and **seq** in its production. We're stuck in a circle: **choice** and **seq** are both made of **cp** elements which are each made of **choice** or **seq** elements.

In the classical approach to parsing computer languages, a regular expression is composed of simpler regular expressions. If a definition has any potential to be circular, then the quest for simpler expressions will eventually take a wrong turn, so nothing taking part in such a circle can be considered a regular expression. The XML spec distinguishes between terms represented by a regular expression and the others by beginning the former with an upper-case letter.

> Within the expression on the right-hand side of a rule, the following expressions are used to match strings of one or more characters:
>
> **#xN**
>
> where N is a hexadecimal integer, the expression matches the character in ISO/IEC 10646 whose canonical (UCS-4) code value, when interpreted as an unsigned binary number, has the value indicated. The number of leading zeros in the #xN form is insignificant; the number of leading zeros in the corresponding code value is governed by the character encoding in use and is not significant for XML.

2.2, "Characters", describes more about ISO/IEC 10646, UCS-4, and hexadecimal numbering. This paragraph tells us that #xN represents the single ISO 10646 character assigned to the number N. Leading zeros don't matter; #x0041 and #x41 both represent an upper-case "A".

> **[a-zA-Z], [#xN-#xN]**
>
> matches any character with a value in the range(s) indicated (inclusive).

Square brackets and other operators that we'll see below are ways to denote flexibility regarding which text can appear at a particular point. Square brackets around a list of characters (or their hexadecimal representations as described above) can match any of those individual characters, so that [aeiou] can match any one of those five letters. The hyphen provides a shorthand way to match a range of characters, so that instead of writing [abcdef] you could write [a-f] to match any of these six. You can include multiple ranges in the list, so that the [a-zA-Z] example shown can match any lower- or upper-case English letter.

> **[^a-z], [^#xN-#xN]**
> matches any character with a value *outside* the range indicated.

The ^ operator applies to everything inside the square brackets, so that [^a-cx-z] would match any characters other than a, b, c, x, y, or z.

> **[^abc], [^#xN#xN#xN]**
> matches any character with a value not among the characters given.

This is actually a simpler case than the one shown just before it.

> **"string"**
> matches a literal string matching that given inside the double quotes.
> **'string'**
> matches a literal string matching that given inside the single quotes.

Text surrounded either in quotation marks ("double quotes") or in apostrophes ("single quotes") must be exactly as shown, in the same case shown. For example, production 75 (reproduced in Example 6.2) shows an expression that must begin with the words SYSTEM or PUBLIC, not system or public.

Example 6.2: A production showing literal strings that must be entered in the case shown

```
[75] ExternalID  ::= 'SYSTEM' S SystemLiteral
                     'PUBLIC' S PubidLiteral S SystemLiteral
```

> These symbols may be combined to match more complex patterns as follows, where A and B represent simple expressions:
>
> **(expression)**
>
> expression is treated as a unit and may be combined as described in this list.

See the description of A | B on page 248 for more on the use of parentheses in regular expressions.

> **A?**
>
> matches A or nothing; optional A.

The question mark comes up a lot after the expression **S**, which matches white space, because white space is optional in so many places in XML. For example, look at production 42, reproduced in Example 6.3.

Example 6.3: Using the ? operator to show that S is optional

```
[42] ETag ::= '</' Name S? '>'
```

The **S?** at the end just before the closing '>' shows that you can include white space before that '>' character, but you don't have to. Examples 6.4 and 6.5 are both legal.

Example 6.4: Using optional white space before an empty-element tag's closing angle bracket

```
</img >
```

Example 6.5: Not using the optional white space before an empty-element tag's angle bracket

```
</img>
```

> **A B**
>
> matches A followed by B.

For example, in the **ETag** production shown in Example 6.3, the **Name** expression has to come right after the `</` that begins the expression, the optional **S** has to be right after that, and the `>` must be last.

> **A | B**
>
> matches A or B but not both.

For example, production 54 (reproduced in Example 6.6) shows that an **AttType** can be a **StringType** or a **TokenizedType** or an **EnumeratedType**.

Example 6.6: Using the "|" ("or") operator in a production

```
[54] AttType ::= StringType | TokenizedType | EnumeratedType
```

Now that we know enough regular expression operators to put them together into something fancier, let's look at production 47 (reproduced in Example 6.7), which shows how to assemble a **children** expression.

Example 6.7: A production using several regular expression operators

```
[47] children ::= (choice | seq) ('?' | '*' | '+')?
```

The parentheses group expressions together. This production shows that a **children** expression is made up of a **choice** or **seq** expression followed by a question mark, asterisk, or plus sign. Actually, the **choice** or **seq** doesn't have to be followed by anything; the question mark at the end shows that the complete second parenthesized expression is optional.

> **A – B**
>
> matches any string that matches A but does not match B.

Production 17, reproduced in Example 6.8, demonstrates this.

Example 6.8: A production using the – operator

```
[17] PITarget ::= Name - (('X' | 'x') ('M' | 'm') ('L' | 'l'))
```

A **PITarget** expression consists of a **Name** expression that isn't an X followed by an M followed by an L, in any combination of upper- and lower-case. (Note the regular expression way of representing the strings xMl or XMl as well as XML and xml.)

> **A+**
>
> matches one or more occurrences of A.

For example, production 3 (reproduced in Example 6.9) shows us the potential components of a white space expression.

Example 6.9: XML's definition of white space characters

```
[3] S ::= (#x20 | #x9 | #xD | #xA)+
```

Using their hexadecimal representations, the parenthesized part shows that we can have a spacebar space, a tab, a carriage return, or a line feed. The plus sign after the right parenthesis shows that any combination of these four characters can be repeated within an **S** expression as many times as you like, but at least one of them must be there.

> **A***
>
>   matches zero or more occurrences of A.

An asterisk in a regular expression is like a combination of a question mark and a plus sign: the expression preceding it is optional, and can be repeated over and over. In other words, it can occur zero or more times. To show that an attribute list declaration doesn't need any attribute definitions (**AttDef**), but can have as many as you want, production 52 (reproduced in Example 6.10) shows its potential structure with an asterisk after the **AttDef** part.

Example 6.10: Showing that an AttDef can occur zero or more times

```
[52] AttlistDecl ::= '<!ATTLIST' S Name AttDef* S? '>'
```

> Other notations used in the productions are:
>
> **/* ... */**
>   comment.

Anything after the /* and before the */ is not to be treated as part of the syntax. Production 2 (reproduced in Example 6.11) shows an example.

Example 6.11: A production with a comment

```
[2] Char ::= #x9 | #xA | #xD |    /* any Unicode
                 [#x20-#xD7FF] |        character excluding
                 [#xE000-#xFFFD] |      the surrogate blocks,
                 [#x10000-#x10FFFF]     FFFE, and FFFF.*/
```

```
[ wfc: ... ]
```
well-formedness constraint; this identifies by name a constraint on well-formed documents associated with a production.

```
[ vc: ... ]
```
validity constraint; this identifies by name a constraint on valid documents associated with a production.

These identify constraints—that is, further rules not expressible in the production syntax. In addition to being named in the production, each constraint is described further in a paragraph or two underneath it. For example, see the "Element Type Match" well-formedness constraint and the "Element Valid" validity constraint identified in and described further under production 39.

References

Appendix

A

This appendix lists additional information on the material described in the specification.

A.1. Normative References

Normative references are works that the XML specification itself depends on. For example, because the XML spec tells you to use IETF RFC 1766 language codes in the `xml:lang` attribute, it also tells you how to find this RFC in this appendix.

Like the W3C, the IETF makes its specs available from its Web site at `http://www.ietf.org`. The ISO and Unicode Consortium have Web sites at `http://www.iso.org` and `http://www.unicode.org`, but do not make their specs available for free.

253

IANA

(Internet Assigned Numbers Authority) *Official Names for Character Sets*, ed. Keld Simonsen et al. See `ftp://ftp.isi.edu/in-notes/iana/assignments/character-sets`.

In the XML specification, this is cited in 2.12, "Language Identification", and 4.3.3, "Character Encoding in Entities".

IETF RFC 1766

IETF (Internet Engineering Task Force). *RFC 1766: Tags for the Identification of Languages*, ed. H. Alvestrand. 1995.

ISO 639

(International Organization for Standardization). *ISO 639:1988 (E). Code for the representation of names of languages.* [Geneva]: International Organization for Standardization, 1988.

ISO 3166

(International Organization for Standardization). *ISO 3166-1:1997 (E). Codes for the representation of names of countries and their subdivisions — Part 1: Country codes* [Geneva]: International Organization for Standardization, 1997.

These three are cited in 1.1, "Origin and Goals" and 2.12, "Language Identification".

ISO/IEC 10646

ISO (International Organization for Standardization). *ISO/IEC 10646-1993 (E). Information technology — Universal Multiple-Octet Coded Character Set (UCS) — Part 1: Architecture and Basic Multilingual Plane.* [Geneva]: International Organization for Standardization, 1993 (plus amendments AM 1 through AM 7).

This is cited in 1.1, "Origin and Goals"; 2.12, "Language Identification"; 2.2, "Characters"; 4.1, "Character and Entity References"; 4.3.3, "Character Encoding in Entities"; and Chapter 6, "Notation".

Unicode
    The Unicode Consortium. *The Unicode Standard, Version 2.0.* Reading,
    Mass.: Addison-Wesley Developers Press, 1996.

Cited in 1.1, "Origin and Goals"; 2.2, "Characters"; and 4.3.3, "Character Encoding in Entities".

A.2. Other References

While the works listed in A.1, "Normative References", are necessary to fully understand every single aspect of the XML specification, this section lists books that are unnecessary but helpful background. In addition to some more IETF Requests for Comment (RFCs) and ISO standards, there are some computer science textbooks and James Clark's concise "Comparison of SGML and XML".

Perhaps the most important non-normative reference is the SGML International Standard, of which XML is a subset. The edition actually used by the XML Working Group is that in the *THE SGML Handbook* (ISBN 0-19-853737-9), which is extensively annotated and cross-referenced by Charles F. Goldfarb, the inventor of SGML and Editor of the International Standard (ISO 8879).

Aho/Ullman
Aho, Alfred V., Ravi Sethi, and Jeffrey D. Ullman. *Compilers: Principles, Techniques, and Tools*. Reading: Addison-Wesley, 1986, rpt. corr. 1988.

Berners-Lee et al.
Berners-Lee, T., R. Fielding, and L. Masinter. *Uniform Resource Identifiers (URI): Generic Syntax and Semantics*. 1997. (Work in progress; see updates to RFC1738.)

Brüggemann-Klein
Brüggemann-Klein, Anne. *Regular Expressions into Finite Automata*. Extended abstract in I. Simon, Hrsg., LATIN 1992, S. 97-98. Springer-Verlag, Berlin 1992. Full Version in Theoretical Computer Science 120: 197-213, 1993.

Brüggemann-Klein and Wood
Brüggemann-Klein, Anne, and Derick Wood. *Deterministic Regular Languages*. Universität Freiburg, Institut für Informatik, Bericht 38, Oktober 1991.

Clark
James Clark. Comparison of SGML and XML. See
`http://www.w3.org/TR/NOTE-sgml-xml-971215`.

IETF RFC1738
IETF (Internet Engineering Task Force). *RFC 1738: Uniform Resource Locators (URL)*, ed. T. Berners-Lee, L. Masinter, M. McCahill. 1994.

IETF RFC1808
IETF (Internet Engineering Task Force). *RFC 1808: Relative Uniform Resource Locators*, ed. R. Fielding. 1995.

IETF RFC2141
IETF (Internet Engineering Task Force). *RFC 2141: URN Syntax*, ed. R. Moats. 1997.

ISO 8879
ISO (International Organization for Standardization). *ISO 8879:1986(E). Information processing — Text and Office Systems — Standard Generalized Markup Language (SGML)*. First edition — 1986-10-15. [Geneva]: International Organization for Standardization, 1986.

ISO/IEC 10744

ISO (International Organization for Standardization). *ISO/IEC 10744-1992 (E). Information technology — Hypermedia/Time-based Structuring Language (HyTime).* [Geneva]: International Organization for Standardization, 1992. *Extended Facilities Annexe.* [Geneva]: International Organization for Standardization, 1996.

Character Classes

- Letters
- Base Characters
- Ideographic Characters
- Combining Characters
- Digits
- Extender Characters

It's easy enough to say, as production 5 does, that a **Name** begins with a **Letter**, but what's a letter? If you're thinking in international terms, it's not such an easy question to answer. In fact, it takes the following two pages for the specification to define it. (If the individual characters were listed instead of ranges, the list would be longer than the rest of the spec.)

Following the characteristics defined in the Unicode standard, characters are classed as base characters (among others, these contain the alphabetic characters of the Latin alphabet, without diacritics), ideographic characters, and combining characters (among others, this class contains most diacritics); these classes combine to form the class of letters. Digits and extenders are also distinguished.

Characters

| [84]**Letter** | ::= | BaseChar | Ideographic |

```
[85]BaseChar   ::=  [#x0041-#x005A] | [#x0061-#x007A] | [#x00C0-#x00D6]
                    | [#x00D8-#x00F6] | [#x00F8-#x00FF] | [#x0100-
                    #x0131] | [#x0134-#x013E] | [#x0141-#x0148]
                    | [#x014A-#x017E] | [#x0180-#x01C3] | [#x01CD-
                    #x01F0] | [#x01F4-#x01F5] | [#x01FA-#x0217]
                    | [#x0250-#x02A8] | [#x02BB-#x02C1] | #x0386
                    | [#x0388-#x038A] | #x038C | [#x038E-#x03A1]
                    | [#x03A3-#x03CE] | [#x03D0-#x03D6] | #x03DA
                    | #x03DC | #x03DE | #x03E0 | [#x03E2-#x03F3]
                    | [#x0401-#x040C] | [#x040E-#x044F] | [#x0451-
                    #x045C] | [#x045E-#x0481] | [#x0490-#x04C4]
                    | [#x04C7-#x04C8] | [#x04CB-#x04CC] | [#x04D0-
                    #x04EB] | [#x04EE-#x04F5] | [#x04F8-#x04F9]
                    | [#x0531-#x0556] | #x0559 | [#x0561-#x0586]
                    | [#x05D0-#x05EA] | [#x05F0-#x05F2] | [#x0621-
                    #x063A] | [#x0641-#x064A] | [#x0671-#x06B7]
                    | [#x06BA-#x06BE] | [#x06C0-#x06CE] | [#x06D0-
                    #x06D3] | #x06D5 | [#x06E5-#x06E6] | [#x0905-#x0939]
                    | #x093D | [#x0958-#x0961] | [#x0985-#x098C]
                    | [#x098F-#x0990] | [#x0993-#x09A8] | [#x09AA-
                    #x09B0] | #x09B2 | [#x09B6-#x09B9] | [#x09DC-#x09DD]
                    | [#x09DF-#x09E1] | [#x09F0-#x09F1] | [#x0A05-
                    #x0A0A] | [#x0A0F-#x0A10] | [#x0A13-#x0A28]
                    | [#x0A2A-#x0A30] | [#x0A32-#x0A33] | [#x0A35-
                    #x0A36] | [#x0A38-#x0A39] | [#x0A59-#x0A5C] | #x0A5E
                    | [#x0A72-#x0A74] | [#x0A85-#x0A8B] | #x0A8D
                    | [#x0A8F-#x0A91] | [#x0A93-#x0AA8] | [#x0AAA-
                    #x0AB0] | [#x0AB2-#x0AB3] | [#x0AB5-#x0AB9] | #x0ABD
                    | #x0AE0 | [#x0B05-#x0B0C] | [#x0B0F-#x0B10]
                    | [#x0B13-#x0B28] | [#x0B2A-#x0B30] | [#x0B32-
                    #x0B33] | [#x0B36-#x0B39] | #x0B3D | [#x0B5C-#x0B5D]
                    | [#x0B5F-#x0B61] | [#x0B85-#x0B8A] | [#x0B8E-
                    #x0B90] | [#x0B92-#x0B95] | [#x0B99-#x0B9A] | #x0B9C
                    | [#x0B9E-#x0B9F] | [#x0BA3-#x0BA4] | [#x0BA8-
                    #x0BAA] | [#x0BAE-#x0BB5] | [#x0BB7-#x0BB9]
                    | [#x0C05-#x0C0C] | [#x0C0E-#x0C10] | [#x0C12-
                    #x0C28] | [#x0C2A-#x0C33] | [#x0C35-#x0C39]
                    | [#x0C60-#x0C61] | [#x0C85-#x0C8C] | [#x0C8E-
                    #x0C90] | [#x0C92-#x0CA8] | [#x0CAA-#x0CB3]
```

```
           | [#x0CB5-#x0CB9] | #x0CDE | [#x0CE0-#x0CE1]
           | [#x0D05-#x0D0C] | [#x0D0E-#x0D10] | [#x0D12-
#x0D28] | [#x0D2A-#x0D39] | [#x0D60-#x0D61]
           | [#x0E01-#x0E2E] | #x0E30 | [#x0E32-#x0E33]
           | [#x0E40-#x0E45] | [#x0E81-#x0E82] | #x0E84
           | [#x0E87-#x0E88] | #x0E8A | #x0E8D | [#x0E94-
#x0E97] | [#x0E99-#x0E9F] | [#x0EA1-#x0EA3] | #x0EA5
           | #x0EA7 | [#x0EAA-#x0EAB] | [#x0EAD-#x0EAE]
           | #x0EB0 | [#x0EB2-#x0EB3] | #x0EBD | [#x0EC0-
#x0EC4] | [#x0F40-#x0F47] | [#x0F49-#x0F69]
           | [#x10A0-#x10C5] | [#x10D0-#x10F6] | #x1100
           | [#x1102-#x1103] | [#x1105-#x1107] | #x1109
           | [#x110B-#x110C] | [#x110E-#x1112] | #x113C
           | #x113E | #x1140 | #x114C | #x114E | #x1150
           | [#x1154-#x1155] | #x1159 | [#x115F-#x1161]
           | #x1163 | #x1165 | #x1167 | #x1169 | [#x116D-
#x116E] | [#x1172-#x1173] | #x1175 | #x119E | #x11A8
           | #x11AB | [#x11AE-#x11AF] | [#x11B7-#x11B8]
           | #x11BA | [#x11BC-#x11C2] | #x11EB | #x11F0
           | #x11F9 | [#x1E00-#x1E9B] | [#x1EA0-#x1EF9]
           | [#x1F00-#x1F15] | [#x1F18-#x1F1D] | [#x1F20-
#x1F45] | [#x1F48-#x1F4D] | [#x1F50-#x1F57] | #x1F59
           | #x1F5B | #x1F5D | [#x1F5F-#x1F7D] | [#x1F80-
#x1FB4] | [#x1FB6-#x1FBC] | #x1FBE | [#x1FC2-#x1FC4]
           | [#x1FC6-#x1FCC] | [#x1FD0-#x1FD3] | [#x1FD6-
#x1FDB] | [#x1FE0-#x1FEC] | [#x1FF2-#x1FF4]
           | [#x1FF6-#x1FFC] | #x2126 | [#x212A-#x212B]
           | #x212E | [#x2180-#x2182] | [#x3041-#x3094]
           | [#x30A1-#x30FA] | [#x3105-#x312C] | [#xAC00-
#xD7A3]
```

As production 84 shows, a **Letter** is either a **BaseChar** or an **Ideographic**. In production 85, the long expression showing the ranges of allowable base characters starts with [#x0041-#x005A], the range of upper-case characters A through Z. The next range, [#x0061-#x007A], matches the lower-case letters a through z. Note how characters like ! (#x0021), 3 (#x0033), and \ (#x005c) don't fall into these ranges, and hence can't be treated as letters.

We don't want to treat !, 3, or \ as letters, but we do want to treat ä ([#x00E4]) and ñ ([#x00F1]) as letters. These both fall in the fourth range shown in production 85: [#x00D8-#x00F6]. The ranges listed for **BaseChar** go all the way to [#xAC00-#xD7A3], used for writing the Korean Hangul script. (In decimal numbers, we've gone from 65 for "A" up to 55,203 for the last Hangul character.)

Production 86 shows that the recognized ideographs are two ranges of numbers for Chinese-Japanese-Korean (CJK) unified ideographs and a single lone ideograph (#x3007) between them.

Production 87 shows us the combining characters that are legal as **NameChar** characters (see production 4). It starts with the accent grave character (#x0300) and includes accents in many different languages ranging up to one in the Japanese Hiragana script (#x309A).

Production 88 lists characters acceptable as numeric digits, from the digits 0 (#x0030) through 9 (#x0039) used in Latin script to the ten used in Tibetan writing ([#x0F20-#x0F29]). Finally, production 89 shows us extenders, a variation on combining characters.

```
[86]Ideographic  ::=  [#x4E00-#x9FA5] | #x3007 | [#x3021-#x3029]
[87]CombiningChar ::=  [#x0300-#x0345] | [#x0360-#x0361] | [#x0483-#x0486]
                       | [#x0591-#x05A1] | [#x05A3-#x05B9] | [#x05BB-
                       #x05BD] | #x05BF | [#x05C1-#x05C2] | #x05C4
                       | [#x064B-#x0652] | #x0670 | [#x06D6-#x06DC]
                       | [#x06DD-#x06DF] | [#x06E0-#x06E4] | [#x06E7-
                       #x06E8] | [#x06EA-#x06ED] | [#x0901-#x0903] | #x093C
                       | [#x093E-#x094C] | #x094D | [#x0951-#x0954]
                       | [#x0962-#x0963] | [#x0981-#x0983] | #x09BC
                       | #x09BE | #x09BF | [#x09C0-#x09C4] | [#x09C7-
                       #x09C8] | [#x09CB-#x09CD] | #x09D7 | [#x09E2-#x09E3]
                       | #x0A02 | #x0A3C | #x0A3E | #x0A3F | [#x0A40-
                       #x0A42] | [#x0A47-#x0A48] | [#x0A4B-#x0A4D]
                       | [#x0A70-#x0A71] | [#x0A81-#x0A83] | #x0ABC
                       | [#x0ABE-#x0AC5] | [#x0AC7-#x0AC9] | [#x0ACB-
                       #x0ACD] | [#x0B01-#x0B03] | #x0B3C | [#x0B3E-#x0B43]
                       | [#x0B47-#x0B48] | [#x0B4B-#x0B4D] | [#x0B56-
                       #x0B57] | [#x0B82-#x0B83] | [#x0BBE-#x0BC2]
                       | [#x0BC6-#x0BC8] | [#x0BCA-#x0BCD] | #x0BD7
                       | [#x0C01-#x0C03] | [#x0C3E-#x0C44] | [#x0C46-
                       #x0C48] | [#x0C4A-#x0C4D] | [#x0C55-#x0C56]
                       | [#x0C82-#x0C83] | [#x0CBE-#x0CC4] | [#x0CC6-
                       #x0CC8] | [#x0CCA-#x0CCD] | [#x0CD5-#x0CD6]
                       | [#x0D02-#x0D03] | [#x0D3E-#x0D43] | [#x0D46-
                       #x0D48] | [#x0D4A-#x0D4D] | #x0D57 | #x0E31
                       | [#x0E34-#x0E3A] | [#x0E47-#x0E4E] | #x0EB1
                       | [#x0EB4-#x0EB9] | [#x0EBB-#x0EBC] | [#x0EC8-
                       #x0ECD] | [#x0F18-#x0F19] | #x0F35 | #x0F37 | #x0F39
                       | #x0F3E | #x0F3F | [#x0F71-#x0F84] | [#x0F86-
                       #x0F8B] | [#x0F90-#x0F95] | #x0F97 | [#x0F99-#x0FAD]
                       | [#x0FB1-#x0FB7] | #x0FB9 | [#x20D0-#x20DC]
                       | #x20E1 | [#x302A-#x302F] | #x3099 | #x309A
```

```
[88]Digit        ::=  [#x0030-#x0039] | [#x0660-#x0669] | [#x06F0-#x06F9]
                      | [#x0966-#x096F] | [#x09E6-#x09EF] | [#x0A66-
                      #x0A6F] | [#x0AE6-#x0AEF] | [#x0B66-#x0B6F]
                      | [#x0BE7-#x0BEF] | [#x0C66-#x0C6F] | [#x0CE6-
                      #x0CEF] | [#x0D66-#x0D6F] | [#x0E50-#x0E59]
                      | [#x0ED0-#x0ED9] | [#x0F20-#x0F29]
[89]Extender     ::=  #x00B7 | #x02D0 | #x02D1 | #x0387 | #x0640 | #x0E46
                      | #x0EC6 | #x3005 | [#x3031-#x3035] | [#x309D-
                      #x309E] | [#x30FC-#x30FE]
```

The character classes defined here can be derived from the Unicode character database as follows:

- Name start characters must have one of the categories Ll, Lu, Lo, Lt, Nl.

- Name characters other than Name-start characters must have one of the categories Mc, Me, Mn, Lm, or Nd.

- Characters in the compatibility area (i.e. with character code greater than #xF900 and less than #xFFFE) are not allowed in XML names.

- Characters which have a font or compatibility decomposition (i.e. those with a "compatibility formatting tag" in field 5 of the database - - marked by field 5 beginning with a "<") are not allowed.

- The following characters are treated as name-start characters rather than name characters, because the property file classifies them as Alphabetic: [#x02BB-#x02C1], #x0559, #x06E5, #x06E6.

- Characters #x20DD-#x20E0 are excluded (in accordance with Unicode, section 5.14).

- Character #x00B7 is classified as an extender, because the property list so identifies it.

- Character #x0387 is added as a name character, because #x00B7 is its canonical equivalent.

- Characters ':' and '_' are allowed as name-start characters.

- Characters '-' and '.' are allowed as name characters.

In the Unicode standard, characters fall into categories labeled by two-letter names. The list above shows the correspondence between these categories and XML character classes.

XML and SGML (Non-Normative)

■ Treating XML Documents as SGML Documents

This appendix describes where to find detailed information on treating XML documents as SGML documents.

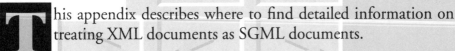

XML is designed to be a subset of SGML, in that every valid XML document should also be a conformant SGML document. For a detailed comparison of the additional restrictions that XML places on documents beyond those of SGML, see [Clark].

The normative parts of a standard are those that actually spell out the official standard. "Non-normative" parts only provide background information. This particular non-normative part reiterates what the spec said in Chapter 1, "Introduction", about how XML is a subset of SGML. It also tells how you'll find more information in James Clark's detailed comparison mentioned in Appendix A, "References". This comparison is available at `http://www.w3.org/TR/NOTE-sgml-xml-971215`.

Expansion of Entity and Character References (Non-Normative)

 Entity and Character Reference Expansion: Two Examples

This appendix steps through the XML processor's actions as it deals with two examples of entity usage. They're fairly tricky examples, with some explanation; I've added some more explanation.

This appendix contains some examples illustrating the sequence of entity- and character-reference recognition and expansion, as specified in **Section 4.4: XML Processor Treatment of Entities and References**.

If the DTD contains the declaration

```
<!ENTITY example "<p>An ampersand (&#38;#38;) may be escaped
numerically (&#38;#38;#38;) or with a general entity
(&amp;amp;).</p>" >
```

> then the XML processor will recognize the character references when it
> parses the entity declaration, and resolve them before storing the follow-
> ing string as the value of the entity "example":
>
> ```
> <p>An ampersand (&#38;) may be escaped
> numerically (&#38;#38;) or with a general entity
> (&amp;amp;).</p>
> ```

& is a character reference to the ampersand character. The first
and second lines of the example each have only one of these; the other
occurrences of #38; don't have an ampersand (&) in front of them.

The description of the example tells us that the XML processor will
replace each & with an ampersand as it reads the entity declaration. There are more replacements to make, but it won't do those
until it finds a reference to the example entity in the document element. Until then, it stores the text shown above as this entity's
replacement text.

One entity reference in particular that it leaves alone at this time is
the & near the end. This is a general-entity reference, and parsing
of entity declarations only replaces character references (like &)
and parameter-entity references, as we'll see in the next example.

> A reference in the document to "&example;" will cause the text to be rep-
> arsed, at which time the start- and end-tags of the "p" element will be
> recognized and the three references will be recognized and expanded,
> resulting in a "p" element with the following content (all data, no delimiters
> or markup):
>
> ```
> An ampersand (&) may be escaped
> numerically (&#38;) or with a general entity
> (&amp;).
> ```

When the XML processor finds a reference to the example entity in
the document (that is, when it finds &example;) it's time to reparse
its text. Before this point, it didn't know that the <p> at the start and
</p> at the end of the entity's replacement text were start- and end-

tags; now, in the context of a document instance, it knows that they serve this purpose.

The processor also takes each `&#38;` (which the initial parse of the `example` entity declaration made out of the `&#38;#38;` strings that it found) and turns them each into an ampersand (`&`).

It also turns the `&amp;` near the end into an ampersand, which had been left alone up to this point. This, along with the two `&#38;` references before it, are the "three references" that the specification paragraph refers to.

At this point, it's done. It looks like the final example text you see above has a literal ampersand (`&`), a character reference (`&#38;`) and an entity reference (`&amp;`). This is how the document's author wants it to look.

Obviously, tricks like this are often necessary when you're writing about XML to demonstrate markup. I've certainly had to use them myself plenty of times in the last few paragraphs!

A more complex example will illustrate the rules and their effects fully. In the following example, the line numbers are solely for reference.

```
1 <?xml version='1.0'?>
2 <!DOCTYPE test [
3 <!ELEMENT test (#PCDATA) >
4 <!ENTITY % xx '&#37;zz;'>
5 <!ENTITY % zz '&#60;!ENTITY tricky "error-prone" >' >
6 %xx;
7 ]>
8 <test>This sample shows a &tricky; method.</test>
```

This produces the following:

- in line 4, the reference to character 37 is expanded immediately, and the parameter entity "`xx`" is stored in the symbol table with the value "`%zz;`". Since the replacement text is not rescanned, the reference to parameter entity "`zz`" is not recognized. (And it would be an error if it were, since "`zz`" is not yet declared.)

Recall that, while a general entity holds text to be used in a document element, a parameter entity holds text to be used in a DTD.

Character 37 is the percent sign (%). After `&#37;` is replaced by %, the xx parameter entity stores the text `%zz;`, a reference to the parameter entity zz. As the description above tells us, the processor doesn't yet know that `%zz;` is a valid parameter-entity reference, because (unlike the resolution of general-entity references in a document element) the processor doesn't rescan and rescan a DTD until all parameter entity references are resolved.

> • in line 5, the character reference "`&#60;`" is expanded immediately and the parameter entity "zz" is stored with the replacement text "`<!ENTITY tricky "error-prone" >`", which is a well-formed entity declaration.

This tells us that the first pass also replaces the `&#60;` in line 5 with the < character that it represents, making the zz parameter entity's replacement text into the entity declaration shown in Example D.1.

Example D.1: Line 5 from the spec's example, after parameter entity replacements

```
<!ENTITY tricky "error-prone">
```

Note that, to allow double quotes around the text error-prone in the zz parameter entity's replacement text, the entity value is delimited by single quotes.

> • in line 6, the reference to "xx" is recognized, and the replacement text of "xx" (namely "`%zz;`") is parsed. The reference to "zz" is recognized in its turn, and its replacement text ("`<!ENTITY tricky "error-prone" >`") is parsed. The general entity "tricky" has now been declared, with the replacement text "error-prone".

The xx entity's replacement text was declared on line 4, and that text happens to be a parameter-entity reference to the zz parameter entity. zz was declared on line 5; its replacement text is a declaration of the general entity `tricky`. So ultimately, line 6 is declaring the general entity `tricky`.

> • in line 8, the reference to the general entity "`tricky`" is recognized, and it is expanded, so the full content of the "`test`" element is the self-describing (and ungrammatical) string *This sample shows a error-prone method.*

At first glance, one sees the `&tricky;` general-entity reference on line 8 but no declaration for it in the DTD. Now we know that the declaration was there, or at least it was there after the XML processor made a complicated series of parameter entity replacements. (By the way, the `test` element is "ungrammatical" because it should say "an error-prone method" and not "a error-prone method".)

This example is intentionally complicated to demonstrate how an XML processor approaches entity replacement. Real entity structures are rarely this complicated.

Tip   As with any markup or programming language, avoid confusion over complicated constructs by adding comments and using names more meaningful than xx and zz.

Deterministic Content Models (Non-Normative)

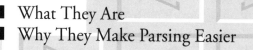

- What They Are
- Why They Make Parsing Easier

Perhaps the toughest part of a validating XML processor's job is to figure out, as it reads each element in a document, whether that element fits the content model declared for it. This is the key reason that XML software is easier to write when it only worries about whether a document is well-formed, because it doesn't have to perform this validation task.

> For compatibility, it is required that content models in element type declarations be deterministic.
>
> SGML requires deterministic content models (it calls them "unambiguous"); XML processors built using SGML systems may flag non-deterministic content models as errors.

Content models often allow flexibility in an element's structure; that's why we use symbols like +, * and | to specify them. Too much flexibility can confuse the parser, and "for compatibility" XML draws the line at the same point that SGML does: a content model must be

273

"deterministic" or "unambiguous". As 3.2.1, "Element Content", tells us, a non-deterministic content model is one in which "an element in the document can match more than one occurrence of an element type in the content model".

> For example, the content model `((b, c) | (b, d))` is non-deterministic, because given an initial b the parser cannot know which b in the model is being matched without looking ahead to see which element follows the b. In this case, the two references to b can be collapsed into a single reference, making the model read `(b, (c | d))`. An initial b now clearly matches only a single name in the content model. The parser doesn't need to look ahead to see what follows; either c or d would be accepted.

Example E.1 demonstrates this. Let's say an XML parser had begun to parse it and had read the first 8 lines. It knows that everything is fine, and reads line 9, which has the b element that must start all a elements. The a element type has a choice of two expressions to match, as shown by the two parenthesized expressions with a "|" character between them on line 3. Which one should the parser try to fit this document to: (b, c) or (b, d)?

Example E.1: A document with a nondeterministic content model

```
1. <?xml version="1.0"?>
2. <!DOCTYPE a [
3. <!ELEMENT a ((b,c) | (b,d))>
4. <!ELEMENT b    (#PCDATA)>
5. <!ELEMENT c    (#PCDATA)>
6. <!ELEMENT d    (#PCDATA)>
7. ]>
8. <a>
9. <b>Here is a b.</b>
10. <!-- valid up to here? -->
```

It can't tell, as the description tells us, "without looking ahead" to see whether a c or a d element follows line 9's b element.

Looking ahead to figure out what's going on is not impossible for a parser. Some of the books listed under "Other References" in Appendix A, "References", explain techniques used by programming language compilers for doing this. Not having to worry about it, however, makes a parser much easier to write, and design goal 4 listed in 1.1, "Origin and Goals", tells us that "It shall be easy to write programs which process XML documents".

Problematic content models like this can often be reworked to express the same element type structure without being ambiguous; the spec paragraph above shows how to revise this particular one.

> More formally: a finite state automaton may be constructed from the content model using the standard algorithms, e.g. algorithm 3.5 in section 3.9 of Aho, Sethi, and Ullman [Aho/Ullman]. In many such algorithms, a follow set is constructed for each position in the regular expression (i.e., each leaf node in the syntax tree for the regular expression); if any position has a follow set in which more than one following position is labeled with the same element type name, then the content model is in error and may be reported as an error.

By "more formally" this means "in computer science talk generalized beyond XML". Using this terminology makes it easier for programmers who understand it to write software that implements the checking of content models.

> Algorithms exist which allow many but not all non-deterministic content models to be reduced automatically to equivalent deterministic models; see Brüggemann-Klein 1991 [Brüggemann-Klein].

This is good news. It means that rewriting ambiguous content models to be deterministic isn't a matter of luck; someone has figured out a way to either do it, or to establish that it can't be done, automatically for a given content model.

Autodetection of Character Encodings (Non-Normative)

■ Special Problems and Their Solution

This appendix and 4.3.3, "Character Encoding in Entities" tells us that an XML declaration that starts an external entity can include an encoding declaration to tell the XML processor which set of character encodings is used for that particular entity.

For example, the encoding declaration in Example F.1 shows that its entity uses the 4-octet version of the ISO 10646 UCS standard.

Example F.1: A sample encoding declaration

```
<?xml version="1.0" encoding="ISO-10646-UCS-4" ?>
```

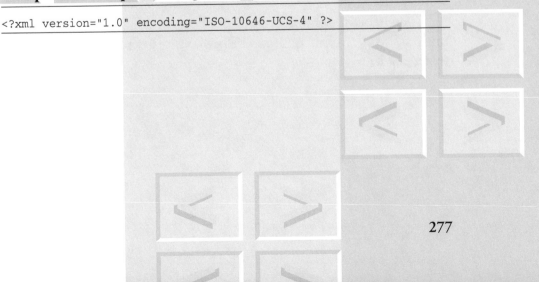

The XML encoding declaration functions as an internal label on each entity, indicating which character encoding is in use. Before an XML processor can read the internal label, however, it apparently has to know what character encoding is in use—which is what the internal label is trying to indicate. In the general case, this is a hopeless situation. It is not entirely hopeless in XML, however, because XML limits the general case in two ways: each implementation is assumed to support only a finite set of character encodings, and the XML encoding declaration is restricted in position and content in order to make it feasible to autodetect the character encoding in use in each entity in normal cases. Also, in many cases other sources of information are available in addition to the XML data stream itself. Two cases may be distinguished, depending on whether the XML entity is presented to the processor without, or with, any accompanying (external) information. We consider the first case first.

There's a slight catch-22 at work here: a processor has to know an external entity's encoding as it reads it, but doesn't know the encoding until it's read up to the first ?>. How does it know how to interpret the octets that represent those first forty or fifty characters? As the spec tells us, "it is not entirely hopeless", because a processor can figure out out much of what it needs to know after reading two or four octets.

The rest of this appendix describes how to interpret those first few octets and the potential role of additional information about the encoding that may be sent by the file system or network protocol along with the file.

In general, a programmer who develops multi-lingual software will understand the rules and hints below, and other people don't have to worry about it.

Because each XML entity not in UTF-8 or UTF-16 format *must* begin with an XML encoding declaration, in which the first characters must be '<?xml', any conforming processor can detect, after two to four octets of input, which of the following cases apply. In reading this list, it may help to know that in UCS-4, '<' is "#x0000003C" and '?' is "#x0000003F", and the Byte Order Mark required of UTF-16 data streams is "#xFEFF".

- 00 00 00 3C: UCS-4, big-endian machine (1234 order)
- 3C 00 00 00: UCS-4, little-endian machine (4321 order)
- 00 00 3C 00: UCS-4, unusual octet order (2143)
- 00 3C 00 00: UCS-4, unusual octet order (3412)
- FE FF: UTF-16, big-endian
- FF FE: UTF-16, little-endian
- 00 3C 00 3F: UTF-16, big-endian, no Byte Order Mark (and thus, strictly speaking, in error)
- 3C 00 3F 00: UTF-16, little-endian, no Byte Order Mark (and thus, strictly speaking, in error)
- 3C 3F 78 6D: UTF-8, ISO 646, ASCII, some part of ISO 8859, Shift-JIS, EUC, or any other 7-bit, 8-bit, or mixed-width encoding which ensures that the characters of ASCII have their normal positions, width, and values; the actual encoding declaration must be read to detect which of these applies, but since all of these encodings use the same bit patterns for the ASCII characters, the encoding declaration itself may be read reliably
- 4C 6F A7 94: EBCDIC (in some flavor; the full encoding declaration must be read to tell which code page is in use)
- other: UTF-8 without an encoding declaration, or else the data stream is corrupt, fragmentary, or enclosed in a wrapper of some kind

This level of autodetection is enough to read the XML encoding declaration and parse the character-encoding identifier, which is still necessary to distinguish the individual members of each family of encodings (e.g. to tell UTF-8 from 8859, and the parts of 8859 from each other, or to distinguish the specific EBCDIC code page in use, and so on).

Because the contents of the encoding declaration are restricted to ASCII characters, a processor can reliably read the entire encoding declaration as soon as it has detected which family of encodings is in use. Since in practice, all widely used character encodings fall into one of the categories above, the XML encoding declaration allows reasonably reliable in-band labeling of character encodings, even when external sources of information at the operating-system or transport-protocol level are unreliable.

Once the processor has detected the character encoding in use, it can act appropriately, whether by invoking a separate input routine for each case, or by calling the proper conversion function on each character of input.

Like any self-labeling system, the XML encoding declaration will not work if any software changes the entity's character set or encoding without updating the encoding declaration. Implementors of character-encoding routines should be careful to ensure the accuracy of the internal and external information used to label the entity.

The second possible case occurs when the XML entity is accompanied by encoding information, as in some file systems and some network protocols. When multiple sources of information are available, their relative priority and the preferred method of handling conflict should be specified as part of the higher-level protocol used to deliver XML. Rules for the relative priority of the internal label and the MIME-type label in an external header, for example, should be part of the RFC document defining the text/xml and application/xml MIME types. In the interests of interoperability, however, the following rules are recommended.

- If an XML entity is in a file, the Byte-Order Mark and encoding-declaration PI are used (if present) to determine the character encoding. All other heuristics and sources of information are solely for error recovery.

- If an XML entity is delivered with a MIME type of text/xml, then the `charset` parameter on the MIME type determines the character encoding method; all other heuristics and sources of information are solely for error recovery.

- If an XML entity is delivered with a MIME type of application/xml, then the Byte-Order Mark and encoding-declaration PI are used (if present) to determine the character encoding. All other heuristics and sources of information are solely for error recovery.

These rules apply only in the absence of protocol-level documentation; in particular, when the MIME types text/xml and application/xml are defined, the recommendations of the relevant RFC will supersede these rules.

W3C XML Working Group (Non-Normative)

■ Members and Their Affiliations

Appendix

G

This appendix tells us about the people who, as representatives of their respective organizations, debated and voted on the details of the XML spec. There are two interesting things about this list:

- The companies represented were clearly interested in XML very early in its history if they allowed such expert employees to devote so much time and energy to its development. This commitment to XML from such big names sent a strong signal to the world that XML was more than just a fad.
- Those familiar with the SGML world will recognize some of its best-known experts on the list. Many others took part in the e-mail development of the XML specs, which should put to rest the misconception that XML is somehow a competitor to SGML.

Having read through much of the e-mail myself, I can tell you that it's impossible not to be somewhat awed by the level of expertise, dedication, and commitment that these people brought to the spec's development.

This specification was prepared and approved for publication by the W3C XML Working Group (WG). WG approval of this specification does not necessarily imply that all WG members voted for its approval. The current and former members of the XML WG are:

Jon Bosak, Sun*(Chair)*; James Clark*(Technical Lead)*; Tim Bray, Textuality and Netscape*(XML Co-editor)*; Jean Paoli, Microsoft*(XML Co-editor)*; C. M. Sperberg-McQueen, U. of Ill.*(XML Co-editor)*; Dan Connolly, W3C*(W3C Liaison)*; Paula Angerstein, Texcel; Steve DeRose, INSO; Dave Hollander, HP; Eliot Kimber, ISOGEN; Eve Maler, ArborText; Tom Magliery, NCSA; Murray Maloney, Muzmo and Grif; Makoto Murata, Fuji Xerox Information Systems; Joel Nava, Adobe; Conleth O'Connell, Vignette; Peter Sharpe, SoftQuad; John Tigue, DataChannel.

Supplementary
Annotations

- Grammars, Productions, and Computer Languages
- Becoming a W3C Recommendation
- W3C Document Copyright Notice

Grammars, Productions, and Computer Languages

A specification for a computer language, whether a programming language such as Java or a markup language such as XML, is defined by a grammar. For spoken languages, grammar is the collection of rules we deduce by analyzing the patterns in sentences that people speak and write. With computer languages, the rules come first, and something written in a particular language must completely conform to those rules if a program that processes it is to be able to do its job properly.

A computer language's grammar has four parts:

- The vocabulary of "words" that we can use. These are known as *terminals* or *tokens*.
- The language components that we create by combining the tokens. In the English language, a sentence is one

287

such component. Others would be a subject (for example, "the brown horse"), a gerund phrase ("walking the dog"), or an adverb clause ("after walking the dog"). We call these combinations *nonterminals*. Nonterminals aren't always combinations of terminals; they can include other nonterminals, just as the adverb clause "after walking the dog" includes the gerund phrase "walking the dog". (We'll see what's so "non" about nonterminals shortly.)

- Rules for combining terminals and nonterminals into new nonterminals. In English, you have one rule saying that a definite article nonterminal is always the word "the" and another rule saying that you can create a subject nonterminal by combining definite article, adjective, and noun nonterminals—for example, "the brown horse". A different language may have a different rule to create the same thing; for example, the same nonterminal in Spanish puts the adjective after the noun: "el caballo maron".

In computer languages, such rules are called *productions*. The above rule for constructing a sentence's subject in English might be written as shown in Example 12.

Example 12: A "production" for assembling an English-language sentence subject

```
Subject := DefiniteArticle Adjective Noun
```

The := essentially means "is made of the following components". On the left side of this := we see the nonterminal whose construction is defined by this rule, and on the right are its components and their order.

- A special nonterminal, called a *starting nonterminal*, that can stand on its own. The goal of combining any selection of terminals and nonterminals is to create this particular nonterminal. In English, this would be a sentence. In most programming languages, it's usually a complete program, and a program nonterminal's production rule shows the syntax used to indicate the program's beginning and end as well as the necessary and optional components between these. In XML, the starting nonterminal is the document, and its production is the first one in the spec.

Terminals and Nonterminals

What is it that a starting nonterminal starts? What's so terminal about a token, and what quality does it have that a nonterminal lacks?

When a program reads a unit of information, whether an English sentence or a line of C++ code that adds the number 3 to some stored value, it must figure out this information unit's components and their relationships. You probably had to do this by hand with English sentences in your early school years, and you probably hated it: they called it "diagramming sentences". (In both computer languages and spoken languages, we also call it *parsing*.) Figure 1 shows one of of these diagrams.

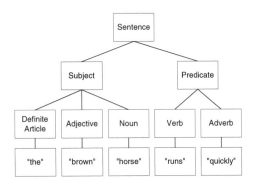

Figure 1 Sample sentence diagram.

(It's a bit simplified, but will serve our purpose.) Working from the top, sentence is the first nonterminal. A parser determining the information's components begins with this, the starting nonterminal. Once it works its way down to the actual words of the sentence, it can't break them down into component parts, so it's reached the end of the decomposition for these parts of the sentence. Each vocabulary word is the end, or "terminal" of one decomposition path, while a "nonterminal" is a part that can be broken down further.

The most important part of a specification is often the productions that show how you combine terminals and nonterminals into new nonterminals, because when you come across an unfamiliar construction in a particular language, these productions serve as a reference to describe exactly (and I mean exactly) how this construction is assembled.

For example, if you're not sure what XML "content" is, production 43 shows that it's a combination of zero or more elements, and **Char-Data**, **Reference**, **CDSect**, **PI**, and **Comment** nonterminals. (Throughout these annotations, symbols defined by productions are shown in a bold Courier font, like **CharData** and the other four nonterminals mentioned in the previous sentence.) If any of these are unfamiliar, you can look up their productions as well. To make all this looking up easier, the *Index of Productions* in this book provides an alphabetical index showing the page number where you will find each production.

Syntax of Productions

The production that we saw in Example 12 is oversimplified. A subject is not always made of these three parts. For example, an adjective is not necessary, and you can have multiple adjectives if you like ("the big brown thoroughbred horse").

Describing such potential complexity in a production rule requires its own syntax. In the 1950s, Noam Chomsky developed Chomsky Normal Form, or CNF, the first language widely used to formally describe the rules of languages. Building on Chomsky's work, in 1960 John W. Backus developed a syntax for describing the productions of FORTRAN, the first popular high-level programming language. This syntax for describing a language's productions was originally called BNF, for "Backus Normal Form", but after Peter Naur revised it, (mostly to limit the syntax to characters already on the typical keyboard) the BNF stood for "Backus-Naur Form". As various researchers added symbols to make it more flexible, instead of adding all of their names as well, the language became known as "Extended Backus-Naur Form", or just EBNF.

EBNF has become such a standard that you can find grammars of EBNF productions for SGML and for many programming languages on the Internet. Using them, you can take advantage of the many tools that exist to create new parsing tools right from these grammars. You feed in a text file of EBNF productions (or something very similar such as the yacc program's own language) as input, and these programs output code in one language or another that can parse something conforming to the rules enumerated by those productions. For example, the parser development tools yacc, Bison, and Flex read the productions for a language and produce C code to parse that language; Bison++ and Flex++ produce C++ code; ayacc produces Ada code; and Sun's JavaCC produces Java code.

The XML specification defines its grammar using productions written in EBNF notation. Chapter 6, "Notation", describes the details of the EBNF used in the spec's productions, and this book includes annotations to that section with examples that demonstrate the use of the various options.

Becoming a W3C Recommendation

The World Wide Web Consortium was founded by MIT's Laboratory for Computer Science and the European Laboratory for Particle Physics (CERN) in Switzerland. Although the W3C offers no individual memberships, over 230 companies and universities around the world are now institutional members.

The W3C can't force anyone to do anything, but once a specification carries official W3C "Recommendation" status, you know that a wide variety of universities, hardware and software companies, banks, publishers, entertainment giants and others voted on it and took part in its development. These organizations have a vested interest in ensuring that their products conform to the standard, because their products will then work more cooperatively with other companies' products. After all, this is what standards are for.

What if you have your own idea for a standard? How does it become a W3C Recommendation? First, you have to be a member. You can't say "I, Joe Guy, think it would be valuable to have a common standard for delivering recipes over the Web". You have to say "We at Guyco, a W3C member company, think it would be valuable to have a common standard for delivering recipes over the Web".

If you have a proposed draft of the standard, you may submit it as an official W3C Submission; if you don't, the W3C may put together a workshop to discuss the scope of the idea and the goals for a Working Group. Once a Working Group is formed, they may work with an Editorial Review Board (a group of expert consultants elected from nominations made by W3C members) as they develop a draft specification.

From an officially Acknowledged Submission by a member organization or a draft created by a Working Group, the next step is a Working Draft. These works-in-progress are publicly available via the Web for review by anyone. As the Working Group revises its Working Draft, it especially considers comments from other W3C members. Nothing remains a Working Draft forever; it may be promoted to Proposed Recommendation status, or it might be dropped—especially if its ideas are absorbed into another evolving standard.

XML received so much publicity in its year as a Working Draft (for example, a full-page article in Time Magazine in November of 1997) that many people started writing books about XML and developing software for it even though it was still evolving. As I write this, XLink, XPointer and XSL are still Working Drafts.

Figure 2 Becoming a W3C standard: promotion through the ranks of W3C Technical Reports.

When a Working Group is happy with its draft specification, the Group submits it to the W3C Director, who decides whether it can be considered a Proposed Recommendation. If so, representatives of all the W3C member organizations vote on whether to make it an official Recommendation or not. They may approve it, with or without minor changes; they may send it back to being a Working Draft; or they can drop it as a W3C work item. This stage doesn't take long, because when a recommendation is proposed, a specific voting period is announced. Members had six weeks to review and vote on XML.

Once a specification reaches Recommendation status, it is an official standard. According to the W3C, such specifications "are stable, contribute to Web interoperability, and are supported for industry-wide adoption by the W3C".

W3C Document Copyright Notice

(This document is stored at `http://www.w3.org/Consortium/Legal/copyright-documents.html`.)

DOCUMENT NOTICE

Copyright © 1995-1998 World Wide Web Consortium, (Massachusetts Institute of Technology, Institut National de Recherche en Informatique et en Automatique, Keio University). All Rights Reserved.

`http://www.w3.org/Consortium/Legal/`

Documents on the W3C site are provided by the copyright holders under the following license. By obtaining, using and/or copying this document, or the W3C document from which this statement is linked, you (the licensee) agree that you have read, understood, and will comply with the following terms and conditions:

Permission to use, copy, and distribute the contents of this document, or the W3C document from which this statement is linked, in any medium for any purpose and without fee or royalty is hereby granted, provided that you include the following on *ALL* copies of the document, or portions thereof, that you use:

1. A link or URL to the original W3C document.[†]
2. The pre-existing copyright notice of the original author, if it doesn't exist, a notice of the form: "Copyright © World Wide Web Consortium, (Massachusetts Institute of Technology, Institut National de Recherche en Informatique et en Automatique, Keio University). All Rights Reserved. http://www.w3.org/Consortium/Legal/" (Hypertext is preferred, but a textual representation is permitted.)

---

† The original W3C XML specification is at `http://www.w3.org/TR/REC-xml`.

3. *If it exists*, the STATUS of the W3C document.

When space permits, inclusion of the full text of this **NOTICE** should be provided. We request that authorship attribution be provided in any software, documents, or other items or products that you create pursuant to the implementation of the contents of this document, or any portion thereof.

No right to create modifications or derivatives of W3C documents is granted pursuant to this license.

THIS DOCUMENT IS PROVIDED "AS IS", AND COPYRIGHT HOLDERS MAKE NO REPRESENTATIONS OR WARRANTIES, EXPRESS OR IMPLIED, INCLUDING, BUT NOT LIMITED TO, WARRANTIES OF MERCHANTABILITY, FITNESS FOR A PARTICULAR PURPOSE, NON-INFRINGEMENT, OR TITLE; THAT THE CONTENTS OF THE DOCUMENT ARE SUITABLE FOR ANY PURPOSE; NOR THAT THE IMPLEMENTATION OF SUCH CONTENTS WILL NOT INFRINGE ANY THIRD PARTY PATENTS, COPYRIGHTS, TRADEMARKS OR OTHER RIGHTS.

COPYRIGHT HOLDERS WILL NOT BE LIABLE FOR ANY DIRECT, INDIRECT, SPECIAL OR CONSEQUENTIAL DAMAGES ARISING OUT OF ANY USE OF THE DOCUMENT OR THE PERFORMANCE OR IMPLEMENTATION OF THE CONTENTS THEREOF.

The name and trademarks of copyright holders may NOT be used in advertising or publicity pertaining to this document or its contents without specific, written prior permission. Title to copyright in this document will at all times remain with copyright holders.

Please see our Copyright FAQ (http://www.w3.org/Consortium/Legal/IPR-FAQ.html) for common questions about using materials from our site, including specific terms and conditions for packages like libwww, Amaya, and Jigsaw. Other questions about this notice can be directed to site-policy@w3.org.

Glossary

See the index for pointers to more information on each of these terms.

application, XML application

An XML application is a reason for using XML, such as a comparative shopping service on the Web. The term is also applied to the software that implements an application.

See also: *processor, XML processor*

ASCII

The American Standard Code for Information Interchange, the most popular character set for representing characters on non-mainframe computers. Because ASCII only includes 128 characters, it's inadequate for representing documents that are not limited to the Latin alphabet.

attribute, attribute specification

Attributes are properties of elements. They are specified as named pieces of information in an element's *start-tag* or *empty-element tag*. For example, the single attribute specification of the following empty a element pairs the attribute value "http://www.snee.com" with the href attribute name.

```
<a href="http://www.snee.com">The Snee Group</a>
```

See also: *attribute-list declaration*

attribute list

The *attribute specifications* included in a given *tag*.

See also: *attribute-list declaration*

attribute-list declaration

An attribute-list declaration defines the attributes for the elements of a given type.

See 3.3, "Attribute-List Declarations", for more information.

See also: *DTD, document type declaration, element type declaration, attribute type*

attribute specification

See *attribute, attribute specification*

attribute type

A category of information to which the value of a given *attribute* is restricted. For example, an attribute value can be limited to whole numbers or specific strings. See 3.3.1, "Attribute Types", for more information.

big-endian

A *byte* is a series of bits. Different operating systems consider either end of this series to be the "first" bit, so the terms big-endian and little-endian are used to distinguish the two approaches.

binary notation

A method of representing data that is based on binary digits (ones and zeroes) rather than characters.

byte

A collection of bits used to represent a single unit of information. On personal computers, this is typically eight bits (an "octet"), and is often used to represent each character of a text file. (For example, the word "cat" can be three bytes—one for each letter.) However, despite a popular misconception, a byte isn't always eight bits.

CDATA sections

A specially marked section of an XML document within which all characters, including those usually treated as markup (for example, < and &) are treated as data. See 2.7, "CDATA Sections", for more.

character

According to Section 2.2 of the XML specification, an "atomic unit of text as specified by ISO/IEC 10646". In general, this means a letter, digit, or punctuation character from some language whose alphabet is represented by *Unicode* and *ISO 10646* (which both include *ASCII* as a subset). The standard also accounts for symbols from many non-Western languages.

See also: *character data, character encoding*

character-based notation
See *binary notation*

character data

According to 2.4, "Character Data and Markup", "All text that is not *markup* constitutes the character data of the document".

character encoding

The association of a *character* with a bit pattern representing that character in computer storage.

See 4.3.3, "Character Encoding in Entities", for more information.

character reference

A method for representing characters in an XML *document* even if they are not available on your keyboard.

See 4.1, "Character and Entity References", for more information.

child elements

Also, "sub-elements". Elements contained within another, *parent* element. In the following, `adjective` and `noun` are children of the `nounPhrase` element.

```
<nounPhrase><adjective>Red</adjective>
<noun>sails</noun></nounPhrase>
```

classes

In object-oriented development, a class of objects is a group of things having the same structure and behavior. In XML, a class of documents is called a *document type*. Memos, menus, and recipes would be three examples.

See also: *element type*

comment

Comments in an XML document, like those in a programming language, are messages for humans reading the source. They are ignored by the processing software.

See 4.1, "Character and Entity References", for more information.

content

The text between an element's *start-tag* and *end-tag*. This can include *character data* and *markup*.

content model

According to the XML specification, "a simple *grammar* governing the allowed types of the *child elements* and the order in which they are allowed to appear". This is the part of an *element type declaration* that describes the possible content of elements of that type.

See 3.2, "Element Type Declarations", for more information.

content particle

In a specification *production*, a "building block" that represents a unit of content. See 3.2.1, "Element Content", for more information.

declaration

Declarations are instructions to the XML processor that govern the parsing and processing of the document.

See also: *document type declaration, standalone document declaration, element type declaration, attribute-list declaration, encoding declaration, entity declaration, text declaration, notation declaration, XML declaration*

delimited text

Text surrounded by *delimiters*; "these three words" are delimited by quotation marks.

See also: *delimiter*

delimiter

A special character that identifies the beginning or end of a *string*. In a normal English sentence, spaces and punctuation serve as delimiters.

See also: *delimited text*

document

The XML specification merely defines XML documents as a *"class of data objects"*. It also says that "XML documents are conforming *SGML* documents", so we'll go with the SGML ISO 8879 definition of "document": "a collection of information that is processed as a unit". Note that this collection is not necessarily *stored* as a unit; storage arrangements are determined by a document's *entity* structure.

See Chapter 2, "Documents", for more information.

document element, root element

The single *element* containing all the other elements in a document. The document element is the only element that has no *parent element*. The *document type declaration*, if present, *identifies* the *element type* of the document element.

See Chapter 2, "Documents", for more information.

See also: *document entity, document instance*

document entity

The main *entity* of a *document*; the entity in which parsing begins. By following any *entity references* in the document entity (and any references in the referenced entities, and so on), a *parser* will eventually find all the entities in which parts of the document are stored.

See also: *document element, root element, document instance*

document instance

Everything in a document after the prolog. Generally, this means the *document element*, but may include *comments*, *processing instructions*, and extra *white space* following the document element.

See also: *document entity*

document type

A *class* of documents with similar properties. Memos, purchase orders, and algebra textbooks are three potential document types.

See also: *document type declaration*

document type declaration

A *declaration* identifying the *document type*. It contains the declarations for the *document type definition*, either directly within its *internal subset*, through a reference to an *external entity* containing such declarations known as an *external subset*, or both. The following document type declaration has both a reference to an external subset and three declarations in its internal subset:

```
<!DOCTYPE glossary SYSTEM "gloss.dtd" [
<!ELEMENT annotation (#PCDATA)>
<!ATTLIST annotation author NMTOKEN #IMPLIED>
<!ENTITY rfd "rosy fingered dawn">
]>
```

See 2.8, "Prolog and Document Type Declaration", for more information.

See also: *document type, element type declaration, attribute-list declaration, entity declaration, notation declaration, external subset*

document type definition

See *DTD*

DTD

"Document Type Definition". The rules for applying XML to documents of a given type. It is expressed by markup declarations in the *document type declaration*. (Note that DTD does not refer to a *document type declaration*.)

See also: *document type*

EBNF

"Extended Backus-Naur Form", the notation often used to describe the syntax of markup and programming languages. See "Syntax of Productions", and Chapter 6, "Notation", for more on its history and use.

element type

An element type is a *class* of *elements* with similar properties, including their structure and element type name. In HTML documents, all h1 elements belong to the h1 element type; all img elements belong to the img element type.

See 3.2, "Element Type Declarations", for more information.

element type declaration

An element type declaration is the markup used to define an element type—in other words, it's how you say "here's an element type that can be used in this document, and here is its structure". For example, the following declaration for the book element type shows that a book element consists of a title element, an author element, an optional TOC element, and one or more chapter elements:

```
<!ELEMENT book (title,author,TOC?,chapter+)>
```

See 3.2, "Element Type Declarations", for more information.

See also: *DTD, document type declaration*

elements

The logical components of a *document*. *Start-tags* and *end-tags* show the beginning and end of elements; *empty-element tags* are sometimes used to represent *empty elements*.

For example, the following has two elements, setup and punchline, inside of a third element, joke:

```
<joke>
<setup>My apartment is so small</setup>
<punchline>The mice are round-shouldered</punchline>
</joke>
```

See also: *element type*

empty element, empty-element tag

An empty element has no content. XML represents it with either a start-tag immediately followed by an end-tag or by an empty-element tag, which looks like a start-tag with a slash before its closing ">":

```
<img src="stoppages.jpg"/>
```

encoding

See *character encoding*

encoding declaration

The part of the *XML declaration* or *text declaration* identifying the *character encoding* used for that *document entity* or *external entity*. In the following encoding declaration, ISO-10646-UCS-4 is the encoding.

```
<?xml version="1.0" encoding="ISO-10646-UCS-4" ?>
```

See 4.3.3, "Character Encoding in Entities", for more information.

See also: *text declaration, XML declaration*

end-tag
See *tags*

entity

According to Chapter 4, "Physical Structures", a "virtual storage unit". This is often a file, but can be a database record, network resource, etc.

See also: *external entity, internal entity, general entity, parameter entity, parsed entity, unparsed entity*

entity declaration

A *declaration* that defines an *entity* by associating a name with either a character string (*internal entity*) or a storage location (*external entity*) where text or data are found.
See 4.2, "Entity Declarations", for more information.

See also: *general entity, parameter entity, parsed entity, unparsed entity, document type declaration*

entity reference

An ampersand, entity name, and semicolon indicating that the named *entity* should replace the entity reference. The entity reference in the following will be replaced by the replacement text of the `tax-time` entity:

```
&taxtime; is the cruelest month
```

See 4.1, "Character and Entity References", for more information.

entity value
The literal text in an internal entity declaration.

See also: *replacement text*

escaped text

Text whose *markup* instructs the processor to treat it as data even if it includes characters normally used for markup. For example, while a < character normally begins a start- or end-tag, when escaped by a *CDATA section*, an XML processor treats it as just another data character. Most markup and programming languages offer some way to escape text.

Extended Backus Naur Form
See *EBNF*

external entity

An entity whose content is stored outside the entity where its declaration is stored. The following declares an external *general entity*:

```
<!ENTITY cpinfo SYSTEM "cpinfo.xml">
```

See 4.2.2, "External Entities", for more information.

See also: *internal entity*

external subset

An external subset of a *Document Type Declaration* is a collection of *DTD* declarations stored in the unnamed *external entity* declared by the external parameter of a a document type declaration. (Compare *internal subset*.)

general entity
An entity that can be used in the *document element*.

See also: *parameter entity*

generic identifier

Sometimes abbreviated "GI". The part of a *start-tag* or *end-tag* that identifies an element as a member of a particular *element type*. It is "generic" because it identifies the element as a member of a particular *class* of elements, unlike a *unique identifier* that identifies one specific element. In the following example, the strings "verse" and "illus" are the generic identifiers:

```
<verse><illus pic="pic17"/>Hurry up please it's time</verse>
```

GI

See *generic identifier*

grammar

The rules for creating the components of a particular language.

IETF

The "Internet Engineering Task Force", the group that develops and propagates Internet standards by coordinating the *RFCs* that have accumulated since 1969.

internal entity

An entity whose replacement text is defined by an *entity value* in its declaration. The following declares an internal entity called sss with a entity value of "Shantih shantih shantih":

```
<!ENTITY sss "Shantih shantih shantih">
```

See also: *external entity*

internal subset

The *DTD declarations* included between square brackets in the *document type declaration*. In the following example, the internal subset has three declarations:

```
<?xml version="1.0"?>
<!DOCTYPE redecl SYSTEM "extdecl.dtd" [
<!ELEMENT redecl (#PCDATA)>
<!ATTLIST redecl flavor CDATA "lemon">
<!ENTITY rutle "Barry">
]>
<redecl>My favorite Rutle was &rutle;.</redecl>
```

See also: *external subset*

interoperability

In the spec, this refers to the ability to use a particular XML document with *SGML* systems developed before the *WebSGML* adaptations to the SGML standard.

See 1.2, "Terminology", for more information.

ISO

The International Organization for Standardization. (Note that the name isn't an acronym, but a coinage derived from the Greek "isos", for "equal".) It creates standards for everything from the aluminum used in aerospace construction (ISO 8591-1:1989) to character sets (ISO 10646). SGML is ISO standard 8879.

See also: *ISO 10646*

ISO 10646

An international *character set* standard for representing characters from alphabets used around the world.

See also: *Unicode*

language

In addition to the sense of spoken or written languages (for example, Spanish or Chinese) and computer programming and markup languages (Java, C++, XML, HTML), this word has a specific technical meaning in computer science: the possible combinations of symbols and terms that can be generated by a set of rules known as *productions*.

markup

Text of a document that describes properties of the document and its data. According to 2.8, "Prolog and Document Type Declaration", "the function of the markup in an XML document is to describe its storage and logical structure and to associate attribute-value pairs with its logical structures". *Tags* and *entity references* are types of markup.

See also: *character data*

name token

An *attribute type* that allows only letters, digits, and certain punctuation characters to be used in the attribute value.

namespace

A set of unique names.

nesting

The storing of one container inside another, which may in turn be inside another, as with Russian nesting dolls. Proper nesting is the assurance that if one *element* or *entity* begins inside of another, the contained one ends before its container does. In the following, `element2` nests properly within `element1`:

```
<element1>Here is element 1
<element2>Here is element 2
</element2>
</element1>
```

In this erroneous example, however, the elements are not properly nested:

```
<element1>Here is element 1
<element2>Here is element 2
</element1>  <!-- wrong place for this tag! -->
</element2>
```

Proper nesting of entities and elements is a key requirement of *well-formed documents*.

nmtoken
See *name token*

non-validating parser
A *parser* only responsible for checking that a document is *well-formed*.

See also: *validating parser*

nonterminal
See *terminal*

normative
The normative parts of a standard are those that must be followed. The parts labeled as "informative", such as Appendix C, "XML and SGML (Non-Normative)", and Appendix D, "Expansion of Entity and Character References (Non-Normative)", provide background, explanations, and examples.

notation declaration
A declaration that associates a notation name with information that may locate an interpreter of the notation. For example, when an *unparsed entity* uses a format of JPEG, the following declaration provides further information on this format:

```
<!NOTATION JPEG SYSTEM "Joint Photographic Experts Group">
```

See 4.7, "Notation Declarations", for more information.

See also: *DTD, document type declaration*

octet
See *byte*

parameter entity
An *entity* that can be referenced in parameters of a markup *declaration*.

See also: *general entity*

parent element
An element containing other elements called *child elements* or *subelements*. In the following, the `nounPhrase` element is the parent of the `adjective` and `noun` child elements:

```
<nounPhrase><adjective>Red</adjective>
<noun>sails</noun></nounPhrase>
```

parsed entity
An *entity* whose *replacement text* will be parsed as part of the document in which a reference to it occurs. See 4.3, "Parsed Entities", for more information.

See also: *entity reference, unparsed entity*

parser, XML parser
The component of an XML processor that analyses the markup and determines the structure and other properties of the data.

See also: *validating parser, non-validating parser*

PCDATA

Parsed Character Data: data remaining after the *processor* has parsed text for *comments* and *processing instructions*. PCDATA differs from the data in *CDATA sections*, in which the parser will only look for the]]> that ends a CDATA section.

processing instruction

Markup containing information for *applications*. Unlike *elements*, there is no way to indicate specific places where they are allowed or not allowed, so their use is more flexible. The following is a processing instruction for the `stinker` application:

```
<?stinker scent="newcar.sml" time="5 secs" ?>
```

See 2.6, "Processing Instructions", for more.

processor, XML processor

When discussing XML, these terms are often used interchangeably (though incorrectly) with "XML parser". To quote the spec, "a software module called an XML processor is used to read XML documents and provide access to their content and structure. It is assumed that an XML processor is doing its work on behalf of another module, called the application".

From an end-user's perspective, the same program may serve as the XML processor and the application, but the distinction helps developers know what to expect from a processor when they build an application around an existing processor.

See also: *parser, XML parser*

production

A rule for creating a *nonterminal* from *terminals* and other nonterminals in a language's *grammar*. In other words, a rule for combining certain pieces and constructs of a language to create a new piece. In the XML specification, the first production shows which nonterminals combine to create an XML document; all the other productions show how a document's components break down into their own components.

prolog

The initial portion of a document that precedes the *document instance*. It contains only *declarations*, *white space*, *comments*, and *processing instructions*. See 2.8, "Prolog and Document Type Declaration", for more information.

regular expression

A *grammar* for describing a family of character strings with something in common. Chapter 6, "Notation", describes the regular expression syntax used in the spec's productions.

replacement text

The text ultimately substituted for an *entity reference*. After an XML processor replaces an internal entity reference with its *entity value*, it then processes any markup (including additional entity references and *character references* in that entity value) recursively until there are no more to process. The result is the replacement text.

See also: *entity value*

RFC

A "Request for Comment" document maintained by the *IETF* to define a standard for some aspect of the Internet. Each RFC has a number assigned to it; for example, RFC 1738, "Uniform Resource Locators", specifies how *URLs* work, and RFC 959 contains the specification for FTP, "File Transfer Protocol".

See also: *IETF*

root element

See *document element*

SGML

The Standard Generalized Markup Language, an *ISO* standard for representing the logical and physical structure of documents in order to ease automated processing without information loss. The XML specification describes XML as an "application profile or restricted form of SGML", meaning that it is a simplified version that leaves out many SGML features to make it more suitable for a particular class of applications. This makes XML software much easier to develop than full SGML software.

standalone document declaration

The standalone document declaration, found in the *XML declaration* (as shown in the example below) answers the question "can we use this document without paying attention to declarations outside this entity?" See 2.9, "Standalone Document Declaration", for more information.

```
<?xml version="1.0" standalone="yes"?>
```

start-tag

See *tags*

string

A sequence of characters. Strings are often delimited by quotation marks "like this" or by apostrophes 'like this'. (Programmers refer to quotation marks as "double quotes" and apostrophes as "single quotes".)

sub-elements

See *child elements*

tags

A category of markup used to identify either the start and end of elements, or, in the case of some *empty elements*, the entire element.

See also: *attribute specification*

terminal

A terminal, or token, is one of the indivisible units of a *grammar*. These are combined according to the rules of a grammar's *productions* into *nonterminals*, which combine into larger nonterminals. Eventually, in XML, these form the most important XML nonterminal of them all: the *document*.

text declaration

An optional declaration at the beginning of a *parsed entity* that identifies the *character encoding* used for that entity and, optionally, the version of XML that it conforms to. For example:

```
<?xml version="1.0" encoding="ISO-8859-1"?>
```

See 4.3.1, "The Text Declaration", for more information.

token
See *terminal*

UCS

Universal Multiple-Octet Coded Character Set, a family of subsets of the ISO/IEC 10646 standard for representing international character sets. They use multiple octets (groups of eight bits) because the 256 possible values of a single octet, like the *ASCII* byte used on typical PCs, just aren't enough (especially when ASCII only uses seven of those eight bits). 10646's UCS-2 uses two octets per character and UCS-4 uses 4.

See also: *character encoding*

Unicode

A standard for representing characters from the alphabets of the world. While Unicode is a separate standard from *ISO 10646*, the Unicode Consortium and the *ISO* have worked to keep Unicode's related standards synchronized with the *UCS-2* subset of *ISO 10646*.

Uniform Resource Identifier

See *URI*

Uniform Resource Locator

See *URL*

unique identifier

A name for an element that can be used to refer to it unequivocally. It is assigned using an attribute of type ID.

See also: *generic identifier*

unparsed entity

An *external entity* that the *XML processor* should not parse as XML in the current document. A document can use these to store data such as image or sound files. A document identifies unparsed entities by naming them in *attributes* of type ENTITY or ENTITIES after declaring them with an associated *notation* to identify their format.

See also: *parsed entity*

URI

Uniform Resource Identifier, the system used for naming resources on the Web. This includes URLs and future categories of resources.

See also: *URL*

URL

Uniform Resource Locator, known more popularly as a Web address—for example, `http://www.w3c.org` or `ftp://ftp.snee.com/public`.

See also: *URI*

UTF-8, UTF-16

UCS Transformation Formats 8 and 16: specific *ISO 10646 character encodings* that use multiples of 8 and 16 bits for each character. In the words of the XML specification, "All XML processors must accept the UTF-8 and UTF-16 encodings of 10646".

valid

A valid XML *document* has an associated *document type declaration* and follows all the rules specified by that declaration. A document that isn't valid may still be *well-formed*, and therefore still a conforming XML document.

See also: *parser, XML parser, validating parser, validity constraint, well-formedness constraint*

validating parser

A parser that goes beyond checking a document for *well-formedness* by also checking whether the document is *valid*. Much of the XML specification details the additional responsibilities of a *validating parser*. See 5.1, "Validating and Non-Validating Processors", for more information.

See also: *parser, XML parser*

validity constraint, well-formedness constraint

In the XML specification, a condition accompanying a *production*. This condition imposes further requirements to be met by the component being defined by the production. For a parser to consider the component's containing *element* or *entity* to be *valid*, that component must conform to any validity constraints; to be considered well-formed, it must meet any well-formedness constraints.

For example, XML production 29 shows the constraint vc: `Root Element Type`, and production 39 shows the constraint wfc: `Element Type Match`.

See 1.2, "Terminology", for more information.

vc
See *validity constraint, well-formedness constraint*

Web server
A program that responds to requests from Web browsers by sending Web documents over a network (usually, the Internet).

WebSGML
A revision to the *SGML* standard that, among other things, allows non-valid *well-formed* XML documents to be conforming SGML documents.

well-formed
A well-formed XML document is one that conforms to the XML specification, but not necessarily to its validity constraints.

See also: *validity constraint, well-formedness constraint*

well-formedness constraint
See *validity constraint, well-formedness constraint*

wfc
See *validity constraint, well-formedness constraint*

white space
Any combination of the tab character, carriage return, line feed, and the character produced by the keyboard's space bar.

XML

The Extensible Markup Language. Like its parent *SGML*, XML allows the definition of the logical and physical structure of *documents* in order to ease automated processing of those documents; special care was taken to ensure that XML documents (and associated information) would transmit across the Internet easily.

XML application

See *processor, XML processor*

XML declaration

An optional declaration at the beginning of an XML document that identifies the version of XML being used, and possibly includes an *encoding declaration* and a *standalone document declaration*. For example:

```
<?xml version="1.0" encoding="SO-10646-UCS-4" ?>
```

See 2.8, "Prolog and Document Type Declaration", for more information.

Production Indexes

Alphabetically

By Production Number

Index

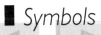

B

C